The Tale of Matsura

Michigan Monograph Series in Japanese Studies, Number 9

Center for Japanese Studies
The University of Michigan

The Tale of Matsura
Fujiwara Teika's Experiment in Fiction

Translated with an Introduction and Notes
by Wayne P. Lammers

Ann Arbor
Center for Japanese Studies
The University of Michigan
1992

The paper used in this publication meets the requirements of the ANSI Standard Z39.48-1984 (Permanence of Paper).

Library of Congress Cataloging-in-Publication Data
Matsura no Miya monogatari. English
       The tale of Matsura: Fujiwara Teika's experiment in fiction / translated with an introduction and notes by Wayne P. Lammers.
             p. cm.—(Michigan monograph series in Japanese studies ; no. 9)
       Translation of: Matsura no Miya monogatari.
       Includes bibliographical references and index.
       ISBN 0-939512-48-3 (alk. paper)
       I. Fujiwara, Sadaie, 1162–1241. II. Lammers, Wayne P., 1951–. III. Title. IV. Series.
PL790.M34E5 1992
895.6′322—dc20
                                                                                    90–42197
                                                                                         CIP

A Note on the Type
This book was set in Caslon 540, a modern adaptation of a type designed by William Caslon (1692–1766), greatest of English letter founders. The Caslon face, an artistic, easily read type, has enjoyed two centuries of ever-increasing popularity in our own country. The first copies of the Declaration of Independence and the first paper currency distributed to the citizens of the newborn nation were printed in this type face.

Book design by Lisa Jacobs
Composed by The Composing Room of Michigan, Inc., Grand Rapids, Michigan
Printed and bound by Braun-Brumfield, Inc., Ann Arbor, Michigan

∞
Printed in the United States of America

This book is dedicated to the memory of
Robert H. Brower
1923–1988

Contents

List of Charts

Preface

This book derives from my doctoral dissertation, "A Poetic Ideal in a Narrative Context: Fujiwara Teika and *The Tale of Matsura* (*Matsura no miya monogatari*)," submitted to the University of Michigan in 1987. I have expanded chapter one to include brief remarks on aspects of the tale left untouched in my dissertation, and have added further elaboration at several places in chapter two. I have condensed former chapters three through six and combined them with the crucial analytical portions of the three original appendixes into two, much shorter, new appendixes; the analysis here supersedes the earlier in several respects but does not affect the essence of the argument. The translation has also seen minor adjustments throughout.

The translation is based on Hagitani Boku, ed., *Matsura no miya monogatari* (Kadokawa, 1970), which is the only edition of the text to supply annotations and a complete modern Japanese translation. Further information on this text can be found in chapter three. My translation and notes owe a considerable debt to Hagitani's work even where I have not provided explicit references; in general, I have given individual citations only where it seemed particularly important to underscore my adherence to, or signal my departure from, his reading of a passage.

Although I have striven to make the translation readable entirely on its own, without reference to notes, I have also made no effort to minimize the notes either in number or in size. The tale presumes a vast knowledge of prior Japanese and Chinese literature on the part of the reader, and it cannot be appreciated in its full complexity, even by the specialist, without supplementary information close at hand. My hope is that this has resulted in a work more useful to advanced students and specialists of Japanese literature.

In Romanizing Japanese I have followed the modified Hepburn system (*n* rather than *m* immediately before *b*, *p*, and *m*), and for Chinese I have used Wade-Giles. All Japanese and Chinese names have been given in their native order, surname first. For Japanese, I have preserved the particle *no* when it appears between surname and personal name in the translation, but in the introduction and notes I have followed the recent practice of retaining it only after surnames of one or two syllables—thus, Abe no Nakamaro, but Fujiwara Teika. For Chinese personal names and titles of works I have consulted *The Indiana Companion to Traditional Chinese Literature* (William H. Nienhauser, Jr., ed.) where possible.

I wish to acknowledge with deepest gratitude the generous encouragement and help I received from the late Robert H. Brower in preparing this translation and study. I benefited immeasurably from his learned counsel through many years of graduate study and dissertation research, and had hoped to profit from many more years as I made my way out from under his wing to establish myself as a full-fledged member of the scholarly community, getting to know him better as a colleague and friend and not just as a teacher. His sudden illness and death thus came as a particularly severe blow to me. His critical eye saved me from many an embarrassing mistake in writing my dissertation, and I do not doubt that it would have further improved this book had the manuscript been ready in time for him to review. In hope that what has resulted without benefit of his continued guidance is nevertheless worthy of him, it is to his memory that I dedicate this book.

I would also like to thank several other individuals for their various contributions: Tsai-fa Cheng, Tse-tsung Chow, and Joseph S. M. Lau for kindly answering questions about matters Chinese; James O'Brien for his invaluable comments on the translation; Robert Danly for his always helpful advice; and my wife Cheryl and son Michael for their patient and understanding support through all the years it has taken to bring this work to completion. Needless to say, I alone must bear the burden of any errors or infelicities that remain uncorrected.

Finally, I am most grateful for the support provided this study at the dissertation stage by grants from the Fulbright-Hays Doctoral Dissertation Research Abroad Program and the Horace H. Rackham School of Graduate Studies at the University of Michigan.

Matsura no Miya Monogatari:
A Critical Introduction

Chapter One: Fujiwara Teika and *Matsura no Miya Monogatari*

Matsura no miya monogatari ("The Tale of Matsura," ca. 1190) is a classical Japanese tale or romance that belongs to the same category of courtly fiction as Murasaki Shikibu's unsurpassed masterpiece, *Genji monogatari* ("The Tale of Genji," ca. 1010). When compared with most of the best-known works of its genre, however, *Matsura no miya monogatari* stands out in striking contrast: Whereas the typical *monogatari* is set in the Heian period (794–1185) and in the Japanese capital of that time, *Matsura no miya monogatari* is set in the period before Japan's first "permanent" capital was established at present-day Nara in 710, and most of its action takes place in China. Whereas the typical *monogatari* centers almost entirely on affairs of the heart between men and women, nearly half of *Matsura no miya monogatari* is devoted to politics and government, including a violent succession struggle with armies marching halfway across China and back. And whereas the typical *monogatari* is fundamentally realistic, with only minor intrusions of the supernatural, the progress of *Matsura no miya monogatari* depends on supernatural interventions almost from beginning to end.

The work is in three *maki* ("scrolls" or "books"—in this case the latter), but, for purposes of outlining, the plot may be divided into five parts. First comes a sort of prologue, introducing the protagonist Ujitada as a child and in brief order taking him past the usual milestones in the early life of an idealized *monogatari* hero: he excels in Chinese poetry at the age of seven, demonstrates precocious mastery of musical instruments, undergoes a coming-of-age ceremony at the age of twelve, receives appointment to three highly demanding offices at the age of sixteen, and then experiences the awakening of first love. Ujitada's hopes in love are stopped short, however, when the mother of the lady who holds his heart captive accedes to the emperor's wish that she send her daughter to court. A short time later Ujitada is appointed deputy ambassador of an embassy scheduled to go to China the following year.

The second part tells of Ujitada's early experiences in China, including the immediate and special favor he receives from the emperor for demonstrating his superior talents and great knowledge. On a night away from court, he meets an old man playing the *kin*, the seven-stringed Chinese koto, or zither,[1] and the

---

1. Two kinds of Chinese koto are commonly mentioned in *monogatari*: the seven-stringed *kin*, and the thirteen-stringed *shō*. The *kin* was considered especially difficult to play, and at least in Japan had developed a certain association with mysterious supernatural forces (see Lammers 1982, 139–40 and passim, and Pollack 1983, 372–73 for discussions of the use of the *kin* in *Utsuho monogatari* and *Genji monogatari*; also see translation, n. 87).

old man tells him that he is destined to transmit the secrets of the instrument to Japan. Following the old man's instructions, Ujitada goes to Mount Shang, a place protected by divine sages, to receive the teachings from the beautiful Princess Hua-yang. Predictably, he falls in love with her, and she returns the sentiment, but this love, too, is destined to be short-lived and unfulfilled. One night not long after the transmission of the teachings has been accomplished, the princess reveals that she will soon die, and tells Ujitada that when he returns to Japan he must go to Hatsuse and conduct a certain series of services before the image of Kannon there to ensure that they will meet again. Back in her own apartments, she sends her zither flying off into the heavens, then lies down as the life rapidly ebbs from her body. By morning she is dead.

In the meantime, the Chinese emperor, who has been ailing, has spoken to Ujitada prophetically about his own impending death, exhorting Ujitada not to shrink from the role that will be thrust upon him by subsequent events. The emperor's death follows closely on the princess's, and marks the beginning of the third part of the tale: a violent succession struggle between the emperor's brother and his son, the rightful successor. The new emperor, who is still a child, is forced to flee the capital with his mother, the empress dowager, and they are pursued to the west by the rebel armies as their own loyalist armies dwindle rapidly along the way. Ujitada goes with the loyalists in this flight. When all looks hopeless, the empress dowager appeals to him to lead the imperial armies in a counterattack. He does so, and with the help of the Japanese god of Sumiyoshi, who suddenly appears at his side in the form of nine identical mounted warriors, vanquishes the previously invincible rebel general Yü-wen Hui, along with seven or eight of his stalwarts. Struck with terror at the sight, the entire rebel army takes to its heels, and the imperial train returns to the capital in triumph. The last rebel holdouts who would stand in the way of their entering the city are routed by Ujitada and his phantom assistants as summarily as the main rebel force had been.

Having escaped what seemed certain death at the hands of the rebels, Ujitada is now anxious to return home to his loved ones in Japan. But soon he becomes involved in a love affair with a mysterious lady who comes and goes like the morning clouds on the mountain peak and who will not tell him who she is or where she lives. His heart is torn between two desires: the desire to set sail for home as soon as possible, and the desire to extend his stay in China until he can learn who the lady is. After considerable delay—this fourth part of the tale, with its several dreamlike meetings between Ujitada and the lady, comprises nearly half the tale's length—her identity is revealed as none other than the empress dowager herself, who is in fact not an ordinary mortal, but a lady sent from the Second Heaven of Buddhism to rescue China from disaster. The empress dowager tells Ujitada that he, too, was sent from heaven, to assist her in this charge.

In the final part of the tale, Ujitada returns to Japan to be reunited with his family as well as with the magically reincarnated Princess Hua-yang. They begin a happy life together, and before long the princess is with child. Then, with a hint of stormier times to come as the princess concludes that Ujitada must be seeing another woman (he has been gazing through a magical mirror at the empress dowager, and her perfume has transferred to his robes), the tale breaks off with a note that the rest of the text is missing: "The manuscript states: 'Here, too, the binding is damaged and the remaining pages have been lost.'"[2]

The title of the tale presumably derives from events surrounding Ujitada's departure for China, when his mother arranges for a palace to be built on a mountainside in Matsura (the area of Saga and Nagasaki prefectures in Kyushu today) so that she can await her son's return at the point in Japan closest to China. The word *miya* in the title may refer either to the palace or to the lady who goes to live there, but neither plays any significant role in the story; and though it might well have done so, especially in the long fourth part of the tale, the narrative does not develop or draw on the association between Ujitada's waiting mother and the meaning "to wait" (*matsu*) embedded in the title.[3] We may observe that the title refers to the episode commencing the main action of the tale, but even then we cannot escape the sense that the reference is pointless and the episode undistinguished.[4] The puzzle of how and why *Matsura no*

2. Another lacuna is noted some twelve manuscript pages earlier: "The manuscript states: 'The binding is damaged and some pages are missing.'" The page count is from the Go-Kōgon manuscript. See chapter three for details on the manuscripts and texts.

3. Misumi (1975, 1–3) believes the title is indeed intended to suggest the presence of a lady who waits, but does not discuss how, if at all, the narrative draws upon that suggestion, or how the suggestion otherwise affects our understanding of the tale. Arguing by analogy with *Hamamatsu Chūnagon monogatari* ("Tale of the Hamamatsu Middle Counselor," ca. 1060s), which in its alternate title of *Mitsu no hamamatsu* ("Waiting by the Pines on Mitsu Beach"—if *matsu* is rendered in both of its meanings, "pine" and "to wait") undoubtedly refers to a lady who waits, Misumi asserts that naming tales after someone other than the hero or heroine was an accepted practice. The analogy misses the mark, however, for Ujitada's mother has almost no role at all, while Taishō no Kimi in *Hamamatsu Chūnagon monogatari* plays a prominent role throughout. In an apparent attempt to satisfy those who would insist on a title referring to the main character, Misumi also stretches for a way to construe "Matsura no Miya" as an indirect reference to Ujitada himself, but in this, too, the analogy he draws with *Mitsu no hamamatsu* is too loose to persuade.

Nishiki (1988, 139–40) observes that all of the ladies in Ujitada's life must wait for him in one sense or another, and, by contrasting the experiences of the various ladies, attempts to find a special thematic place for Ujitada's mother's waiting, such as to justify a title reference to her. There are a number of problems with the reading he provides, but most fundamental among them are that he cannot alter the utterly minor role Ujitada's mother plays in the narrative, and that he does not explain the failure of the narrative itself to draw on an association between her (or any of the other women who wait) and the title.

4. The title seems tangential even by comparison to *Utsuho monogatari* ("The Tale of the Hollow Tree," ca. 983), which similarly takes its name from a minor episode early in the tale. The episode involving the hollow tree (see Kōno Tama 1959–62, vol. 1, 78ff.; Harada 1969, vol. 1, 47ff.) is one of considerable charm in itself, and it plays an important role not only in introducing the hero of the subsequent action but also in establishing the tale's most important motif—the magical *kin* music and its transmission. In fact, the episode may even be considered a thematic encapsulation of the tale as a whole. Nothing of this kind can be said about the events surrounding Ujitada's departure for China in *Matsura no miya monogatari*.

miya monogatari gained such an opaque title will probably never be satisfactorily explained.

An intriguing four-part colophon is found at the end of all manuscripts of the tale, and reads as follows (I have added letters to permit easier reference to each of the four entries later):

A.   This tale is about events that took place long ago, and, indeed, both the poetry and the language are pleasantly old-fashioned. Beginning with the flight to Mount Shu, however, the text appears to have been revised by some clever fellow of our own age, and contains many unsightly passages. I wonder what the truth of the matter is? And when the grand lady of China speaks of drifting onto the path of dreams—what a charming tale within a tale it is!

[new page]

B.   Jōgan 3, Fourth Month, Eighteenth Day.
     Finished writing [copying] in the western wing of the Somedono Palace.

C.   She seems a flower, but is not; she seems a mist, but is not.
     In the deep of night, she comes; as the heavens dawn, she departs.
     She comes like a spring night's dream, for but a fleeting moment;
     She departs like a morning cloud, leaving no trace to follow.

[blank page]

D.   How true it is! But I am mystified why one so sober of heart—one who preferred not to meet beauty such as can topple cities— would have left such a poem behind him. Or is it that in China a mist like this really does exist?[5]

The date given in entry B, Jōgan 3, corresponds to the year 861 on the Western calendar. If A and B were written by the same hand, that year must be a copy date, and the remarks in A suggest a date of original composition sufficiently earlier that the tale has had time to go through a revision that sets off the language in the early, unrevised part of the tale as distinctly "old fashioned" in contrast to the revised portions, which are written in the idiom of the colophon writer's "own age," ca. 861. The extant version of *Matsura no miya monogatari* then would be roughly contemporary with *Taketori monogatari* ("The Tale of the

5. The manuscript known as "the manuscript in imitation of the copy by Retired Emperor Go-Hanazono" ("Den Go-Hanazono In shinkan mohon") carries the only variant colophon noted by any of the scholars who have pursued the questions associated with the manuscript tradition. In addition to the entries translated here, it bears the dated signatures of two copyists of later centuries. See Hachisuka 1935, 130–31. The reference to Retired Emperor Go-Hanazono in the traditional name for this manuscript is probably an error for Retired Emperor Go-Kōgon. See chapter three.

Bamboo Cutter"), which scholars have placed variously between the early ninth century and the mid-tenth century, and which is called the "progenitor of all tales"—*monogatari no idekihajime no oya*—in the "Eawase" chapter of *Genji monogatari*.[6] The original *Ur-Matsura no miya monogatari* would antedate *Taketori monogatari* by as much as a century, perhaps even a little more.

Alternatively, if entry A is viewed as a later interpolation, 861 can be considered the date of original composition. In that year, the Somedono Palace was the residence of Chancellor Fujiwara Yoshifusa (804–72),[7] and we may imagine that the western wing was occupied by his daughter, Meishi (or Akirakeiko, 829–900), consort of Emperor Montoku (827–58, r. 850–58) and mother of then-reigning Emperor Seiwa (850–80, r. 858–76).[8] The designation of the western wing of the Somedono Palace as the place of writing would therefore suggest that the Somedono Empress (as Meishi was known) or a lady in her service was the author of the manuscript.[9] We might also imagine that Yoshifusa played a sponsoring role, much as Fujiwara Michinaga (966–1027), in a later century, sponsored the literary endeavors of such women as Murasaki Shikibu and Izumi Shikibu, who were in service to his daughter, Shōshi (or Akiko, 988–1074), consort of Emperor Ichijō (980–1011, r. 986–1011). Because so few writings survive from the ninth and early tenth centuries, this view would not substantially change the historical position of the *Ur-Matsura no miya monogatari* in early Japanese literature: the only change would be in its historical

6. Efforts to determine the date of *Taketori monogatari* are complicated by the fact that parts of the tale must have existed in a different form, or perhaps even several different forms, before the tale was written down in its present redaction. Most evidence points to the late ninth century or very early tenth century for the tale as it has come down to the present.

For the relevant passage in *Genji monogatari*, see Abe et al. 1970–76, vol. 2, 370.

7. After crushing rival families vying with the Fujiwara for power at court, Yoshifusa became the first man not of royal blood to serve as chancellor and as regent to the emperor. He established, decisively, the ascendancy of the Fujiwara that was to continue virtually unchallenged for some two centuries.

8. Hagitani 1970, 122, n. 4.

9. Another choice might be to associate the task of writing with Meishi's cousin, Kōshi (or Takaiko, 842–910). With Yoshifusa as her adoptive father, Kōshi apparently was close to Meishi and spent much time with her. In 866, at the age of twenty-four, she became consort to Meishi's son, the sixteen-year-old Emperor Seiwa, and later came to be known as "the Empress from the Second Ward." Her lasting fame, however, comes from a legendary liaison several years earlier—it could well have been around 861, though possibly as much as five years before— with Ariwara Narihira (825–80), undistinguished in rank but one of the most colorful lovers of the Heian court. According to one account, Narihira visited Kōshi at Meishi's residence and on one occasion actually managed to steal her away (*Ise monogatari* ["Tales of Ise," ca. 935], episode 6). When the affair was discovered, Kōshi was placed out of Narihira's reach so as not to further jeopardize Yoshifusa's plans to send her to court once Emperor Seiwa came of age. Although the historicity of the affair remains uncertain, it was given a lasting place in literature by *Kokinshū* (or *Kokin wakashū*, "Collection of Ancient and Modern Poetry," ca. 905), in the headnotes to poems 632 and 747; and by *Ise monogatari*, in episodes 3–6 (episode 4 is cited in chapter two, p. 30), 26, 29, 65, and 76. For a discussion of the affair and a translation of the account given in *Ise monogatari*, see Helen McCullough 1968, 45–49 and the episodes indicated. Also see brief discussion of colophon entry B on pp. 24–25, below.

relationship to *Taketori monogatari*—if a particularly early date for that tale were assumed. On the other hand, the historical position of the extant version of the tale, with two of its three books dating from an indeterminate period after 861, would need to be evaluated quite apart from what is said in colophon entry B.

As anyone familiar with the historical development of classical Japanese fiction will immediately recognize upon reading the tale, the suggestion that *Matsura no miya monogatari* as it is known today might have been completed in or before the year 861 is beyond all credibility. Naive though the tale is in some of its features, it is in the end far too sophisticated a work to have been created in the eighth or ninth century. The reader might wonder momentarily if it perhaps represented a flash of genius far ahead of its time, but he would quickly realize that such a work could not possibly have existed for so many centuries without once being mentioned in any later work. Had the tale really been in circulation since 861 and before, surely it, instead of *Taketori monogatari*, would have been the one called progenitor of the genre by the author of *Genji monogatari*.[10]

Indeed, the earliest mention of the tale in any secondary source is found in *Mumyōzōshi* ("Untitled Leaves," ca. 1201), the first work of criticism to survey and discuss methodically, if impressionistically, the *monogatari* of the Heian period (794–1185) and the opening years of the Kamakura period (1185–1333). This work has long been placed by modern scholars at the turn of the thirteenth century, between 1196 and 1202; in a relatively recent study, Higuchi Yoshimaro has narrowed the span convincingly to between 1198 and 1201, and with some caution to a period of one year and several months running from 1200 to 1201.[11] Scholars agree that the work was written by someone close to Fujiwara Shunzei (1114–1204) and his son Teika (1162–1241), and although some doubt remains, the likeliest candidate is the lady known as Shunzei's Daughter (ca. 1171–after 1252)—in fact Shunzei's granddaughter, brought up in her grandparents' care from a young age.[12]

10. Readers familiar with *Genji monogatari* will recall that the reference to *Taketori monogatari* as "progenitor of all tales" appears in the context of a picture contest in which illustrations of different tales are pitted one against another (see Abe et al. 1970–76, vol. 2, 370–72; Seidensticker 1976, 311–13). Whether we imagine *Matsura no miya monogatari* matched in such a contest with *Utsuho monogatari*, to compare an older and newer treatment of a similar plot and bring out the strengths of each, or matched with *Taketori monogatari*, to compare two older works of very different plots, *Matsura no miya monogatari* would in either case have to be the one given the distinction of "progenitor"—if any work be given it at all.

    It is often emphasized (e.g., Nakano 1969; Akiyama et al. 1975, 107) that the remark about *Taketori monogatari* as progenitor appears in a contest between a tale of long ago and a tale that is more or less contemporary, and in this context should not be taken as literal truth. Murasaki Shikibu could not have had precise records indicating the dates of composition of the various early tales circulating among court circles in her day. Her characterization of *Taketori monogatari* is better taken as a critical statement (that the tale was the best—the most accomplished, impressive, and memorable—of the early tales) rather than a historical one (that the tale was necessarily the very first tale).

11. Higuchi 1970.iv, 81–88.

12. Although some doubt remains, for the sake of convenience I will refer to the author of *Mumyōzōshi* using feminine pronouns.

The passage of interest in *Mumyōzōshi* reads as follows:

> As for all those tales that have been appearing one after another in recent years, although some of them do seem to improve on earlier tales in style and form, it is not possible to find any that compares to *Nezame, Sagoromo,* or *Hamamatsu.* In *Ukinami,* written by Takanobu, one is moved to a certain extent by the obvious effort and feeling the author has put into the writing, but the style is so awkward that one cannot really enjoy reading the story. The several works written by Minor Captain Teika are nothing but empty forms, lacking any semblance of reality. The only exception is the tale known as *Matsura no miya*: this tale is in the style of *Man'yōshū* and reminds one of *Utsuho*; it is beyond anything a simpleminded person could have imagined.[13]

Mumyōzōshi is generally considered a reliable testament for such matters as are stated unambiguously in its pages,[14] and there is no ambiguity here with regard to the approximate date its author assigns the tale. The passage cited, speaking of numerous tales from "recent years" (*konogoro idekitaru mono amata*), is itself part of a more extended discussion of tales belonging to the late Heian period. "Recent" is an elastic term, of course, but even in a survey of tales spanning several centuries, we would not normally expect it to extend beyond four or five decades. The other tale mentioned here, *Ukinami* by Fujiwara Takanobu (1142–1205, half brother of Teika), has been dated between 1160 and 1180.[15] The absence of a consistent chronological order for the tales discussed before and after this passage prevents the immediate conclusion that *Matsura no miya monogatari* must have appeared after these dates, but they can be taken as a rough measure of what the author of *Mumyōzōshi* meant by "recent years." In any case, it is quite clear that she lends no credence to the colophon date, for if she did, she would have discussed the tale in an altogether different section of her work, and would more likely have noted that *Utsuho monogatari* ("Tale of the Hollow Tree," ca. 983) was reminiscent of *Matsura no miya*

13. Or, "it seems beyond the comprehension of a simpleminded reader (like myself)." Likewise, "nothing but empty forms" (*keshiki-bakari*) could be "nothing but atmosphere or flights of fancy," or perhaps merely a reference to the brevity and insubstantiality of the stories.

   The two ascriptions, *tsukuritaru tote*, might more literally be rendered as "said to be written by," which potentially suggests uncertainty; but *tote*, like the modern *to iu*, often indicates indirect knowledge on which no doubt is to be cast, and given the discussion below a straightforward "written by" seems to be the appropriate translation here.

   There are other ambiguities in the passage as well. See Kuwabara 1976, 97–98; Tomikura 1954, 248–50; Marra 1984, 418; Keene 1989, 4. Translations are my own unless indicated otherwise.

14. For example, to my knowledge no one has questioned the accuracy of the ascription of *Ukinami* to Fujiwara Takanobu. Ishida (1940, 66–67) expresses his confidence in *Mumyōzōshi* directly, saying it "does not seem at present to be a document whose word must be doubted." Additionally, the general consensus that *Mumyōzōshi* was written by Shunzei's Daughter or by someone else close to Teika and Shunzei tends to instill even greater faith in its reliability for matters relating to Teika, since for such matters, presumably, whoever the author may be, his or her remarks are based on firsthand knowledge.

15. Higuchi 1970.ii, 21.

monogatari rather than vice versa. At the same time, the very mention of *Matsura no miya monogatari* in this passage provides the same terminus ad quem for the tale as for *Mumyōzōshi*, namely 1201.[16]

In searching through the sources scholars have found no further secondary reference explicitly addressing the date of the tale, but the absence of any other secondary mention before *Mumyōzōshi*, coupled with the relatively regular (though not frequent) mention thereafter, serves as strong corroboration of a late twelfth-century date. The date is also supported by a wide assortment of internal evidence, ranging from individual linguistic items, to general historical features, to poetic allusions and other textual precedents dating from the tenth through twelfth centuries.[17] So as not to overburden and delay the present discussion, a summary of all such evidence pertaining to the date of the tale has been placed in appendix A.

While the ascription of the tale to the hand of Fujiwara Teika found in this same passage of *Mumyōzōshi* would seem in itself to confirm a late twelfth-century date, a slight linguistic ambiguity in the passage, more pronounced in the original than in the translation given above, long left the door open for scholars to question that an ascription to Teika was intended at all: Is *Matsura no miya monogatari* being singled out as the best among "the several works written by Teika," or as a work of unspecified authorship that is the best of all recent works? An article written by Tesaki Masao in 1940, however, presented several observations about the discursive style of *Mumyōzōshi* and argued persuasively that the author must indeed be speaking of *Matsura no miya monogatari* as a product of Teika's hand.[18] The tale is thus one of the few examples of classical fiction for which we possess a contemporary record of authorship.

Having such a record does not immediately assure us of its reliability, however, and scholars of the tale have sought independent confirmation through a variety of means. The most important supporting evidence comes from articles by Ishida Yoshisada and Hagitani Boku, written in 1940 and 1941,

16. The terminus ad quem of 1201 will change little even if it should be determined that certain parts of *Mumyōzōshi* contain later interpolations, since the designation of Fujiwara Teika as a minor captain (*shōshō*) in the passage quoted is one of the primary reasons why 1202 was long given as the terminus ad quem for *Mumyōzōshi*: it was in the intercalary Tenth Month of that year that Teika was promoted to acting middle captain (*gon no chūjō*).

17. See notes to translation, passim.

18. One effect of the ambiguity was to allow the possibility of Teika's authorship to go entirely unremarked, at least in print, until Shida Gishū suggested it in a 1926 article; Edo, Meiji, and Taishō period scholars of the tale had noted only the sentence referring to *Matsura no miya monogatari* and ignored the previous sentence telling of Teika's fiction writing. This is no reason to conclude that the latter reading of the two sentences is the more natural one, however. Neither the tale nor *Mumyōzōshi* had yet received more than perfunctory attention from scholars, within broad historical surveys that went little further than to describe the works and place them in their proper place on the literary chronology. Printed editions existed for both works, but in neither case with any substantial annotation or commentary; so far as I have been able to determine, the first articles to take these works as their particular focus appeared in 1929 (Sugiyama) and 1933 (Sakurai).

See appendix B for a brief outline of Tesaki's argument.

respectively. Hagitani documents the Chinese sources reflected in *Matsura no miya monogatari*, many of which would not have been known to the average Heian courtier, and demonstrates in great detail that Teika was familiar with them—thus establishing with certainty that he indeed *could have* written the tale. He shows also that there is a very close correlation between the Chinese features of the tale and the things Teika found of special interest in his Chinese studies—a correlation so close that it is difficult to imagine it being duplicated by any other man. Ishida focuses upon poetic style, examining the poems in the tale and in Teika's oeuvre for usage of identical or similar expressions, and finds what he believes to be a set of matching "fingerprints" that confirm Teika's authorship even more positively. While many readers have found these arguments persuasive, however, apparent irregularities of method in Ishida's study, together with the essentially circumstantial nature of Hagitani's evidence, have also left room for others to continue questioning the ascription on one ground or another. Some of these grounds for doubt are sufficiently plausible, in fact, that most scholars of the tale still speak of Teika as the possible, or at most probable, author, rather than as confirmed author. As a consequence, *Matsura no miya monogatari* has remained, in effect, an isolated curiosity, worthy of some discussion in and of itself—including how Teika's aesthetic inclinations may (possibly) be reflected in it—but not of sufficiently certain provenance to be treated as an integral part of Teika's literary legacy such as can cast new light on our understanding of his other work.[19]

I first came across the name of *Matsura no miya monogatari* while compiling a bibliography of materials on Teika—which is to say, in effect, that I was introduced to the tale by way of its authorship. Initially, I assumed the ascription to Teika must be like most others I had encountered in my reading of Heian and Kamakura *monogatari*: the evidence would be vague and circumstantial at best, unable to support anything other than speculative claims, perhaps even allowing different scholars starting from the same point to argue in opposite directions. In fact, one of my first decisions when I began this project was not to get

---

19. Although Higuchi Yoshimaro and Misumi Yōichi have both written articles suggesting they fully accept Teika's authorship (Higuchi 1980; Misumi 1974, 1975, 1979), they nevertheless feel compelled to use a more cautious locution in their brief entry on the tale for *Shinpen kokka taikan* (Henshū Iinkai, 1983–87, vol. 5), saying "Fujiwara Teika saku *ka*" ("By Fujiwara Teika?"—my emphasis). Nakano Kōichi (1971a, 260–61) asserts Teika probably was not the author. Nishiki Hitoshi (1988, 136–39) thinks Teika most likely *was* the author, but raises a number of questions about the evidence and asserts that we must stop short of considering the ascription confirmed. Donald Keene (1989, 4) says, "At one time doubts were expressed about his authorship, but no scholar now seriously questions the attribution," but it appears he is merely passing on the judgment of Hagitani 1970. My own dissertation took up the question precisely because a careful survey of the scholarship showed that the matter could not be considered resolved. Ishida Yoshisada, specialist on Teika that he is (Hagitani has not continued to focus on Teika), is the only scholar I know of who has used *Matsura no miya monogatari* as a bona fide source for the study of Teika's poetics (1970, 1979). Others—even those who appear to have accepted Teika's authorship—have felt inhibited from discussing the tale as anything other than an isolated entity, rather than as a work that has bearing on our better understanding of Teika.

caught up in the authorship controversy. Upon surveying the secondary literature, however, I discovered a remarkable convergence of evidence in support of
the ascription—a convergence that struck me as being truly rare, if not altogether unique, for studies of this nature. Further, although the procedural irregularities in Ishida's study prevented it from closing the case as conclusively
as he (and a number of his readers) clearly believed, the premises and the basic
method of the study appeared sound: I thought it quite possible that a careful
review of Ishida's data with a more rigorous and consistent treatment of the
control group would show that the apparent irregularities were merely infelicities of presentation, or that they involved only incidental matters with no
bearing on the essential validity of the main argument. That is to say, here was a
case in which a genuine chance for positive confirmation of the ascription
appeared to exist, unlike other authorship studies I had encountered, and I
found myself drawn in by that tantalizing possibility. Thus it was that I set
about retracing Ishida's steps, carefully evaluating his methods, checking and
updating his evidence, and expanding the control portion of his study so as to
gain a more accurate perspective on the observations he makes regarding
Teika's particular poetic usage.

A summary of my review and expansion of Ishida's work has been placed in
appendix B, along with descriptions of the other principal evidence regarding
authorship of the tale. Here I will state only my conclusion: The review might
well have revealed that fundamental irregularities of method rendered Ishida's
evidence meaningless, but it did not. Though I did indeed dismiss one entire
section of his study, the bulk of his data and argument stood intact, confirming
the essential soundness of his conclusion. On this basis, I would assert that the
case may now be considered closed. When the full range of evidence on both
date and authorship is examined together, there can be little doubt that
scholars' attention would sooner or later have turned to Teika as one of the
possible authors of *Matsura no miya monogatari* even without the testimony of
Mumyōzōshi; with that testimony, we may be as certain of his authorship of
Matsura no miya monogatari as we are of Murasaki Shikibu's authorship of *Genji
monogatari*.

We may now return briefly to the question of date: Since Teika was born in
1162, the terminus a quo for the tale could not be much before 1180; the
terminus ad quem of 1201, established above, remains unaffected. The apparent modeling of the child emperor's flight from the Chinese capital on Emperor
Antoku's flight from the Japanese capital (modern Kyoto) in 1183 narrows the
span slightly.[20] Efforts to pinpoint more exactly the tale's date of composition
based on what is known of Teika's life and literary career have remained in-
conclusive, but most speculations fall within a year or two on either side of
1190. The principal arguments have been summarized in appendix A along
with the other evidence pertaining to the date of the tale.

20. Ishida 1940, 82–83. See translation, p. 98 and n. 95.

Fujiwara Teika

Fujiwara Teika is one of the giants of classical Japanese literature, a figure who has been called "the single most important influence in the entire history of classical poetry."[21] He was heir to the Mikohidari house of poetry, whose preeminence in poetic circles at the end of the twelfth century had been established by his father, Shunzei, following the death of the leading poets of the rival Rokujō house of poetry. It is from this Mikohidari house that the major poetic houses of the remainder of the court-poetry period can be said to have issued. Teika was a leader among the compilers of *Shinkokinshū* ("New Collection of Ancient and Modern Poetry," 1205), the eighth imperial anthology, and was sole compiler of the following one as well, which was given the title *Shinchokusenshū* ("New Imperial Anthology," 1232). He was the first poet to have a role in the compilation of more than one such collection. Although as a young poet, especially in his twenties, he suffered derision from other poets owing to his penchant for innovation and experimentation, after winning the favor of Retired Emperor Go-Toba in *Shōji ninen shodo hyakushu* ("First Hundred-Poem Sequences of the Shōji Era," 1200), he remained for many years at the center of poetic developments both as a poet and a critic: he was a regular participant in poetry contests, often serving as judge, and he wrote several important poetic treatises that set down prescriptions and proscriptions for successful poetic composition, which continued to be cited and followed for generations. Such was Teika's stature and poetic legacy that the fifteenth-century poet Shōtetsu was led to declare, "He who dares cast aspersions upon Teika in the Way of Poetry, may he be denied the protection of the gods and buddhas and condemned to the punishments of hell."[22]

Teika was also an important scholar, editor, and transmitter of prose texts from the Heian period. Most modern editions of *Genji monogatari* are based on manuscripts descended from one copied and edited by Teika, and manuscript lines emanating from a copy made by Teika (*Teika-bon*) exist for numerous other courtly tales and literary diaries. Even where Teika's copies have not been accepted as the best among several available, they provide valuable references for determining more accurately what the original text must have been like. In some cases, notes written by Teika in commentaries or in colophons provide important information about manuscripts and texts, including evidence regarding authorship.

Teika's immense stature within Japanese literature makes it potentially of much greater interest to learn that he wrote a fictional tale than to learn that Takanobu or some otherwise undistinguished aristocrat did, for it adds yet another dimension to a figure who already looms large and complex in our understanding—a dimension that, if fully recognized and studied, could even

---

21. Brower 1981, 447.
22. Hisamatsu and Nishio 1961, 166. Translation adapted from unpublished manuscript of *Shōtetsu monogatari* ("Conversations with Shōtetsu," ca. 1448) by Robert H. Brower.

lead us to alter previous understandings of that figure.[23] Yet, perhaps owing precisely to his great eminence, which makes anything less than a masterpiece seem unworthy of him, even those scholars who for some time have accepted *Matsura no miya monogatari* as a product of his hand have been slow to consider how the tale might shed light upon Teika's life and work as a whole—both his pronouncements upon, and his actual practice in, the composition of poetry—and in turn upon the poetics of the late Heian and early Kamakura age. Although a full discussion of such questions is beyond the scope of the present work, it is worth noting three points in particular where our understandings may be altered once scholars of Teika and midclassical poetry begin treating *Matsura no miya monogatari* as an integral part of Teika's oeuvre.

Early in his career, Teika was something of a controversial figure. He was an innovator, and some of his poetry was sufficiently unconventional to earn the label of *darumauta*, "poems like Zen gibberish,"[24] from other poets, who found them incomprehensible. In time, Teika's experiments yielded to what may be described as more traditional and conventional compositions, though still colored by techniques he had gained in his experimental period. Among the fruits of the period was the aesthetic of *yōen*—"ethereal beauty" or "ethereal charm"[25]—the origins of which have been traced to Chinese poetry.[26] As discussed in chapter two, the qualities of this particular ideal of beauty are quite prominent in *Matsura no miya monogatari*. Although it is not possible at present to determine which came first in Teika's work, *yōen* in his poetry or *yōen* in his tale, a connection between the two must be assumed. Studies taking full account of the place of *Matsura no miya monogatari* in Teika's literary development could well alter our understanding of how the aesthetic of *yōen* evolved and changed in late twelfth-century Japan.[27]

A second point relates to Teika's views on the technique of *honkadori*, "allusive variation," in which a poet makes reference to an earlier poem or poems in such a way that the meaning of the new poem expands to include the older poem(s). This technique saw its greatest development in the time of Shunzei and Teika, and several statements of how the technique should be used are found in Teika's poetic treatises.[28] Among the rules he sets down for

---

23. The discovery, in 1940, of the diary *Towazugatari* ("Confessions of Lady Nijo," 1313), written by one of Emperor Go-Fukakusa's consorts, offers an example to contrast with Teika. Lady Nijo was previously unknown as a literary figure, and even now is known only for (and by) her composition of this single work.

24. Brower 1978, 18.

25. Brower 1978, 18.

26. Konishi 1953 provides a useful discussion of these origins, finding them in qualities of late T'ang poetry considerably broader than those generally associated with Chinese usage of the term *yao-yen* (*yōen*).

27. The discussion in chapter two is concerned with how *yōen* works within the tale, and does not venture into considerations of the relationship between the *yōen* in the tale and in Teika's poetry—though see chapter two, n. 77. Ishida 1979 engages to some degree with the latter question.

28. The most detailed statement is in his *Maigetsushō* ("Monthly Notes," ca. 1213–19). See Fujihira 1975b, 522–24; Brower 1985, 417–19 and n. 56.

honkadori is the following, found in his *Kindai shūka* ("Superior Poems of Our Time," ca. 1209):

> Next, with regard to poems by one's fellow poets, even if they are no longer living, if they have been composed so recently that they might be said to have been written yesterday or today, I think it essential to avoid using any part of such a poem, even a single line, that is distinctive enough to be recognized as the work of a particular poet.[29]

These statements notwithstanding, some of the evidence offered in support of Teika's authorship appears to indicate that he was quite willing to use lines from *Matsura no miya monogatari* in his compositions, either in the form of direct borrowing of language, or as the basis for allusive variation.[30] If this is indeed the case, then it would seem to indicate a gap between his prescription and practice, or at least that he viewed the rule considerably more flexibly than many scholars believe.[31] A complete investigation of this apparent disjunction between theory and practice, including an effort to distinguish more carefully among the many different ways in which a poet might draw upon an earlier poem or prose text, could well alter our understanding of the statements Teika makes on the subject of *honkadori* in his treatises.

The third point lies in the qualities that have led scholars to describe many of Teika's poems as *monogatari-teki*, "talelike," meaning not that they are narrative poems embodying a brief story in themselves, but rather that they have dramatic qualities—like poems composed, say, between lovers in a romance. Such poems in one way or another suggest that they are part of a complex circumstance, drawing upon that circumstance and interacting with it. The precise nature of the qualities Japanese scholars are referring to when they use this label remains to be fully and clearly articulated. But if Teika experimented with romantic fiction in his youth, it is reasonable to assume that the qualities of his poems that have been labeled *monogatari-teki* are in some way related to those experiments. This is another area where previously held views could be altered by studies that treat *Matsura no miya monogatari* as a wholly legitimate source for studying the development of Teika's poetics.[32]

29. As translated in Brower and Miner 1967, 45–46. The original text may be found in Fujihira 1975a, 472.
30. Possibly it is the other way around in some cases—i.e., Teika appropriated lines from his already published compositions when he wrote the tale—but it seems less likely. See appendix B, p. 187.
31. If we assume that Shōtetsu knew Teika had written *Matsura no miya monogatari*—not an improbable assumption when considered that he was trained by Teika's poetic heirs—or that he at least knew its approximate date, it would appear that he viewed Teika's rule on *honkadori* more flexibly than such modern scholars as Ishida Yoshisada (see appendix B, p. 186) and Nakano Kōichi (see appendix B, pp. 190–91). In *Shōtetsu monogatari*, far from assuming that Teika would not have drawn on a contemporary tale for his own compositions, Shōtetsu pointedly calls our attention to how he did indeed do so—by citing two poems Teika wrote based on *Matsura no miya monogatari*. See Hisamatsu and Nishio 1961, 211–12.
32. Ishida 1970 touches on this issue to some extent.

Some Features of the Tale

In spite of earning special attention from the author of *Mumyōzōshi* in a manner that suggests it was the best among Teika's works of fiction, *Matsura no miya monogatari* cannot be considered a resounding success. Perhaps the greatest problem lies in its fragmentary character. The three women Ujitada loves each occupy a different portion of the tale, without interaction and with virtually no interplay even in Ujitada's mind; each love effectively comes to a full stop before the next begins, and, in spite of the intensity of the passion attributed to Ujitada while he is with each woman, only in two or three instances does he think of her later. By the time the women are finally brought together, after a fashion, at the end of the tale, the story is in rapid decline, with obvious signs that Teika has lost interest in it. The introduction of a military tale into the middle of it all further fragments the work, as do the various political discussions interspersed distractingly amongst the otherwise highly romantic developments of the long, fourth part of the tale (see below). Although some scholars have attempted to interpret the tale as a more coherent whole by viewing the fragments as deliberately contrastive modules of a larger conceptual unity, none is very persuasive, and in fact the very diversity of interpretations advanced serves rather to underscore the tale's failure as a unified and coherent work of art.[33]

The tale nevertheless has a number of interesting features that set it apart from other fictional works of the Heian and early Kamakura periods. One of these is the extensive use Teika makes of imagery associated with his poetic ideal of *yōen*, a subject that is treated at length in chapter two. Several others may be mentioned more briefly here.

Given the genre to which the tale belongs, the most immediately obvious feature of interest is the military episode at the center of the tale. *Monogatari* of the Heian period had been strictly a courtly genre focusing on the elegant lives of noblemen and women at or near the pinnacle of the aristocratic society of the time.[34] Although many of the principal male characters appearing in them had military titles, they were never depicted in military roles. Among extant tales only two early cases can be found where military activities are mentioned at all: in *Taketori monogatari*, two thousand guardsmen are sent by the emperor to the bamboo cutter's house to prevent the heroine, Kaguyahime, from being taken back to the moon; and in the first chapter of *Utsuho monogatari*, the presence of

---

33. See Sasaki 1940; Hagitani 1969; Misumi 1974, 1975; and Nishiki 1988 for interpretations attempting to see coherence. Ishii Yukio 1977 and Toyoshima 1980 are not persuaded. Kikuchi 1981 states his concurrence with Ishii, but then develops a reading of his own that could be considered one of the former group.

34. Here as elsewhere in this volume, I use *monogatari* in the conventional manner, to mean the group of tales that are sometimes called, more specifically, *tsukuri-monogatari* (fictional tales), to distinguish them from other genres of prose writings that are of varying degrees of fictionality: *uta-monogatari* (poem tales), *gunki-monogatari* (military tales), *setsuwa* (legendary and anecdotal tales, often exemplary), and *nikki* (diaries).

armies in nearby mountains is given as reason for Toshikage's daughter to take out the magical *kin* that can be played only in times of supreme happiness or extreme distress. In neither of these cases are individual military men or their actions actually depicted, and in the latter case the armies mentioned do not even appear on the scene. Individual men of military character as well as military incidents of various kinds did appear in legendary or anecdotal tales (*setsuwa*) and military chronicles from at least the tenth century onward, and in the middle of the twelfth century the rising fortunes of the provincial military clans gave rise also to a new genre of literature that has come to be called *gunki-monogatari*, or military tale. Until *Matsura no miya monogatari*, however, these forms of writing remained entirely distinct from the mainstream of *monogatari* literature, the tale of aristocratic elegance and love.

The military tales of the twelfth century chronicled true historical events, recounting clashes between vast armies as well as combat between individual warriors. In some cases there are glimpses into the private lives of the warriors as well, adding dimension to the characters, and in such scenes these tales take on some of the romantic conventions of the courtly tale. Both in battle scenes and in more private episodes, fiction is frequently mixed with fact, but in plot outline the narratives provide a roughly accurate accounting of the turbulent events that changed the political face of Japan.

By contrast, *Matsura no miya monogatari* is a purely fictional tale that begins in the conventional manner of the elegant love-tale, and it is into the middle of such a work that Teika merges a segment of narrative essentially equivalent to the military tale—except that in this case the military events are also purely fictional. The character of Ujitada, son of a major counselor and a princess of the blood, is introduced and developed in the manner we would expect for *mono-gatari* heroes: as a prodigy of all the most refined aristocratic accomplishments but without a hint of any martial skills. Yet, with the help of supernatural inter-vention, he is made into a military hero who saves the Chinese dynasty from over-throw by rebel armies. The combination is unprecedented, and it may be seen as a precursor of the much increased presence of military men in the *giko-monogatari* ("pseudoclassical tales" or "tales after the manner of the tales of old") of the thirteenth century—a presence undoubtedly reflecting the changed times and the expanded influence military matters had on the lives of the aristocracy.

This is not to suggest that *Matsura no miya monogatari* affirms the new ascendancy of the military classes, for in fact the story depicts military men of all ranks and loyalties as useless cowards. The one fearless exception is the rebel general Yü-wen Hui, and he, of course, is even worse than a coward—a traitor. It is the paragon of aristocratic virtue, Ujitada, who saves the day, in spite of his total lack of military training or experience—thanks to supernatural assistance. When all of this is set against the historical events taking place in Japan around the time the tale was written, it looms like a wishful fantasy: a wish that someone or something would come forth to reverse the tide of the times and return to the aristocracy the power and prestige that rightfully belonged to it. Such sentiments indeed were held and kept alive among certain members of the court well into the thirteenth century, and resulted in an abortive attempt by former emperor Go-Toba to overthrow the Kamakura regime in 1221.[35] Though Teika is known to have opposed Go-Toba's plans, or at least declared himself indifferent to them,[36] this does not rule out the possibility that he once may have engaged in similar wishful thinking—at a younger age, and at a time closer to the disturbances that so clearly marked the loss of aristocratic prestige.[37]

Also unusual for a courtly tale are the repeated glimpses we receive of the sovereign's daily audiences in which the business of government is conducted—scenes more reminiscent of episodes in the Chinese dynastic histories in which the emperor is advised or remonstrated with than of anything found in prior works of fiction. Both the emperor who first welcomes Ujitada to Ch'ang-an and the empress dowager who rules in the name of her infant son after the first emperor's death appear in such scenes, seeking and responding to the advice of their counselors. Specific policy actions are mentioned, and historical precedents are cited in support of decisions made. None of these scenes go on at great length, or turn into full-scale treatises on good government, but from their cumulative effect the empress dowager emerges as an enlightened and benevolent ruler, fit to be ranked with the sage emperors of old. In this, too, one senses Teika's longing for a more stable age, free of the upheavals caused by powerful and ruthless men whose only concern is their own self-interest.[38]

To judge from *Taketori monogatari*, *Utsuho monogatari* (especially the first chapter), and what is known of other tales that no longer survive, at one time many *monogatari* were built on supernatural premises.[39] From the late tenth century onward, however, including the bulk of *Utsuho monogatari*, the *monogatari*

---

35. In the Shōkyū War of 1221, members of the imperial court led by Go-Toba attempted to dislodge the Kamakura shogunate from power by taking advantage of discord within the shogunate that had persisted since Minamoto Yoritomo's death in 1199. See Ishii Susumu 1974, mainly pp. 348–92; also William McCullough 1964 and 1968.

36. Tsuji 1977, 94–99.

37. In spite of the resemblances between Emperor Antoku's flight from the Japanese capital in 1183 and the Chinese emperor's similar flight in the tale, the uniformly uncomplimentary treatment of military men on both sides of the Chinese conflict prevent the conclusion that Teika intended direct parallels between the Heike and the loyalists on the one hand, and the Genji and the rebels on the other, and was thus taking sides in the Genpei War—i.e., expressing his regrets over the Heike defeat.

38. Imai (1954, 20–21) speaks in very general terms of the military and political matter in the tale as an expression of Teika's dissatisfaction with the state of the imperial court and the turn of recent events.

39. An often cited source in this regard is the preface of Minamoto Tamenori's (d. 1011) *Sanbō ekotoba* ("The Three Jewels," 984), which states: "[*Monogatari*] attribute speech to trees and plants, mountains and rivers, birds and beasts, fish and insects that cannot speak; they invest

was a fundamentally realistic genre, with intrusions of the fantastic or incredible occurring rarely. When such intrusions did occur, as in the events surrounding Prince Genji's move from Suma to Akashi, or the descent from heaven of Amewakahiko in the opening chapter of *Sagoromo monogatari* ("The Tale of Sagoromo," ca. 1070s), they generally required only a momentary suspension of disbelief, on the order of the unlikely coincidences found in many novels of our own day, before returning to wholly believable sequences of events. Even some of the elements that might seem unrealistic to a modern reader, such as the spirit possessions in *Genji monogatari* or the role that dreams and reincarnation play in *Hamamatsu Chūnagon monogatari* ("Tale of the Hamamatsu Middle Counselor," ca. 1060s), were probably accepted by contemporary readers as representative of the real world, and therefore believable.[40]

Once past its opening section, *Matsura no miya monogatari* breaks sharply away from this realistic tradition, with a plot that is built almost entirely upon supernatural premises. The circumstances of Ujitada's zither lessons with Princess Hua-yang are linked repeatedly to otherworldly powers, both by the old zither player who directs Ujitada to the princess, and by the princess herself. Excessive idealizations of the characters notwithstanding, the lesson scenes may have been within the realm of believability for contemporary readers, but the manner of the princess's sudden demise, including the release of her zither into the sky, must have gone beyond. The military episode that comes next begins realistically enough, but then rises to its fantastic climax involving phantom warriors, and it ultimately becomes clear that this entire episode, as well as the love affair between Ujitada and the mysterious lady that follows, are founded from start to finish on a fantasy quite beyond the belief of even twelfth-century readers. Major portions of the tale do remain verisimilar in detail, like many works of modern day science fiction, but the verisimilitude no longer serves the ends that it did in previous tales: representational, true-to-life portrayal (or, in some cases, parody) of the lives and loves of Heian nobility. *Matsura no miya monogatari* is instead the product of a creative imagination that has consciously turned away from the received tradition of realism in *monogatari*, toward fantasy. This quality of the tale can be seen most clearly in those aspects, discussed in chapter two, relating to the evocation of *yōen*.

Another way in which Teika breaks with what had become a standard practice for writers of *monogatari* is his readily apparent determination to avoid

unfeeling objects with human feelings and ramble on and on with meaningless phrases like so much flotsam in the sea. . . . [They] depict relations between men and women just as if they were so many flowers or butterflies. . . ." (Kamens 1988, 93). Ogi (1973, 6–7) concludes from this passage, and from what little is known of tales now lost, that many of the tales written before the last two decades of the tenth century were juvenile fairy tales, fables, stories of marvelous princesses from Immortal Mountain, and the like.

40. For possession, see William McCullough 1973 and Bowring 1982, 51–57. For dreams, see introduction to Rohlich 1983, passim, and Saigō 1972.

imitating *Genji monogatari* as other writers of the eleventh and twelfth centuries had done. Since he nevertheless drew heavily on two major tales for his central plot elements, *Utsuho monogatari* and *Hamamatsu Chūnagon monogatari*, he cannot have objected to the practice of imitating earlier works in itself.[41] In fact, quite the contrary, so open and unabashed is his borrowing from these two tales—in some cases following details found in them so closely that we can only imagine he had the works spread open before him as he wrote—one even wonders if he thought of his father's poetic dictum, "old words, new heart," as applying equally to fiction: a writer was *supposed* to build his tale on foundation stones taken from the fiction and poetry of the past.[42] *Genji monogatari*, however, had already been imitated repeatedly, and Teika may well have felt it had been overworked as a source of foundation stones.[43]

On the other hand, it is quite obvious, too, that Teika's selection of sources reflects the same turn toward fantasy, and away from realism, described above. His borrowing from *Utsuho monogatari* comes from its most fantastic section, which tells of Toshikage's sojourn in the marvelous land of Hashi where almost nothing bears even the remotest resemblance to the real world. His borrowing from *Hamamatsu Chūnagon monogatari* comes from one of its most highly romantic episodes involving the Hoyang Consort, which, though essentially realistic, contains an element of mystery that lends it to being transformed into something akin to a Chinese *ch'uan-ch'i* (tale of the supernatural). While in the latter case nothing dictates that the story materials *must* be shaped into a fantasy, the germ is there, and given the nature of the tale that he created, one can little

41. With regard to borrowing from *Utsuho monogatari*, see notes to the translation 4, 60, 87, and 89; for borrowing from *Hamamatsu Chūnagon monogatari*, see notes 48, 50, 62, 65, 68, 69, 71, 78, 148, and 182.

42. Rohlich (1983, 16–17) notes in his discussion of what *Mumyōzōshi* has to say about *Hamamatsu Chūnagon monogatari* that implicit praise is directed at scenes and situations representing familiar, well-known patterns. Rohlich's discussion is concerned mainly with individual scenes and character types rather than with broader plot structures, but the same must have held true to some extent for the latter as well. At the very least, to judge from the kinds of tales written, as well as from the nature of their treatment in *Mumyōzōshi*—i.e., no negative remarks about their borrowing from *Genji monogatari*—it seems doubtful that readers of the time disapproved of the imitative qualities of late-Heian tales as much as moderns do. Novelty was not a condition of *monogatari* to the extent it has become for modern fiction. Readers were more interested in variations on familiar themes than in altogether new themes.

Kuge 1981 provides a brief but interesting discussion of various ways in which the medieval writers of *giko-monogatari* quite unabashedly borrowed from earlier tales (*monogatari-tori*)—always adding something of their own in a manner at least partially paralleling the technique of *honkadori* in poetry.

43. On a more local level, several scenes in the tale contain allusions and descriptions echoing *Genji monogatari*. For example, see translation notes 33, 69, 143, 152, 154, and 175, as well as Hagitani 1970, passim. Where such echoes served his purpose, Teika did not go out of his way to avoid the influence of *Genji monogatari* altogether. However, the manner in which he drew on *Genji monogatari* is wholly different from his imitation of the other tales, as well as from other authors' imitations of *Genji monogatari*.

doubt that that germ is what caught Teika's imagination. Teika's other sources reflect the same inclination toward the fantastic and otherworldly, from "Kao-t'ang fu," which provides a constant allusive refrain and plays a significant role in shaping the narrative throughout the latter part of the tale, to poems, tales, and legends that receive only passing reference or allusion, such as *The Tale of the Magic Cape*, the story of Princess Lung-yü, and Po Chü-i's "Lady Li." *Genji monogatari*, as not only the greatest but the most realistic of tales, was the logical model for writers of the late Heian wishing to create stories about true-to-life characters in true-to-life situations, but it was not so for an author more interested in fantasy than realism.[44]

Finally, the tale's unusual ending—the lacunae and the colophon—requires a few remarks. The time of the tale, set at the turn of the eighth century, and the heavy use of Man'yō diction, especially in the poetry in book one, reveal clearly that Teika was attempting, in effect, to forge an ancient tale; and we can see just as clearly that the colophon belongs to the same artifice. Of course, a counterfeit colophon is not strictly necessary for a forgery: the success of the forgery actually rides on consistent adherence to an appropriate time frame for everything included in the story, from material descriptions, to historical references and language. On the other hand, a counterfeit colophon can assist the forgery by pointing the reader in the desired direction, or by stating a specific date of composition that is consistent with what is suggested by the story itself.

Though we can never know how much, if any, of the present colophon was part of Teika's original plan, scholars have enjoyed speculating on the matter. Since most scholars think of the shift in style from Man'yō diction to a more contemporary (i.e., late-Heian) idiom near the end of book one as an abandonment of initial intent, most of them likewise see the colophon as an invention necessitated by that abandonment. That is to say, they view entry A, which notes the style shift and suggests that the work has been revised by a contemporary hand, as having been conceived to cover up Teika's inability to sustain the archaic style through the entire work.[45] Regardless of when or why Teika conceived of this contrivance, however, what we have in the first entry of the colophon is an attempt to fabricate a textual history for the tale—attributing the current state of the tale to changes made during a centuries-long transmission of the manuscript.

Even if the style shift is seen as largely involuntary, a counterfeit colophon is not strictly necessary. Teika could have left it to the reader to devise an explanation for the stylistic inconsistency. But if he had originally set out

---

44. For "Kao-t'ang fu," see notes to the translation 139, 153, 157, 158, and 170; for *The Tale of the Magic Cape*, n. 142; for Princess Lung-yü, n. 132; and for "Lady Li," n. 211.
45. Thought of in this way, entry B may have been of late conception as well, since the unplanned mixing of two styles would have suddenly increased the need—or perceived need—to support the forgery with an explicitly stated, counterfeit date.

intending the entire tale to be in an archaic, Man'yō style, and was feeling somewhat chagrined at having to change his plan—whether because of particular lapses he had noticed, because it was more generally failing to live up to his expectations, or because it had simply become too much trouble—one can understand why he might have wanted to provide his own explanation or excuse.[46]

At this point it will be useful to pause for a closer look at the lacunae before proceeding with the colophon. With proof that the colophon is false, and that the tale was actually written around 1190, we may be certain that the lacunae are also counterfeit. Our suspicions would have been aroused in any case because the lacunae are so utterly benign. Instead of leaving the reader hanging in midsentence or midscene, as one would expect if the binding had broken and pages fallen out, the lacunae come conveniently at the end of sentences, and at logical stopping points for the scenes leading up to them. Nothing really seems to be lacking: the only indications of anything amiss in the text are the two double glosses announcing the lacunae themselves; take them out, and the reader would read on with no sense of anything lost (in the first instance), or close the book thinking he had reached the end of the tale (in the second).

The narrative between the two lacunae is obviously hurried and perfunctory, as if Teika had tired of the story and wanted to finish it up as quickly as possible. Some have asserted that the lacunae fit the same temper: they allowed Teika to dispense with material he would otherwise have had to include. If this were so, however, we would expect to find some obvious gaps in the narrative.

---

46. Though I am inclined to believe the colophon was conceived out of necessity following an involuntary style shift, it remains possible that the style shift and fictitious textual history were in fact part of Teika's plan from the beginning.

Hagitani 1969, for example, argues that Teika was using the tale as a backdrop for experimentation with three different styles of poetry—of the Man'yō period (eighth century and before), the Kokin period (ninth to early tenth centuries), and the Shinkokin period (around the turn of the twelfth century)—and attempts to divide the tale into three distinct sections accordingly. Misumi 1975 quite clearly accepts this view, and Keene 1989 appears to find it plausible. I remain unpersuaded. The chart Hagitani provides shows substantial intermixing of styles between sections, making it difficult to see them as all that distinct (though the first shift is relatively clear—from Man'yō to "contemporary" idiom); and even the vague divisions that can be discerned do not occur at the breaks between books or at other logical points in the narrative, as we would expect if any such systematic experimentation were the aim. Further, under such a plan one would expect entry A to suggest a more complex history for the text, speaking not of a single "clever fellow of our own age" but of several "later copyists."

The shift from Man'yō to contemporary idiom could, by itself, still be viewed as part of an original master plan to forge an ancient tale with a history of revision. In this case, too, however, we would expect the shift to occur in a more logical place. This depends to some extent on the nature of the revision we imagine, of course. But Teika's handling of the lacunae (discussed below) shows that his narrative contrivances remained on a relatively naive and simple level.

Perhaps, for example, we would suddenly find the action of the story returned to Japan without having been told of the return journey, and then there would be a fragmentary reference or two to a poem that was composed or an event that occurred on that journey. Since the story has no such gaps, it is inappropriate to think of the lacunae as helping to speed the end of the story. That task is accomplished entirely by the hurried section of narrative found between the two lacunae, which very efficiently gets Ujitada home, picks up the loose ends left by his previous relationships, and ties them up in the open ended way so often favored among Japanese writers old and new—not with a clear resolution, but with a hint of trials to come. As already stated, if no lacuna had been noted to make the reader think that there was originally more to the tale, he would little doubt that this was the intended ending—even if he found it a bit too hasty and perfunctory in manner to be really satisfying.[47]

Most likely, then, the lacunae were conceived to work together with the colophon in providing a sense of history for the tale: a manuscript is not only likely to be *revised* in the course of time, it is also likely to be *damaged*, and so the appearance of damage to the manuscript helps to authenticate the antiquity of the story by showing the effects of a long transmission. In this case, the sense of history is further enhanced by indications that the present copy of the tale is already at least two manuscript generations removed from the one to which the damage occurred: *"The manuscript states*: 'The binding is damaged . . .'" (my emphasis).

There is, in fact, a small problem: the damage occurs in the part of the tale that is said to have been recently revised. On the one hand, we would normally expect that anyone spending the time and effort to revise a tale would also mend any damage he discovered; no matter how ancient the tale, it should not show the ravages of time in this way if it had been just recently revised. On the other hand, if we are to believe that the manuscript has already been damaged after recent revision, then the damage does not serve to authenticate the tale's antiquity and long transmission. These internal contradictions ultimately prevent the lacunae from assisting the colophon in the intended manner, and instead help tip Teika's hand of contrivances. Even so, there can be little doubt of the intent: the lacunae were to join the colophon in creating the impression that the text had a long history of transmission.

We may now return to the colophon. As a rule, the colophons found at the end of *monogatari* manuscripts of this period are entries placed there not by the author, but by later readers or copyists, responding in some way to the tale or recording bibliographical information about its provenance and transmission. Entry A has precisely such an appearance. It declares the antiquity of the tale in a general way, and points out the shift in style from which it infers recent

---

47. It is therefore also inappropriate to call the tale unfinished, as Keene (1989, 4) does. Teika did not simply abandon the story when he tired of it; he stayed with it long enough to complete the circle of Ujitada's journey and to establish this open-ended conclusion.

revision. It is to be taken as a note added by a late reader in the space that happened to be available in the manuscript between the end of the tale and entry B.

Entry B, we are apparently to believe, is the original colophon by the author himself: the date and place of completion. There are difficulties, however, in reconciling this with the final lacuna: how is it that the original colophon has survived while the end of the tale has not? That the manuscript was in book form, which would allow individual pages to fall out, makes this slightly easier to imagine than if it had been in scrolls, but even so it tries one's credulity. Also, since entries of this kind by the author were quite standard for nonfiction but not for fiction, one wonders if it might not potentially be seen as a source of suspicion instead of as confirmation of the tale's antiquity. Perhaps, then, entry B should be taken as coming from the hand of a copyist rather than of the original author. Whatever the case may be, there can be no doubt that the intent of this entry was to certify a very early date for the tale.[48]

Why the year 861, and why Somedono? We cannot be certain of the answer, but the date and place are both associated with Ariwara Narihira's legendary, forbidden love affair with the future imperial consort, Fujiwara Kōshi (or Takai-ko, 842–910)—including the famous episode in which Narihira returns to the place where he had met with her the previous year, to gaze at the moon and think of the lady who has now disappeared. The parallels between this affair and the affair of Ujitada with the mysterious lady—a forbidden love with a lady "from above the clouds," and repeated disappearances of that lady, which leave Ujitada gazing forlornly at the moon—may be only very loose, but one imagines they must have had something to do with Teika's choice of date and place.[49] At the same time, given the repeated emphasis on benevolent rule found in the

48. This is obviously true even if 861 is viewed as a copy date, by which time the tale had already been damaged and revised—as I suggested in first introducing the colophon. Blatant internal contradictions—especially poetic influences and allusions that any reasonably well-versed reader would have recognized as belonging to a much later age—make it impossible to believe that Teika intended it to be taken that way, however. By contrast, the difficulties with viewing entry B as giving the original date of the tale are of a kind easily overlooked; in fact, it is quite possible that Teika himself overlooked them, and was unaware (at least initially) of the contradictions he had introduced between the lacunae and the colophon.

49. See n. 9, above, regarding Narihira's affair with Kōshi (for the date, the association is only approximate). Also see chapter two, p. 30, for the famous episode here mentioned. Narihira's implicit questioning of reality in his poem—which allows Brower and Miner (1961, 193) to offer a different translation that begins with the line "What now is real?"—provides an additional parallel with Ujitada's confusion between dream and reality. The appropriateness of associating Ujitada with Narihira is further heightened when we note that perhaps the next most famous story about him, found in episode 69 of *Ise Monogatari*, is also one involving a forbidden love, and contains another much celebrated exchange of poems centering on confusion between sleeping and waking, dream and reality. See Fukui Teisuke 1972; Helen McCullough 1968, 115–17.

portrayal of the empress dowager, the idea that the Jōgan eras of both China (627–49) and Japan (859–76) were times of prosperity and order brought by wise government—in the Japanese case, under the leadership of Chancellor Yoshifusa—must also have played a role in determining the date and place indicated in entry B.

Since neither entry C nor entry D addresses itself to the antiquity of the tale, or otherwise gives itself away as false, we cannot be quite so certain that they are deliberate contrivances coming from Teika's hand. It is possible that they are in fact remarks added by later readers or copyists, as with colophons found in manuscripts of other tales from this period, and as with two additional colophon entries that appear in only one of the extant manuscripts of *Matsura no miya monogatari*.[50] The best explanation would seem to be, however, that they are of a piece with entries A and B and the lacunae: an integral part of Teika's forgery of an ancient tale.

Proceeding on this assumption, it remains somewhat ambiguous how Teika wished the reader to view entry C, a poem by the Chinese poet Po Chü-i (772–846). On the one hand, the poem seems to stand in relation to the tale almost like the *tanka* envoys found at the end of many *chōka*, so perfectly encapsulating the story of the affair between Ujitada and the mysterious lady that it is difficult to think it could have been put there by anyone but the author. One can readily imagine that the author had this poem in his mind as he wrote the entire fourth part of the tale, and that it even had a part in shaping the tale. In the Go-Kōgon manuscript the poem appears immediately after entry B, on the same page: perhaps we are meant to think that the author himself set down this poem here as a way of revealing the inspiration, or the foundation, for his story.[51] On the other hand, the poem's affinities to the story can be seen as accidental, and its entry here as the work of a later reader who happened to be reminded of it when he read the story. This would have to be the preferred view of entry C if Teika intended his readers to think of the author as a lady residing in Somedono (that is to say, the second circumstance suggested when we first looked at the colophon, above, pp. 6–7), for the normal assumption was that women did not

50. See n. 5, above.
51. An author writing in 861 could indeed have been quite familiar with the works of Po Chü-i (though, by common assumption, only if he was male—see following note). *Montoku jitsuroku* ("Actual Records of Emperor Montoku," one of the *Rikkokushi*, or "Six National Histories"), entry for Ninju 1[851].ix.26, records that an edition of *Po-shih wen-chi* (Japanese *Hakushi monjū*, "The Collected Works of Master Po"; the final seventy-five-volume version was completed in 845) was presented to Emperor Ninmyō (r. 833–50) in 838. A less reliable record, an anecdote included in the *setsuwa* collection *Gōdanshō* (ca. 1111), suggests editions of Po's works circulated in Japan as early as in the time of Emperor Saga (r. 809–23). See Maruyama 1964, 86; Oka 1972, 19–20; *Nihon koten bungaku daijiten* 1983–85, vol. 5, 51–52. In fact, since the mid-ninth century was a time of great popularity for Chinese poetry in Japan, Po's works were probably more widely known among courtiers of that time than of the late twelfth century.

read Chinese.[52] In this case, it becomes a further extension of Teika's effort to fabricate a textual history for his tale. If the entire colophon is counterfeit, we can have it both ways: we can affirm our feeling that it could not have been placed there by anyone but the author, but as part of the fictitious textual history attached to the story, we can still look upon it as the response of a later reader.

Entry D is more obviously cast as the words of a later reader or copyist, responding most directly to Po Chü-i's poem, but also through it to the tale itself. It adds yet another voice to the fictitious textual history, and in its ultimate question becomes the final tongue-in-cheek remark of Teika's great hoax—which apparently fooled no one, if we are to judge from *Mumyōzōshi*.

As a whole, then, whatever its flaws—and here one might add weak characterization and an at-times repetitious style to the fragmentation of plot mentioned earlier—*Matsura no miya monogatari* emerges as one of the most interesting of the minor tales surviving from the Heian and Kamakura periods. In its military episode, its portrayal of public business, its enthusiastic embrace of the supernatural, its unabashed borrowing from *Utsuho monogatari* and *Hamamatsu Chūnagon monogatari*, and its false antiquity and textual history, *Matsura no miya monogatari* does not lack for engaging and clever new departures—in some cases, perhaps too clever for their own good—that make it an unusual and different work from the standard *monogatari*. There is plenty here to justify the remark made by the author of *Mumyōzōshi* at the end of the passage cited above, that *Matsura no miya monogatari* is "beyond anything a simpleminded person could have imagined." This introduction has touched only the surface of some of the most salient of the tale's features; the next chapter will take a closer look at those qualities that have led some scholars to call it a *"yōen* romance."

---

52. Modern scholars agreed that the author must be male even before Hagitani's detailed documentation of the Chinese sources the author had to have known. This conclusion was largely based on the amount of material in the tale that any reader could see must have come from Chinese sources, even if he did not know from exactly which ones: while noblewomen of the time may have been familiar with *some* Chinese sources (mostly literary—see appendix B, p. 176), we may be certain that none had the broader Chinese knowledge displayed in the tale. When we consider that Kamakura readers would probably have drawn the same conclusion, the question arises: could Teika have intended his reader to think of the author as Yoshifusa himself? The specification of the *western wing* of Somedono Palace makes this doubtful, however, since Yoshifusa surely would have occupied the main hall of his own palace. With most, though not all, of the material deriving from more specialized Chinese sources appearing in the sections after the style shift, perhaps Teika hoped colophon entry A would lead readers to think of an original author who was female and a reviser who was male: it would then be the reviser who appended the poem, either as a reader responding to the story of Ujitada's affair with the mysterious lady, or as the original author of that section of the tale. In any case we have here another element in Teika's attempted forgery that he failed to think through in all its implications, and that prevents a full reconciliation of his various contrivances within a single explanation.

Chapter Two: The Aesthetic of *Yōen* in a Narrative Context

Yōen is an aesthetic term whose use has traditionally been restricted to poetry. Scholars of *Matsura no miya monogatari*, however, have found frequent occasion to speak of the work as a "*yōen* romance" because the effects and overtones created by the imagery and incidents in several scenes in the tale show strong affinities to those of *yōen* poetry. Although it is impossible to know at present which came earlier, *yōen* in poetry or in the tale, it will be useful here to look first at how *yōen* has been described and defined in connection with poetry.

Robert H. Brower and Earl Miner, in their several discussions of Japanese court poetry, translate the term as "ethereal charm" or "ethereal beauty" and, in one case, describe it as:

> the romantic idealization of a delicate, dreamlike beauty—the beauty of a peony or of an exquisite heavenly maiden descending to earth on a hazy[, moonlit] spring night. Such beauty was elusive, ephemeral, the stuff that dreams are made on, and while the typical imagery of yōen had the delicate lightness of cherry petals, it was often used to convey a tone of sadness—of lovers parting or of nostalgia for the vision of a beauty not of this world.[53]

They also note an emphasis on overtones, frequently through the use of allusion; the "evocation of a romantic atmosphere of mysterious beauty"; and a relative ornateness in comparison to another midclassical ideal, *yūgen*, which otherwise contained some of the same emphases on overtones, allusive depth, and mystery.[54] Elsewhere they add that *yōen* is "characterized by complexity of technique," tends to "express subtle shades of pathos," combines "elements of more sombre styles with 'beautiful' imagery and an ethereal atmosphere," and presents an "aura of magic."[55]

The following famous poem by Teika, found in *Shinkokinshū*, is used as an example of *yōen* probably more frequently than any other. Brower and Miner

53. Brower and Miner 1961, 262, with the word "moonlit" collated from a similar description on p. 513.
54. Brower and Miner 1961, 268.
55. Brower and Miner 1961, 512; Miner 1968, 165.

present it as their premier illustration of the *yōen* style, and it is their translation that I quote:

A. *Shinkokinshū* 38, Fujiwara Teika:

Haru no yo no	The bridge of dreams
Yume no ukihashi	Floating on the brief spring night
Todae shite	Soon breaks off:
Mine ni wakaruru	Now from the mountaintop a cloud
Yokogumo no sora	Takes leave into the open sky.[56]

The speaker of the poem has been dreaming on this spring night, and by tradition it is to be assumed that it is a dream of love. This dream is cut short by the approach of dawn, just as real lovers' trysts are interrupted, especially in the spring—or felt more acutely in the spring—because of the shortening of the nights, and the speaker awakes to see in the loveliness of the spring dawn what is in effect a metaphorical conclusion to his dream: a cloud "taking leave" of the mountaintop, just as he would take leave of his beloved. Thus, a bridge has been formed between dream and reality; they have become fused.

Allusions add complexity and depth to the poem. The bridge of dreams referred to in the second line of the poem (the first line of the translation) alludes to the last chapter of *Genji monogatari*, where the story of the broken love between Ukifune and Kaoru seems itself to break off like an unfinished dream. This allusion evokes the romantic atmosphere of their story for the poem, including all the complications of the heart that came with Prince Niou's involvement, and serves as a bridge between the fictional world of the tale and the real world described in the poem. The final two lines add further to the romantic overtones of the poem through an allusion to *Kokinshū* (or *Kokin wakashū*, "Collection of Ancient and Modern Poetry," ca. 905) 601, by Mibu no Tadamine:

Kaze fukeba	Before the gusting winds,
Mine ni wakaruru	From the mountaintop takes leave
Shirakumo no	A tall white cloud,
Taete tsurenaki	To be broken apart, as am I
Kimi ga kokoro ka	By the endless cruelty of your heart.

These allusions, together with the overtones of the poem itself, suggest that the speaker is thinking of, and was dreaming of, a real love that suffered the same fate as the broken love between the lovers of Tadamine's poem, or between Kaoru and Ukifune of *Genji monogatari*. The latter in particular suggests a love that was broken off not just for the moment, by the dawn, but forever, by a "leave-taking" that is no more reversible than the course of the cloud that drifts off into nothingness in the open sky. Thus, a fusion takes

---

56. Brower and Miner 1961, 262. Much of my commentary on this poem follows their discussion as well.

place, a bridge is formed, between man and nature as well. The scene described in nature is one of supreme loveliness, and yet it carries a tone of wistful sadness because of its metaphorical value.[57]

A full discussion of the aesthetic of *yōen* in poetry is beyond the scope of this study. Among the poems frequently noted by scholars and critics for their *yōen* qualities, however, are several that show affinities to certain scenes and developments in *Matsura no miya monogatari* even more strikingly than the poem cited above—not only in their natural imagery but also in their total effect and overtones. These few poems cannot be considered fully representative of *yōen* in all of its dimensions, but they do represent an important group of *yōen* poems, and can provide useful points of reference for the discussion of similar characteristics found in the tale. They may be discussed briefly, as a group.

B. *Shinkokinshū* 112, Shunzei's Daughter:
<table>
<tr><td>Kaze kayou</td><td>The wind breathes softly,</td></tr>
<tr><td>Nezame no sode zo</td><td>Bringing the scent of flowers to my sleeve,</td></tr>
<tr><td>Hana no ka ni</td><td>And calls me from my sleep;</td></tr>
<tr><td>Kaoru makura no</td><td>And, my pillow redolent with spring,</td></tr>
<tr><td>Haru no yo no yume</td><td>I waken from a night of fragrant dreams.[58]</td></tr>
</table>

C. *Shinkokinshū* 45, Fujiwara Ietaka:
<table>
<tr><td>Ume ga ka ni</td><td>Stirred by the fragrance</td></tr>
<tr><td>Mukashi o toeba</td><td>Of the flowering plum, I ask about the past,</td></tr>
<tr><td>Haru no tsuki</td><td>But the soft spring moon</td></tr>
<tr><td>Kotaenu kage zo</td><td>Beams unchanged with enigmatic radiance</td></tr>
<tr><td>Sode ni utsureru</td><td>And glistens with a sadness on my sleeve.[59]</td></tr>
</table>

D. *Shinkokinshū* 44, Fujiwara Teika:
<table>
<tr><td>Ume no hana</td><td>Upon my sleeve</td></tr>
<tr><td>Nioi o utsusu</td><td>Plum blossoms pour their fragrance</td></tr>
<tr><td>Sode no ue ni</td><td>Vying in beauty</td></tr>
<tr><td>Noki moru tsuki no</td><td>With moonbeams filtering through the eaves</td></tr>
<tr><td>Kage zo arasou</td><td>And sparkling in the wetness of my tears.[60]</td></tr>
</table>

E. *Shōji ninen shodo hyakushu*, Fujiwara Teika, poem 7:
<table>
<tr><td>Hana no ka no</td><td>So entrancing</td></tr>
<tr><td>Kasumeru tsuki ni</td><td>Is the beauty of the moonlight blurred</td></tr>
<tr><td>Akugarete</td><td>With the scent of blossoms</td></tr>
<tr><td>Yume mo sadaka ni</td><td>That these spring nights are a time</td></tr>
<tr><td>Mienu koro kana</td><td>When even dreams are seen through haze.[61]</td></tr>
</table>

57. The poem contains several other allusions as well. See Kubota 1984, 113–15. Also see discussions of poems 49 and 55 in Lammers 1987, appendix A.
58. Translated in Brower and Miner 1961, 315.
59. Translated in Brower and Miner 1961, 290.
60. Translated in Brower 1978, 41.
61. Translated in Brower 1978, 43. Once again, my commentary draws many of its points from the discussions following these poems in the books from which the translations were taken.

The first and last of these poems repeat the motif of dreams found in poem A—dreams still of a spring night, with a blurring of the distinction between sleeping and waking, dream and reality. They all contain vivid sensual imagery of sight and smell. The fragrance of flowers appears in them all; the moon appears in three, as does the mention of sleeves; and where they appear together (poems C and D) they implicitly suggest tears, since it is only upon a wet sleeve that the moonlight can be caught and reflected. Further, in each case there is a mysterious or magical quality about the imagery: cherry blossoms (the flowers in poem B) do not really have fragrance; the moon is enigmatic and the speaker's question remains unanswered; the fragrance of flowers has an apparently magical hold on the speaker—calling him from sleep, making him ask of the past, putting him in a trance that blurs the moon—or is so powerful as to seem almost visual as it vies in beauty with the moonlight. The mood is of enchantment, of a blur of intoxication, and the atmosphere is dreamlike even where dreams are not mentioned.

Allusions once again give us clues to the circumstances that may have been behind the poems. Poem C alludes to Ariwara Narihira's famous poem about the moon and spring of old and poem D alludes to the story that accompanies the same poem in the fourth episode of *Ise monogatari* ("Tales of Ise," ca. 935):

> Once when the ex-empress was living in the eastern Fifth Ward, a certain lady occupied the western wing of her house. Quite without intending it, a man fell deeply in love with the lady and began to visit her; but around the Tenth of the First Month she moved away without a word, and though he learned where she had gone, it was not a place where ordinary people could come and go. He could do nothing but brood over the wretchedness of life. When the plum blossoms were at their height in the next First Month, poignant memories of the year before drew him back to her old apartments. He stared at the flowers from every conceivable standing and sitting position, but it was quite hopeless to try to recapture the past. Bursting into tears, he flung himself onto the floor of the bare room and lay there until the moon sank low in the sky. As he thought of the year before, he composed this poem:

Tsuki ya aranu	Is not the moon the same?
Haru ya mukashi no	The spring
Haru naranu	The spring of old?
Wa ga mi hitotsu wa	Only this body of mine
Moto no mi ni shite	Is the same body . . .[62]

The last poem by Teika, poem E, also appears to contain an allusion, to none other than a scene from *Matsura no miya monogatari*.[63] In each of these cases,

---

62. Helen McCullough 1968, 71. See n. 49, above.

63. Since *Matsura no miya monogatari* was far from being a well-established source for allusions, and the allusion probably would have been recognized by only a few insiders, it is difficult to

whatever the precise circumstances behind the poem are imagined to be, allusion is an important technique that adds depth and complexity to the poem, giving it strong overtones of sadness, of romance, of lost love and the romantic yearning that goes on without cease in spite of the loss, or even all the more because of the loss; or at least of a love that is hindered by unspecified obstacles and the romantic yearning that comes precisely because of the difficulties that stand in the way of the lovers.

A Night of Enchantment

With this brief glance at what *yōen* signified in the realm of poetry, we may now proceed to the tale. At the center of this discussion will be the very scene to which poem E alludes, midway through book two, after the rebellion has been quelled and peace restored. The peerlessly beautiful empress dowager now rules the Chinese empire wisely and benevolently on behalf of her son, the new emperor, who is still a child. Ujitada has begun to think of returning to Japan.

The evening before the scene in question takes place, the empress dowager has a long conversation with Ujitada amidst a fine spring haze, with the fragrance of plum blossoms filling the air and the bright and enchanting moon overhead. The scene provides a useful contrast to the passage that is the source of Teika's allusion, for, although the sensuous imagery just described is very similar to that in poems B through E above, the scene fails to approach any semblance of the ethereal, dreamlike atmosphere of *yōen*. Instead, the scene is filled with sentimental chatter, centering on a tedious protestation by the empress dowager over the impossible dilemma with which Ujitada has presented her: if she is to reward him properly and fully for the service he has rendered the empire in its time of trial, the rebellion, she should bestow on him vast fiefdoms and turn the affairs of state over to him. Yet to do this, and force him to remain in China against his sincerest wishes, would be a poor way to repay the nation's debt to him. And so on and so forth, ending in the inevitable floods of tears.[64]

Ujitada himself is thoroughly enchanted by the empress dowager, but merely because of her flawless beauty, not because of an ethereal atmosphere or aura of magic. Konishi Jin'ichi and others have noted regarding the etymology of *yōen* that in its earliest appearance in the Chinese sources, the term was simply an adjective used to describe a supremely lovely woman.[65] If this early meaning is to be applied, then perhaps it would be possible to speak of *yōen* here. Then, however, the term would lose virtually all of its usefulness as a term for distinguishing a particular kind of aesthetic quality of the tale, since it would

accept poem E as a legitimate case of *honzetsudori* (taking a foundation passage), in which a poet alludes to a story or other prose passage rather than to another poem. But in its content the poem has all the appearances of this technique, even if we must consider the allusion a mostly private one.

64. See translation, pp. 113–20.
65. Konishi 1953, 9.

have to be applied to every scene in the story where Ujitada is at a loss for words to describe how beautiful one of his ladies is—and there are many of these; further, it would have to be applied to countless scenes in other tales as well. For the present purpose, which is to examine how Teika may have attempted to evoke in *Matsura no miya monogatari* the same kind of atmosphere and effect as is seen in his and others' *yōen* poetry, the word does not apply here: there is no mysterious or magical mood, no suggestion of dreams; there is disappointment and regret and even a touch of resentment, but not the wistful sadness or nostalgia seen in the poems. There has been no lovers' parting, or even a meeting. And, finally, whatever "beautiful" imagery has been presented, its power to evoke an ethereal atmosphere, to charm us with its almost palpable sensuousness and loveliness, has been undermined by the long and tiresome monologue of the empress dowager, which is followed by an equally plodding response from Ujitada. Even the poems that they eventually compose toward the end of the meeting cannot raise the tenor of the scene. They are merely exercises in wit.[66]

Following shortly on this scene comes the one to which the poem from Teika's Shōji sequence alludes. Ujitada has spent his day at court in abstraction, thinking of the empress dowager and the things she said to him the day before. Since she withdraws early, as soon as the official business for the day has been taken care of, he is unable to speak to her on this day. He returns home to gaze at the sky in melancholy reverie:

> As daylight gave way to evening shadows, the dreariness of his interminable reverie grew greater than Ujitada could bear. Restlessly, aimlessly, he set out for a walk, and before long had wandered out of the city into hill country, where the scent of flowering plums came to him from every direction. Proceeding in the direction of the most alluringly scented breath of wind, he arrived at a cluster of dwellings nestled against the side of a small mountain. In the distance he could hear the wind sighing in the pines, and as the last light of the evening faded into darkness the moon rose above the ridge of the mountain to cast its cool, clear brightness across a sky now emptied of clouds. Entranced by the serene beauty of the night, Ujitada pressed on through a large grove of trees.
>
> To his ear came several strains of music. Could it be a *hichiriki*? he wondered. He had never found the tones of the instrument especially to his liking back home in Japan, but it sounded so different here, more beautiful than anything he had ever heard. It was, no doubt, an effect of this place he had come to.[67]

66. Prince Genji's initial encounter with Kokiden's sister, Oborozukiyo, in the "Hana no en" chapter of *Genji monogatari* (Abe et al. 1970–76, vol. 1, 425–29; Seidensticker 1976, 151–53), could be cited as another scene that has some of the right elements, but that does not rise to *yōen*.

67. The passage discussed here is found on pp. 121–23 of the translation, and in Hagitani 1970, 73–76. For *hichiriki*, see following note.

A mood of melancholy is in the air immediately prior to the beginning of the passage and carries over into the events of Ujitada's excursion to the countryside. Opening the passage are a series of sensuous images, of sight, smell, and sound: the moon and the plum blossoms, which were seen in the *yōen* poems; the wind in the pines, which emphasizes the remoteness of the place; and music whose tones are like no other music Ujitada has ever heard, owing to an unspecified but seemingly magical quality of the surroundings. Ujitada senses there is something unusual and different about the mountain region into which he has wandered. In fact, there is a suggestion of magic even before the music, in the entrancing effect that the beauty of the night has on Ujitada. He presses on as though intoxicated with an elixir of plum blossoms or under a spell cast by the moon.

The narrator observes in a parenthetical remark that a *hichiriki* is called a *shō* in China. This is not in fact true, since the names designate two very different wind instruments[68]; but the observation is apparently necessary in order to establish the association that allows him to continue as follows:

> Now I can believe the ancient legend, thought Ujitada, about the princess who was carried away to the realm of the immortals for her playing of the *shō*. Tears of wonder welled in his eyes.
>
> The nation was still in mourning for the deceased emperor, and the sound of strings and pipes had not been heard elsewhere for quite some time. Perhaps it owed to the remoteness of this mountain region that music was being played here. But what kind of person would it be who lived in a place like this?
>
> Still searching for the source of the music, Ujitada came upon a lady dressed most elegantly, standing alone before a simple pinewood gate. Her face was hidden behind a fan and Ujitada could not see clearly what manner of woman she might be.
>
> "Who are you, and why do you stand here before this gate?" he asked.
>
> Without answering, she turned to go inside. Ujitada followed. Although the grounds were in need of care, the building itself stood tall and elegant, not at all like the rustic structure at the desolate estate he had visited on Mount Shang. The pillars seemed new, their color fresh and unweathered. The bamboo blinds, still green, stood out all the more vividly because it was a time when the blinds at the palace had been dulled in observance of the national mourning.

The ancient legend Ujitada alludes to appears in the Chinese collection of folk legends, *Lieh-hsien chuan* ("Biographies of the Immortals," ca. 6 B.C.E.), and among Japanese sources in the extant version of *Kara monogatari* ("Tales from China," ca. 1170): Duke Mu of Ch'in gives his daughter Princess Lung-yü in

---

68. The *hichiriki* is similar to the Western flageolet. The *shō* is a kind of mouth organ, made of bamboo pipes cut to different lengths and arranged in a cylindrical shape above a mouthpiece.

marriage to Hsiao Shih, a virtuoso of the *shō*. The princess learns to play the *shō* as well, with such mastery, in fact, that when she imitates the cry of a phoenix, a phoenix descends upon their house. In the end, after a night of playing the *shō* together beneath the moon, husband and wife fly off to heaven carried by the phoenix.[69]

In the description cited above, Brower and Miner epitomize *yōen* as the beauty of an exquisite heavenly maiden descending to earth on a hazy, moonlit spring night. Here, in the story called to mind by Ujitada's allusion, the image is of an ascent rather than a descent, but in the context of the enchanting moonlight and the intoxicating scent of plum the aesthetic effect is strikingly similar, with its evocation of the heavenly and ethereal, of a beauty not of this world.

More important to note in this portion of the passage are the numerous ways in which this remote dwelling, and Ujitada's experiences there, are wrapped in mystery. One question after another arises in the reader's mind: Why is there music here, in spite of the national mourning? What is a lady of such refinement and elegance doing in this remote and rustic place? Who could she be? Why does she keep her face hidden, and why does she not answer Ujitada's inquiry? The grounds are in need of care—perhaps following the example of some of the more mysteriously or gothically romantic lovers' trysts in earlier *monogatari*.[70] Yet the building seems new. Why? Or is it that the pillars and beams and blinds are fresh in spite of age?—a suggestion of the supernatural and miraculous that takes on new meaning later in the story. And again, the fresh green of the blinds is another thing that is inexplicably out of keeping with the national mourning. The effect is to suggest that Ujitada has entered another world, where the conditions of this world do not obtain. Thus, as the scene unfolds, it moves from the intoxicating, dreamlike enchantment that led Ujitada irresistibly toward first the plum blossoms and then the music, to an otherworldly encounter surrounded by mystery.

The scene continues:

> The fragrance of plum blossoms filled the air, and from within this building came the music Ujitada had heard. He started to follow the woman up the steps into the building, but paused to listen before reaching the top. The place was completely quiet, with no sounds to indicate that anyone else was about. He peeked through a crack in the blinds: the musician was apparently a lady. The wonderful perfume that came from within seemed somehow familiar to him, and Ujitada marveled that it was a remarkable land indeed where there could be another lady like the empress dowager in such a remote place.

69. Hagitani 1970, 275, n. 206. See Geddes 1984, 86–88 for an English translation of the story in *Kara monogatari*.
70. The episode of Toshikage's daughter and Wakakogimi (later known as Kanemasa) in chapter 1 of *Utsuho monogatari* comes to mind, or the episode in chapter 4 of *Genji monogatari*, where Genji takes Yūgao ("the lady of the evening faces") to a deserted villa.

To the scent of the blossoms is added the scent of a wonderful perfume, and then the reader is reminded that not only is this scene taking place in a remote and unusual mountain retreat, but the entire story is taking place in an exotic land of many marvels. There is further mystery: who is this second lady, and why does she call to mind the empress dowager?

After circling the building to see if he can learn anything more about the place, Ujitada enters. At no point is he challenged, nor does anyone emerge to greet him. The lady continues to play her music:

> The tones of the music seemed to rise clearer and purer as the night deepened. Breathing deeply the intoxicating fragrance of plum, Ujitada listened in rapture. Nothing could have induced him to leave; instead, he slid farther into the room.
>
> The lady with the *shō* indicated no surprise at his movement, and played on without interruption. Since the room was deep and she was seated near the back, Ujitada still could not see her clearly. The strangeness of it all brought, for a moment, a twinge of fear, but enticed by the scent that so thickly filled the air, he moved yet closer. Even then the lady seemed not to notice him.
>
> "I came in search of your wondrous music, under the bewitching spell of the moon," he said, but his words were to no avail, for the lady remained silent. Charmed by the uncanny familiarity of her perfume, Ujitada tugged at her sleeve, then took her hand. She showed no alarm, nor did she shrink from his touch. The absence of the slightest indication of shock or rebuff aroused Ujitada to further boldness; he drew her to him. She pliantly yielded to his embrace, and he could no longer restrain himself. He was more helplessly captive to his worldly passions now than he had ever been before.
>
> His meeting with Princess Hua-yang had been like a meeting with the moon that courses the heavens: it had not seemed to be of this world. But the experienced and welcoming manner in which this lady responded to his advances suggested that she was most certainly of this world. Her alluring charm and beauty were beyond compare. Ujitada thought how unbearable it would be to be parted even for a moment from such a lady, but no amount of begging or imploring could bring her to speak. She remained silent, and merely added her own endless flow of tears to Ujitada's.

The perfume that seems so familiar, the complete absence of any surprise or rebuke on the part of the lady, her unbroken silence—all of these factors add to the otherworldly overtones. Yet the lady seems to be very much of this world in her response to the passions of the flesh, and also in her own susceptibility to them, as the following paragraphs will show. She is at once worldly and otherworldly.

Near the end of the last paragraph the tone of the passage turns to sadness. He still lies next to the lady, yet his heart and mind fill with the anticipated grief of separation. It is a heavy, miserable, unbearable sadness, in contrast to the vague and rather light melancholy that had led Ujitada to set out on his nocturnal excursion in the first place. His grief multiplies when the actual time of parting arrives:

> Had the night been as long as a thousand nights, it would not have been long enough, and yet already the cock was crowing. Neither Ujitada nor the lady stirred. Ujitada could think of no place to go even if he should rise. He wished instead that his life might come to an end on that very spot.
>
> The waiting woman—the lady who had been standing by the gate the night before—began noisily clearing her throat to call their attention to the hour, but the lady in Ujitada's arms, perhaps because she, too, was still overcome with emotion, did not try to hurry him away. She went on weeping and said nothing.
>
> The waiting woman came nearer. "It is beginning to grow light," she said. "This is a most disagreeable place in the daytime." She seemed exceedingly anxious that he be on his way.
>
> As they gathered up their garments and began to dress, Ujitada hardly felt alive. In vain would one attempt to describe how bereft of soul he felt by the time he actually departed. He could see from the lady's expression that the parting was as painful to her as it was to him, but even now she did not speak.
>
> Over and over Ujitada repeated his vow to come back again, both to the lady and to the serving woman, and then finally took his leave.
>
> He emerged from the building feeling no more certain of what had taken place than if he had been walking on air, and irrepressible doubts quickly arose in his heart. He called one of his close attendants to his side.
>
> "Stay here and watch this building," he said. "If anyone comes out, follow her and find out where she goes."
>
> Leaving him behind, Ujitada made all haste for the city. It would be unseemly to be seen like this in full daylight.

When the time for parting comes, the highly evocative quality of the scene suddenly seems to evaporate. The cock's crow and the waiting woman's call put an abrupt end to the otherworldly atmosphere: now, once again, real-world conditions are in effect even in this place that had seemed so removed from those conditions in the night. In this final part of the scene is found little more than conventional expressions of the grief of separation, with the narrator's standard (and by now quite tiresome) claim of being at a loss for words. There is still a reminder of the mystery in the lady's continued silence, and in the waiting woman's comment about how disagreeable the place is in the daytime. But the enchantment has been broken, and Ujitada, far from a blur of intoxication, is very quick about his wits now: once he has actually taken his leave, the suspicions of a rational mind make him all business as he arranges for what he hopes will be a means of gaining some confirmable, real-world information about the lady, and as he turns homeward with all due haste so that his nocturnal excursion will not be discovered.

Thus, the scene contains many of the elements that go into the creation of *yōen* in poetry. The presentation of the scene is highly imagistic, suggestive, sensuous—initially with an aura of magic and then moving on to a deep mysteriousness. There is an otherworldly, ethereal atmosphere about the entire encounter. It seems unmistakably an attempt to evoke an atmosphere of *yōen* within prose fiction, and to a large extent it is a successful one. At the same time, the requirements of prose fiction are quite unlike those of poetry, and it need come as no surprise that there are significant differences between the effect achieved here and that achieved in poetry.

To begin with, the brevity of the tanka form means that in a *yōen* poem there is scarcely enough space to create or suggest the desired effect, leaving no room for the effect, so briefly developed, to be displaced by the ongoing narrative, as it is at the end of the passage just examined. Indeed, just as one of the most important conditions for success in any tanka is the ability of the poet, through various technical devices, to expand beyond the thirty-one syllable limit, so the success of a *yōen* poem depends on the use of words and images with a maximum of suggestion, such that the effect of the poem is only beginning to develop when the reader finishes reading the last line. As the images linger and continue to play in the reader's mind, the poem expands and opens out beyond its fifth line, in what Ishida Yoshisada calls an "aesthetic explosion."[71]

Earlier, a number of ways were noted in which the poems cited explicitly evoke mystery through the mention of enigmas and ambiguities. In the overall analysis, however, the thirty-one syllable limit of the tanka form would seem to be one of the most important factors in creating the atmosphere of mystery that surrounds the beauty of these poems. A major component of their powerful effect is that so much is left to suggestion and overtones. Questions suggested by what little is actually stated in the poem arise in the reader's mind, but they cannot be answered. The reader can only guess and wonder what the story is behind the poem, behind the lyricism of the speaker.

In an extended tale, however, there is no such formal limit, and no lack of room to answer the questions, to solve the mysteries. This is certainly the implication of the manner in which the above scene closes, with Ujitada arranging for one of his men to stay behind and follow the lady so that he can find out her identity. In contrast to the unanswerable questions—questions that *cannot* be answered—in the poems or surrounding the poems, the questions that arise from this passage of *Matsura no miya monogatari* are merely unanswered for the moment—not *yet* answered in this particular passage of the tale. And in fact, in a

---

71. Ishida 1979, 50ff. and passim.

narrative context, the questions carry with them the expectation that they will be answered, that the story is not over until they are indeed answered—which is quite the opposite of the expectation in a poem of a limited number of syllables. In essence, then, the mysteriousness associated with the ethereal beauty that is *yōen* becomes an element of narrative suspense, which draws the reader on in the story and moves the action forward. The effect is not an "aesthetic explosion," but merely a tug on one's curiosity.

In the poems cited above, the speaker does not look forward, but backward—nostalgically back to a love that has ended, or at least to a love meeting that is in the past and of which a repetition may be difficult or impossible. In order for this to be the case, the speaker of the poem must be removed from the time of the original event that is the object of his memories, the time of the actual love meeting; he must stand back from it. In the speaker's present he undergoes an aesthetic as well as emotional experience in response to certain natural phenomena, described in the imagery of the poem, that have stimulated his senses. Needless to say, this experience in the speaker's present is aesthetically closer to him than is the experience he remembers; yet, it too has been distanced, for the speaker must stand back even from the experience of remembering in order to be able to see it, especially to see the association between the aesthetic and the emotional, and then to describe it or express it in a poem. Even when the parting scene between the lovers is described in the poem as if it is even now taking place, there is distance, for the speaker could not describe the scene as he does without first standing back to look at it, and himself in it. Thus, the poem itself is an expression of the speaker's experience at the time of remembering, rather than at the time remembered.

The passage in the tale, however, describes the original events—the events "at the time remembered," as it were, though, so far as the narrative is concerned, there has been as yet no lapse of time for there to be any remembering. Ujitada occupies a position equivalent to that of the speakers of the *yōen* poems: he is the one who experiences the enchantment and arousal of passions described. But he is not the speaker of this passage; there is a separate narrator telling of the events. And because this is so, the reader sees Ujitada fully immersed in the events themselves rather than distanced from them. The sensuous imagery of sight and smell and sound belong to the time of the original events rather than to the time in which they are remembered. Thus, whereas in the poems the natural imagery had the power to arouse the memory of a meeting and the wave of nostalgia and sadness that comes with it, in the tale they have the power actually to bring about the meeting.

In fact, they have the power *only* to bring about a meeting—to enchant and arouse passions, but not to strike that note of nostalgic sadness or longing that is so much a part of *yōen* in poetry. Time must pass before this is possible, before Ujitada can compose in his own voice, in reverie, a poem similar to the ones cited at the beginning of this chapter. Within this single scene, there was no room to introduce the retrospective qualities of *yōen*. The sadness expressed here comes in anticipation of the parting, not in remembrance of it. It looks forward to events yet to be narrated, just as do the questions raised by the mysteriousness of the lady, the building, and the place.

The Path So Straight in Dreams

Once the evocative intensity of the scene described above, with its beautiful and intoxicating imagery of sight and sound and smell, has given way to the light of day, apart from the memory of the experience, the principal remaining ✓ *yōen* element is that of mystery. And even this has been changed, reduced from the otherworldly mysteriousness of the night before to the much more pragmatic matter of learning the woman's identity. In fact, in the immediate moments, it seems to be a simple matter of ignorance rather than mystery, easily solved by leaving a man to watch the house and to follow anyone who might emerge from it.

This quickly changes, however. The man left behind by Ujitada returns to report that he saw no one leave the building, but neither did he find anyone inside when he finally tired of waiting and decided to investigate. This confirms the supernatural, otherworldly nature of the experience, and Ujitada is more anxious than ever to find out the truth. When he returns to the place the following night, the building still stands where it did before. This is encouraging, for had the lady been a fox-spirit, such as sometimes appears in the Chinese *ch'uan-ch'i* (tales of the supernatural), Ujitada might have expected to find that the building had vanished altogether or that it was a ruin instead of an elegantly appointed structure; it also confirms that the entire experience was not merely a dream. But it does not explain what manner of being the lady was, that she could vanish without a trace even though she never left the building. Though the building has proved to be real, it embodies a supernatural mystery that Ujitada has no means to explain.

Ujitada finds no indications that anyone has been there, but spends the night, unable to sleep, waiting, hoping for some sign; and he returns again and again on subsequent nights. As the plum blossoms scatter, and he continues to receive no sign, he wonders increasingly whether what he experienced could really have happened. Although the continued existence of the building where it all took place initially seemed sufficient proof of the reality of the experience, as time passes it begins to seem not enough: perhaps the place was real, but the experience nevertheless a dream, induced by the scent of plum and the light of the moon. He longs to see the mysterious lady again if only to confirm that the meeting was real.

After some time, there is indeed another meeting, but it takes place under circumstances no more confirmably—or at least no more understandably—real than the first meeting. As Ujitada gazes at the moon in sad reverie one night, he hears his door drawn shut, and suddenly the wondrous fragrance he remembers from the night of the plum blossoms fills his room. The lady has come to him. He showers her with reproaches for not telling him where she lives or how he can communicate with her, and accuses her of being the spirit of Mount Wu or one of the goddesses of the river Hsiang come to bewitch him. She remains silent this time, too, until just before she goes, then she recites a parting poem, which raises Ujitada's passion for her to a new pitch. Though he knows it would be a scandal to be discovered, he determinedly holds her in his embrace so that she cannot leave:

> He held her tightly in his arms, determined to keep her with him even into the full light of day. For her part, she seemed in no great hurry to depart, and continued to lie pliantly in his embrace.
>
> Then she was gone, vanished without a trace, before Ujitada could realize what was happening. He was stunned. Could she have hidden herself in a magical cape? he wondered, and groped frantically at the space beside him, but to no avail. She was gone, more elusive than a dream, leaving Ujitada in utter darkness as to which direction he might turn his tenderest longings.
>
> Nothing remained but her singlet, scented with the indescribably marvelous perfume that had permeated the room from the moment she entered. No patterned robes of any sort had been worn in the palace since the late emperor's death, but this was a most attractive *zōgan* gossamer. The lady had left no promise of another meeting. If this proved to be their last, was this singlet to be his only memento of her? The thought threatened to send forth a fresh flood of inconsolable tears.[72]

When the lady first appeared, she seemed to have entered the room by the door, in the normal fashion, but when she goes, she vanishes as elusively as a figure in an unfinished and broken dream. Yet Ujitada also has, now, a tangible memento of the lady herself, proof positive that the lady had been there beside him in the flesh, that the lady was real and not merely a dream. Unable to explain this fusion of dream and reality, far from feeling that his earlier meeting has been confirmed real, Ujitada is at a greater loss than ever.

After this, Ujitada increasingly compares his meetings with the lady to an unfinished dream—a spring night's dream. When a sailing date is set for his ship, he greets the announcement with more sorrow than joy:

> Was he destined to row out to sea still feeling as though rudely awakened from an unfinished dream? A new wave of grief came over him. . . . The sleeves of his night clothes still held the scent of the lady's perfume, but even in this he found no comfort, for it pained him the more that he "knew not which way to place his pillow." How had he slept that night when the lady came to him as if in a dream?

Madoromazu	"Since that dream
Nenu yo ni yume no	On a night that brought no sleep,
Mieshi yori	Nor even dozing,
Itodo omoi no	The burning passion in my heart
Samuru hi zo naki	Has not cooled for a single day."[73]

72. Translation, pp. 127–28. Hagitani 1970, 81.
73. Translation, pp. 132–33. Hagitani 1970, 88–89.

The scent that lingers on the sleeve of his nightclothes would seem, as with the lady's own singlet left behind, to provide undeniable evidence of their meeting. But it remains insufficient for certainty because of those aspects of the meeting that, from a rational point of view, cannot truly have happened the way they seem to have happened.

Ujitada's poem suggests once again a fusion of dream and reality. He speaks of a dream that he had while awake—a waking dream. As far as he can determine, especially with the memento of the lady's singlet and her perfume on his sleeve, he experienced the meeting in a waking state, yet the meeting must nevertheless have been a dream, too, for it happened in a manner that can only happen in dreams.

In fact, he seems even to wish it had truly been a dream. His lament that he "knew not which way to place his pillow" is an allusion to *Kokinshū* 516, an anonymous poem:

Yoi yoi ni	Night after night
Makura sadamen	I know not even which way
Kata mo nashi	To place my pillow;
Ika ni neshi yo ka	How did I sleep on that night
Yume ni mieken	When my love came to me in dream?

There would seem to have been a folk belief that the direction of one's pillow would have an effect on one's dreams. Thus, if the meetings were in fact dreams, Ujitada would at least have some small hope of repeating the dream by placing his pillow in the correct position. If it is all waking, then what he has experienced is truly magical and mysterious, truly wondrous; if it is dream, then it is perhaps nothing at all. But even so, Ujitada's allusion seems to say, better a "real" dream—a dream that he can know is nothing but a dream—than this state of complete uncertainty over what is real and what is not.

There are three further meetings between Ujitada and the mysterious lady, and they are repeatedly spoken of as being as much dream as reality. Ujitada continues to express his confusion—his inability to tell how much of his experience is dreaming and how much is waking:

> "Spring nights are short and the cock's crow is not far off," he said. "And still I have no means of knowing whether I hear it crow truly or in dream."[74]

And again:

> When the lady drew the door closed behind her, he quietly slid it open again a crack. Nothing—not even a wisp of cloud drifting off into the empty sky—remained where she had been the briefest instant before. Only the scent of her perfume lingered behind, now a cruel reminder of one who was gone, rather than a longed-for sign of one who had come. As one meeting had followed on another, Ujitada had quite lost the power to free himself of this infatuation, and yet the manner in

74. Translation, p. 135. Hagitani 1970, 90.

which the lady departed left him with scant assurance that it was anything but a fantastic dream.[75]

From the second meeting onwards, within this fusion and confusion of dream and reality one particular motif emerges, deriving from an allusion to *Kokinshū* 558, by Fujiwara Toshiyuki:

Koiwabite	Helpless with yearning,
Uchinuru naka ni	I drifted off to sleep, and then
Yukikayou	Suddenly I was with her;
Yume no tadaji wa	Oh, that the path so straight in dreams
Utsutsu naranan	Could be as straight in reality.

Several references are made in these later meetings to the path of love so straight in dreams, and "dreampath" becomes the unvarying term by which Ujitada and the mysterious lady refer to their love, thus repeatedly underscoring the dreamlike qualities of their meetings. Never, in fact, do they have a "real" love meeting—i.e., one in which Ujitada, knowing the identity of his lover, goes to visit her at night under entirely normal circumstances. Always the lady comes to visit Ujitada, mysteriously, in a manner that can only take place in dreams. And when in the end the lady finally does reveal her identity, it becomes clear why. A love between the empress dowager of China and a young foreigner is not one that can take place in the real, waking world. For them there is no love-path at all in reality, let alone a straight one; their only chance for meeting is in dream. Yet by the power of supernatural forces, their meetings have somehow been made real: a dream cannot leave behind a singlet or perfume—nor take away a peony, as the mysterious lady does in their final dreamlike meeting.

Another important allusion appearing as a recurrent motif throughout these meetings, and underscoring the "*both* dream *and* reality" paradox, is an allusion to the Chinese legend of the spirit of Mount Wu, initially mentioned by Ujitada in the first of the meetings where the lady comes to him at his quarters near the palace. The story is told in the prose preface to "Kao-t'ang fu," by Sung Yü (third century B.C.E.), translated by Arthur Waley as follows. What Waley calls Witches' Hill is Ujitada's Mount Wu:

> Once when Hsiang, King of Ch'u, was walking with Sung Yü on the Cloud-Dream Terrace, he looked up at the Kao T'ang Shrine. Above it was a coil of mist, now pointing steadily skywards like a pinnacle of rock, now suddenly dissolving and in a single moment diffused into a thousand diverse shapes. Then the King questioned Sung Yü, saying, "What Cloud-spirit is this?" And Yü answered: "It is called Morning Cloud." The King said: "Why has it this name?" and Yü answered: "Long ago a former king was wandering upon this mountain of Kao T'ang. When night came he was tired and slept beyond the

75. Translation, p. 137. Hagitani 1970, 92.

dawn. And early in the morning he dreamt that a lady stood before him saying, 'I am a girl from the Witches' Hill. I have come as a stranger to Kao T'ang, and hearing that my lord the King was travelling on this same mountain, I desired to offer him the service of pillow and mat.' So the King lay with her, and when they parted, she said to him: 'My home is on the southern side of the Witches' Hill, where from its rounded summit a sudden chasm falls. At dawn I am the Morning Cloud; at dusk, the Driving Rain. So dawn by dawn and dusk by dusk I dwell beneath the southern crest.'

"Next day at sunrise he looked towards the hill, and it was even as she had said. Therefore he built her a shrine in the place where she had come to him and called it the Temple of the Morning Cloud."

Then King Hsiang questioned Sung Yü, saying, "Tell me of this Morning Cloud, in what guise does she first appear?" And Yü answered: "Still is she and sombre as a forest of tall pines, where tree stands close to tree; but soon she kindles with a shimmering light; as when a beautiful lady, looking for her lover, raises lawn sleeves to shade her eyes from the sun. Suddenly her being is transformed; swiftly now she races as a chariot whirled onward by galloping steeds, with feathery flags outspread. From the rain a dankness she borrows, and from the wind an icy breath. But soon the wind has dropped, the rain has cleared, and Morning Cloud has vanished from the sky."[76]

This story provides a metaphor for Ujitada to use in his reproaches of the mysterious lady each time she returns to him: she has not told him even so much as the cloud spirit of Mount Wu told the King; she comes and goes like the morning clouds without ever revealing to which peak it is that she returns; and so he is left with no means to know whether their dreamlike meetings are in fact dreams, or if they are reality. No matter how many tangible mementoes the lady may leave behind, Ujitada feels he cannot be sure that she is real, he cannot confirm that their meetings are waking rather than dream, so long as she continues to refuse to identify herself.

Yet, paradoxically, it is precisely because she is real, if supernaturally so, that she must continue to conceal her identity. The need for concealment is a condition of the present, human world of which she is a part: her love is forbidden by that world. Were she merely a dream figure, or a being from another world without a particular identity in this world, she could take on any convenient identity she chose for the expediency of the moment. Which is to say, in the final analysis, Ujitada might not truly know whether he is waking or dreaming even if he did learn the lady's identity.

The spirit of Mount Wu stands as a case in point. She is a dream figure, without real-world constraints, and quite ready to identify herself. Yet she is also real, or at least so it seems, for when the emperor awakes and looks up at

76. Waley 1923, 65–66.

the mountain peak, he sees precisely what she has told him he will see. In her case, there is no tangible memento by which the king can confirm her reality. Instead, her identification of herself allows the king to bridge the gap between dream and reality, and to feel that it was indeed a real spirit that came to him in a dream—real enough for him to build a shrine to her. At the same time, for the reader, as for King Hsiang who hears the story from Sung Yü, there is no final confirmation of the reality of the experience. It may have all been the former king's fancy.

There is in the end no way for the experiences Ujitada has had with the mysterious lady to be explained in the rational and natural terms of this world. The lady cannot be both dream and reality, except supernaturally or fantastically, by some power or force beyond this world. The only explanation that can be forthcoming is one that requires Ujitada to accept the fantastic and unbelievable as real. Underlying the fusion of dream and reality is a fusion of the fantastic and the real.[77]

The Spell Is Broken

A review of the characteristics of *yōen* presented at the beginning of this chapter shows that many aspects of the ongoing relationship between Ujitada and the mysterious lady have much in common with *yōen* as seen in poetry. The evocative, ethereal atmosphere of the first meeting on the night of the enchanting moon and intoxicating scent of plum is missing; the almost palpably sensuous imagery of that passage does not reappear in subsequent meetings

---

77. I am not prepared to make a full examination of Chinese usage of the term *yao-yen* (*yōen*) here, but it bears noting that the term would not have been used in reference to the spirit of Mount Wu or her story. In China as in Japan, *yōen* refers to a bewitching kind of beauty, but whereas in Japan the emphasis is on the romantic, in China the emphasis is on the sinister: the word is used to describe supremely beautiful women who can bewitch one and bring one to ruin, perhaps even bring down an entire kingdom as in the story of the famous femme fatale Hsi Shih (fifth century B.C.E.); the word is also used in tales of the supernatural, for fox spirits who disguise themselves as beautiful women (I am indebted to James Crump for this observation; see *Encyclopedic Dictionary of the Chinese Language*, vol. 9, 84). Ishida Yoshisada (1979, 56) speaks of *yōen* in Japanese poetry as ghostly, devilish, corrupting, and destructive, but more as a function of the poems' powerful "intoxicating and paralyzing" effect than of any inherently sinister content. Konishi (1953, 10) is surely correct in asserting that what came to be called *yōen* in Japan has more in common with the *ch'i-mi* (Japanese *kima*) of late T'ang poetry— qualities similar to those described for *yōen* at the beginning of this chapter—than with what the Chinese thought of as *yao-yen*.

In order to discuss the *yōen* aspects of this tale, it has been necessary to analyze the tale in terms of how *yōen* has traditionally been understood in Japanese poetry—as if *yōen* was already clearly established in Teika's mind as a distinct aesthetic ideal, and as if he was deliberately and consciously introducing the qualities he associated with it into a narrative context. In fact, however, the tale may have come first, and may represent a developmental stage before Teika's *yōen* had congealed into a poetic ideal that could be distinctly identified. Considered in this light, Teika's choice of the spirit of Mount Wu as his chief metaphor for the mysterious lady, instead of the fox spirit of a supernatural tale or the story of Hsi Shih, may well have been pivotal in determining that what ultimately came to be identified as *yōen* in Japan would signify the bewitching and romantic rather than the bewitching and sinister.

between the two, nor in any other scene of the narrative. However, although the spell of enchantment seems to break at the end of that first encounter, the truth is that the experience has left Ujitada's heart and soul helplessly captive to the unforgettable lady of that night; the intoxicating, imagistic atmosphere may be gone, but Ujitada remains in a state of powerful enchantment that dominates his entire existence until the spell is finally broken by the revelation of the mysterious lady's identity near the end of the tale.

Further, it is not just that Ujitada is obsessed with discovering the identity of the lady. What seems like a simple mystery at the end of the first meeting, a simple question of identity, quickly takes on complexity as the magical, supernatural quality of that experience is reemphasized, and as increasingly complex overtones are added with each new allusion. Ujitada's quest becomes one of distinguishing dream from reality under circumstances that appear to deny altogether the possibility of such a distinction. The mystery, the magic, the fusion of dream and reality, the continued suggestions of the otherworldly, Ujitada's unbroken enchantment, and the repeated use of allusion to add depth and complexity are all aspects of the aesthetic of *yōen* as it is seen in poetry.

As indicated in chapter one and in several places throughout the notes to the translation, Teika drew heavily upon *Hamamatsu Chūnagon monogatari* in creating his tale, and instructive comparisons can be made on two points here. The manner in which Ujitada first meets the mysterious lady strongly resembles the way in which, in the earlier tale, Chūnagon meets the Hoyang Consort without knowing who she is.[78] Chūnagon's encounter with the unidentified lady, like Ujitada's encounter, begins an important new movement in the plot of *Hamamatsu Chūnagon monogatari*, with Chūnagon longing to meet the lady again, but unable to do so because he does not know who she is or where he can find her. In spite of certain resemblances, however, the encounter lacks the evocative, intoxicating atmosphere of the one in *Matsura no miya monogatari*, and the subsequent plot is essentially handled as a simple matter of hide and seek. There are no subsequent magical meetings of the sort found in *Matsura no miya monogatari*, and there is nothing, either in Chūnagon's thoughts or in his experiences, to suggest a fusion between dream, reality, and magic.

Dreams do figure prominently in *Hamamatsu Chūnagon monogatari*, and given the other ties between that tale and *Matsura no miya monogatari* it is possible that they were among the inspirations for what Teika has done with dreams, or waking dreams, in *Matsura no miya monogatari*. However, the dreams in *Hamamatsu Chūnagon monogatari* are merely devices of prophecy and communication: characters learn from them, and act on them, but they do not enter them, or find that dream and reality seem to be one and the same. Although a more thorough comparison is not possible here, it should be clear even from these brief remarks that Teika was not merely imitating the earlier tale, but instead was transforming materials obtained from it into something altogether different and new.

---

78. See translation, n. 65.

That transformation can justly be called a *yōen* tale, or at least an attempt at one. It may represent an early step in the development of the aesthetic of *yōen*, or it may represent an effort to apply an already developed poetic aesthetic to the medium of fiction. It will not be possible to know which of these views is correct unless a more precise date can be established for the tale. In either case, the essence of what Teika is trying to do remains the same: far from being merely derivative of *Hamamatsu Chūnagon monogatari*, the conceptual under-pinnings of this portion of *Matsura no miya monogatari* are fundamentally similar to those of the aesthetic of *yōen* in poetry. However, in spite of the presence of so many of what would seem to be just the right elements, it must be said that the effect achieved falls short of what Teika achieves in his *yōen* poetry.

The causes are several. While it is possible that a sustained and concen-trated evocation of "beautiful" imagery is not altogether indispensable for the *yōen* effect in narrative, the absence of such imagery certainly contributes to the weakness of the effect achieved in all but the first of the meetings. In a thirty-one syllable poem, beautiful imagery can fill the entire poem, and, as noted before, through its symbolic and metaphorical suggestiveness can create an "explosive" expansion of the poem well beyond its narrow formal limits. It is not so easy to "fill" a narrative tale with imagery in this way, however, either through repeated evocation of the same particular images, which might be necessary if they are to have metaphorical or symbolic meaning, or through the introduction of a wider variety of images in similar concentrations. Not only is this so because of the greater expanse of the form, but there are particular requirements of narrative, of getting the story told, that must be taken care of, and attention to them can easily (though perhaps it does not necessarily) diffuse the effect of the imagery regardless of how concentrated it may be.

In the present case, neither Ujitada's nights of waiting nor even the dream-like meetings themselves are "filled" with beautiful imagery. To be sure, the moon and the wondrous fragrance continue to be present as images in all of the meetings between Ujitada and the mysterious lady, and the allusion to "Kao-t'ang fu" introduces new imagery with metaphorical possibilities as well as the potential to be used in a manner that would heighten the magical or bewitching character of the meetings. On the whole, however, the moon serves merely in its conventional role as a beautiful object that intensifies one's sadness and longing, and when it becomes a metaphor it is a simple, one-dimensional metaphor for the lady rather than a metaphor with more complex symbolic value. The lady's fragrance, which always precedes her appearance, acts merely as an announcement of her coming, not as an agent of enchantment—as it did on the night of the plum blossoms, or as it does in the poems I have cited as examples of *yōen* poetry. Likewise, in spite of its evocative potential, the story of the spirit of Mount Wu is alluded to only in the context of the two lovers' mutual reproaches—their battle of witty banter in which Ujitada tries to shame the lady into divulging her secret while the lady returns fire with accusations of faithlessness. It would seem to have more in common with the conceits of the age of *Kokinshū* than with the *yōen* of the age of *Shinkokinshū*.

If even the scenes that focus on the dreamlike relationship lack the concentration of imagery that could have given them the enchanting, magical quality of *yōen* in poetry, or of the scene in which the fragrance of plum blossoms first leads Ujitada to the mysterious lady, then the scenes that recount political discussions or that show the emperor repeating once again his regrets about Ujitada's impending departure can scarcely be expected to have those qualities. Such pragmatic and mundane matters do not lend themselves to concentrations of rich and evocative imagery.

Perhaps there could be a story that is in its entirety as evocative as the scene where Ujitada first meets the mysterious lady, but one does not imagine it could be very long unless it is a complete fantasy unconstrained by any of the requirements of realism. In the present case, however, though Teika has clearly turned away from sustained realism to experiment with fantasy, he has not given his story completely over to it. In spite of the supernatural premises of much of the story, the narrative remains largely verisimilar in mode. The fantasy is contained within a realistic tale, and must ultimately satisfy the expectations that adhere to such tales.

One of those expectations is that Ujitada must complete his journey and return to Japan. In spite of the famous historical example of Abe no Nakamaro, who, having been blown back to southern China on his only attempt to return to Japan, went back to Ch'ang-an and served the Chinese court for the rest of his life,[79] no fictional tale of a Japanese courtier who travels to China would be complete without a return voyage. Ujitada cannot simply disappear with the mysterious lady into the heavens riding on a phoenix, as Princess Lung-yü and her husband did. Throughout the second half of the tale, Ujitada is tormented by conflicting desires: the wish to go home to Japan as soon as possible to be reunited with his loved ones there, and the wish to stay in China long enough to learn the truth about the dreampath of love on which he has become so helplessly lost. It is in fact the tension between these two desires that keeps the narrative moving—that gives it what little movement it has in its latter half. But the scenes in which Ujitada's plans to return home are the main item of discussion undeniably distract from the scenes in which the dreamlike meetings are portrayed, and they preclude the possibility that there can be any real development in that relationship.

Another expectation, already noted in discussing the scene of Ujitada's first encounter with the lady, is that most if not all of the questions raised by the narrative also will be answered by it before the story is finished. The marvelous, magical fusion of dream and reality developed through the subsequent meetings between Ujitada and the lady cannot be left unresolved, to resonate its mysterious overtones beyond the end of the tale: a solution to the mystery is a precondition for Ujitada's return to Japan, and must be forthcoming unless he is to stay in China permanently. In fact, a solution is necessary even if he were to stay in China permanently, for the relationship cannot go on indefinitely as it is.

79. See translation, n. 45.

Thus, the empress dowager reveals herself to be the mysterious lady, and details at great length the bonds of karma and divine intervention that have brought both her and Ujitada from the Second Heaven to rescue the Chinese empire from the clutches of a diabolical demon. It is an otherworldly explanation, surely enough, to the point of including figures descending from heaven, but it is devoid of any suggestive, imagistic, or sensuous qualities, and it quite dissolves all of the marvelous dreamlike qualities that had been part of the relationship by "rationalizing" it along with all of the other natural and supernatural events in the tale. It is no longer a tale of the marvelous or the supernatural or the fantastic; there is no longer a fusion of dream and reality, for everything has been revealed to be normal and real within the terms that the tale sets for itself. Insofar as the ethereal effect of *yōen* is concerned, the revelation of heavenly causes for all the events of the tale ironically enough brings everything quite down to earth.

In this, the story contrasts sharply with the legend of the spirit of Mount Wu. There, the apparent fusion of dream and reality remains in effect. The cloud on the mountain peak in the morning sufficiently confirms the reality of the meeting for the king to build a shrine to the spirit. But there is no final confirmation of the reality of the experience for the poet of "Kao-t'ang fu," or for the reader. It may all have been the king's fancy. In noting this contrast, one wonders if the disappointing effect of the empress dowager's elaborate explanation had something to do with the great hurry in which the remainder of the narrative proceeds, depicting little more than the barest essentials to complete the full circle of Ujitada's journey.[80]

A final cause of the failure to achieve a fully satisfying *yōen* effect in the tale is the continuing absence of the retrospective quality that has been noted above for the *yōen* poems. From the perspective of *yōen* poetry, the scenes where Ujitada gazes at the moon, longing desperately for the lady to come to him again, would seem to be more likely places for the evocation of *yōen* than the meetings themselves. It is at such times, when he is remembering past meetings, that the moon or the scent of plum or a wisp of cloud might occasion a poem that metaphorically evokes the dreamlike events he remembers. But Ujitada never composes a poem like Teika's *Shinkokinshū* 44 (poem D) or Ietaka's *Shinkokinshū* 45 (poem C), nor like Teika's Shōji poem (poem E), which seems to encapsulate Ujitada's entire experience of an enchantment so powerful that it blurs even his dreams, along with his waking moments.

Neither can it be said that the overtones of wistful sadness and romantic yearning seen in such poems are expressed by Ujitada or the narrator in other ways, as they might well have been. The narrator states that Ujitada is disconsolate and spends his time in endless longing and brooding. Such statements can even be couched in complex allusions, as at the beginning of book three.[81] But, consistent with the expectation that the narrative will answer the questions it

---

80. See translation, pp. 156–58.
81. See translation, pp. 139–40 and nn. 158–63.

has raised, the emphasis in these cases is on Ujitada's doubts and suspicions about the identity of the lady, rather than on his feelings for the lady herself. On this level, in spite of the overtones added to the magical, dreamlike meetings by the various poetic allusions, the mystery does indeed remain one of simple ignorance, and Ujitada's quest is merely to erase that ignorance rather than a quest for a marvelous, magical love. As the narrative itself is witness, the former (an end to the ignorance) is not really a precondition for the latter (attaining the magical love): the love can exist without an end to the mystery—in fact, can only exist in mystery. But so much importance is given to the problem of identity that the balance of emphasis rests on it with distracting heaviness, rather than on the marvelous love itself or Ujitada's memories of it.

In the next to last scene before the story breaks off, Teika has one final chance to bring the full power of *yōen* to his tale, and to do it in a way that resonates mysterious overtones beyond the end of the tale. The scene in which Ujitada gazes at the empress dowager through a magical mirror reprises the marvel and mystery of all their dreamlike meetings in China, with an image of the lady that is no more real than an image in a dream, and a wondrous perfume that cannot be real, yet *must* be real. Ujitada is now indeed looking back in sadness to a lost love, a love that could not continue—which is to say, the moment is right for the retrospective aspects of *yōen* to finally emerge. As noted for the scene of the conversation between Ujitada and the empress dowager on the evening before the night of the plum blossoms, however, having a few of the standard elements of *yōen* is not sufficient to achieve the full effect of *yōen*. This scene contains only the plainest of natural imagery, without color or evocative power, and without metaphorical possibilities or allusive effect; it thus fails to rise even to the level of the scenes it reprises, for which I already have noted a lack of complexity and depth in the treatment of imagery. Further, in spite of its taking place in a special "place of stillness and purity" apart from the world of normal activities, the scene is devoid of the otherworldly and ethereal atmosphere of *yōen*. This owes in part to the plainness of the imagery, but more fundamentally to the outside concern that remains on Ujitada's mind throughout the scene, and, in the end, calls him away from it all too quickly: Princess Hua-yang. Ujitada's thoughts for the princess seriously undermine our sense of any wistfulness or yearning he may be experiencing, and in fact leave us with the impression that, far from being lost once again in the enchantment of his affair with the mysterious lady, he is but perfunctorily doing his duty to the empress dowager.

If this scene had begun with an enchanting moon or scent of plum that aroused Ujitada's memory of the mysterious lady and led him to take out the mirror; if, in turn, the mirror had drawn him into a powerful trance of longing for the empress dowager without a thought for the princess; and if, finally, the story had ended with Ujitada still lost in wistful reverie and perhaps composing a poem like poems A or E—obviously the effect of the scene would then have been much different. Quite possibly, in Teika's hand, or at least in the hand of a Teika not quite so impatient to be done with his tale, such a scene could have made for a highly evocative and suggestive *yōen* ending, which not only would cast a spell of enchantment beyond the end of the tale but restore to the tale itself some of the mysterious and ethereal overtones that were lost when the empress dowager so matter-of-factly revealed the workings of heaven. Instead, Ujitada packs up the mirror and returns to the princess, to an accusation of infidelity and an ending that is suggestive only in its hint of stormier times to come. Far from offering an "aesthetic explosion," it merely leaves the reader wondering what will happen next. Though not an ineffective ending, as I noted in chapter one, it is quite removed from anything that can be called *yōen*.

Some Historical Perspective

Teika's attempt to write a tale embodying in part the same aesthetic conceptions as underlay his *yōen* poetry is certainly a most interesting experiment. He achieves a considerable measure of success in the passage of Ujitada's first encounter with the mysterious lady, where, within the confines of a single scene, it was possible to create an ethereal and magical mood with imagery remarkably like that found in some of the best known *yōen* poetry. His efforts to sustain some of these magical, dreamlike qualities through a longer movement of narrative are less successful, primarily, it would seem, owing to conflicts between the requirements of narrative and the requirements of *yōen*. Whether these conflicts are fundamental, and would inevitably surface in any attempt to evoke the aesthetic of *yōen* in narrative fiction, or are merely a function of the particular story that Teika chose to tell, cannot be determined on the basis of this one example; in envisioning an alternate ending, I have suggested the possibility that the conflicts can be overcome, but the only way to learn whether it would really work would be actually to try out such an ending, along with any necessary adjustments to the rest of the tale. Ishida Yoshisada, in his book-length study of *yōen* in Teika's poetry, mentions modern novelists Enchi Fumiko, Kawabata Yasunari, and Mishima Yukio as writers whose works embody aspects of *yōen*,[82] and it may well be that, belonging as they do to a much more highly developed—or at least more firmly established and respected— tradition of narrative fiction, they in some cases achieve greater success than Teika in applying the conceptions underlying the aesthetic of *yōen* in classical poetry to the medium of fiction. However, an investigation of their work along such lines is beyond the scope of this study.

During the Heian period, fiction had traditionally been accorded second-class status as a literary form. It was regarded mainly as something for the entertainment of women and children, not worthy of the serious attention of educated men.[83] This attitude was changing at the end of the twelfth century:

---

82. Ishida 1979, 55–56.

83. This is not to say, however, that men had never written *monogatari*. Several tales both from before *Genji monogatari* and from during the twelfth century are believed to have been written by men, or with the assistance of men. For particular cases, see authorship studies for *Taketori monogatari*, *Utsuho monogatari*, *Ochikubo monogatari* ("The Tale of the Lady Ochikubo," ca. 996), and *Torikaebaya* ("Would Each Were the Other," ca. 1100). Takanobu's *Ukinami*

Teika's father Shunzei is famous for having publicly stressed the importance of *Genji monogatari* in a poet's training,[84] and both he and Teika composed poems based on allusions to that tale as well as others.[85] Fiction was now gaining a place in poetry, corresponding in some ways to the place poetry had always had in fiction; it was gaining a measure of new respect among men of the court. Whether Teika's experiments with *yōen* in fiction should be regarded as a further sign of heightened respect for fiction is problematical, however, especially since we do not know if the experiment preceded or followed the corresponding innovations in poetry. Had the young Teika perhaps entertained the thought that fiction could be a very serious medium of literary expression, not just in the hands of a woman writer like Murasaki Shikibu but even in the hands of a formally educated male aristocrat like himself? Or was *Matsura no miya monogatari* from the beginning equivalent to an Edo-period *gesaku*—a playful composition, not at all to be taken seriously—written essentially as an escape, for Teika's own entertainment, at a time when he was not receiving the kind of recognition he thought he deserved?[86] On the one hand, to judge from the nature of the work he wrote (by which I mean primarily the playfulness associated with the forgery), the absence of any mention of the work in his diary,[87] and his abandonment of any further experiments in this vein, one is inclined to the latter view. On the other hand, it seems wholly possible that he undertook this essay into the world of fiction, at least initially, in complete seriousness, and

provides an example roughly contemporary with Teika. For some more general views of the process of composition of fictional tales as well as the possible role that men played in that process, see Imai 1967, 49–50; Tamagami 1950 and 1955; Nakano 1963, 1964, and 1967.

84. Konishi 1976, 188.

85. Misumi (1979, 282), with reference to Teramoto (1970, 44–58) and Hagitani 1960, notes that Shunzei composed poems based on passages in *Genji monogatari*, *Sumiyoshi monogatari*, and *Sagoromo monogatari*, as well as on the poems and titles of works included in *Rokujō Sai'in monogatari utaawase* ("*Monogatari*-Poem Contest of the Kamo Shrine Priestess of the Sixth Ward," 1055), and that his compositions also contain phrases echoing poems from several other *monogatari*.

Teika appears to have been an even more avid reader of *monogatari*. Not only did he compile *Monogatari nihyakuban utaawase* ("*Monogatari*-Poem Contest in Two Hundred Rounds," 1195 or 1206—see Higuchi 1980), a mock poetry contest pitting poems from *Genji monogatari* against poems from *Sagoromo monogatari* and ten other tales, but he frequently alluded to *monogatari* in his own compositions, and may be considered responsible at least in part, if not in full, for the sudden, prominent appearance in *Shinkokinshū* of allusive variations based upon prose passages from well-known works of fiction (*honzetsudori*), in addition to the previously more conventional variations upon old poems (*honkadori*). Ishikawa (1958, 280), for example, notes that *honzetsudori* (or *monogatari-tori* as he calls it), was not altogether unknown before Teika's time, but was very rare—including in *Senzaishū* (1188), the imperial anthology compiled by Shunzei, as well as in Shunzei's private collection. By comparison, he observes, both Teika's private collection and *Shinkokinshū*, the imperial anthology of which he was one of the chief compilers, contain many examples of *honzetsudori*.

86. See chapter one, p. 13.

87. Because portions of the diary, *Meigetsuki* ("Record of the Full Moon"), are missing, we cannot know for certain that the tale went entirely unmentioned in it—especially since portions of some of the most likely years for Teika to have written the tale are among those missing: 1182–87, and 1189–90. See appendix B, pp. 189–90.

that he gave up that seriousness only when he saw his efforts failing; had these efforts been more successful, perhaps he would not have abandoned fiction for the rest of his career. Whatever the attitude with which Teika approached this work, however, there can be little doubt that much of what he did here is closely linked to his aesthetic ideal of *yōen* in poetry, and it behooves scholars of Teika and of late classical poetics to take the tale seriously at least on this one count.

Chapter Three: The Manuscripts and Texts

The textual history of *Matsura no miya monogatari* is remarkably uncomplicated. Some twenty individual copies are known to have come down to the modern period in manuscript form; one of these was destroyed by fire during the Second World War, leaving nineteen copies today. The vulgate textual line (*rufubon*), which includes all but one of the extant manuscripts, emanates from a copy believed to have been made personally by Retired Emperor Go-Kōgon (1338–74, r. 1353–71); only the copy said to have been transcribed by Retired Emperor Fushimi (1265–1317, r. 1288–98) reveals sufficient differences to be distinguished by some scholars as a variant (*beppon*), and not all scholars feel it necessary to distinguish even this manuscript from the vulgate line.

In neither the Go-Kōgon nor the Fushimi manuscript does a colophon indicate the identity of the copyist, nor is positive verification of the hand by other means possible from across the centuries. Perhaps in part for this reason, the manuscripts are somewhat more frequently referred to as the Hachisuka and the Takeda (or now the Yoshida) manuscripts, respectively, after the names of the families in whose possession they have resided, instead of by their imperial names, which I have chosen to use. There is in fact some cause to question the identity of the copyist of at least the Go-Kōgon manuscript: the title page of another manuscript that is beyond doubt a copy of this one states the name of Retired Emperor Go-Hanazono (1419–70, r. 1429–64) rather than Go-Kōgon. The general consensus seems to be, however, that the Go-Hanazono ascription is in error, on the grounds that the hand of the Go-Kōgon manuscript is not only in a style that can be dated to the mid-fourteenth century, but also closely resembles the hand of a copy of *Makura no sōshi ekotoba* ("The Pillow Book Picture Scroll") ascribed to Retired Emperor Go-Kōgon. Barring the discovery of further evidence that casts doubt upon the ascriptions, it seems both more just and more convenient to refer to the manuscripts by the names of the emperors by whose hands they are believed to have been copied, rather than by the names of their past or present owners.

Of these two manuscripts, the Fushimi, if its ascription is correct, would date from a period relatively nearer to the time of the original composition of the tale, but it cannot be considered a superior copy. To be sure, in a number of instances it provides more satisfactory readings, and in one case it supplies a poem—poem 27—that is missing from the Go-Kōgon manuscript. In the majority of cases where readings differ, however, the Go-Kōgon version is to be preferred. Further, most to its detriment, the Fushimi manuscript is itself missing substantial portions of the text: in one place approximately one page (half of a folded manuscript sheet); in another, approximately ten pages.

Printed texts include one in *Zoku gunsho ruijū* 502, a typographical edition of the manuscript prepared, apparently in consultation with several different manuscripts of the vulgate line, by the original compiler of *Zoku gunsho ruijū*, Hanawa Hokiichi (1746–1821); one in *Katsuranomiya-bon Sōsho*, volume 16, a faithful transcription of the Old Archives manuscript (*Zushoryō-bon*) of the Imperial Household Archives (Kunaichō Shoryōbu); one in Iwanami Bunko, edited by Hachisuka Fueko, and based solely on the Go-Kōgon manuscript; and one in Kadokawa Bunko, edited by Hagitani Boku, also based primarily on the Go-Kōgon manuscript, but with a number of carefully considered emendations from the Fushimi manuscript. The last of these is fully annotated and contains a modern Japanese translation as well; it is the edition of the text on which I have based my translation and notes. Complete publication information on the texts appears in the bibliography.

Some qualification is necessary with regard to the pedigree of the Kadokawa edition. At the time this edition was published in 1970, the whereabouts of the Go-Kōgon manuscript was in fact unknown. Considering this the best manuscript but being unable to consult it directly, Hagitani based his text on the Iwanami Bunko edition while comparing it with manuscripts other than the Go-Kōgon, including the Fushimi, in an effort to correct some probable errors that had found their way into the Iwanami edition; he hoped that in this way he would be able to arrive at a more accurate transcription of the Go-Kōgon manuscript. The following year, however, the missing manuscript turned up in an exhibition and sale of old manuscripts held at the Nihonbashi branch of the Mitsukoshi Department Store in Tokyo, and in 1974 Hagitani was finally able to inspect it first hand. Subsequently, in 1975 and 1976, he published corrigenda to the text as it appears in the Kadokawa edition, bringing it fully in line (except where he has with good reason found the Fushimi manuscript preferable) with the Go-Kōgon manuscript. Thus, strictly speaking, although the changes called for are all minor, it is only when the text is emended according to Hagitani's later corrigenda that the Kadokawa text can be considered an edition based directly on the Go-Kōgon manuscript.

A beautiful and elegant facsimile reproduction of the Go-Kōgon manuscript was published in 1981 in the *Gensō ei'in kotenseki fukusei sōkan* series, printed on highly decorated paper created in imitation of the paper used in the original, no two sheets of which are alike. The manuscript itself was designated an Important Cultural Property in 1977 and is now in the possession of the Agency of Cultural Affairs of the Japanese government. One presumes there is no longer any danger that it will be lost.

The Tale of Matsura: A Translation
of *Matsura no Miya Monogatari*

Book One

Long ago, in the days when the emperor's palace was at Fujiwara,[1] a certain nobleman of the senior third rank held concurrently the offices of major counselor and major captain of the Imperial Bodyguards. His name was Tachibana no Fuyuaki, and he had a son named Ujitada,[2] borne to him by his wife Princess Asuka. The boy, an only child, was from birth unparalleled in beauty and temperament, and as he grew older not only his father but the entire court sang his praises as a beacon of light for this unhappy world. He learned to compose Chinese poetry by the age of seven, and of the many skills and arts there was none that he did not master.[3]

"Surely these are not the accomplishments of an ordinary boy," the emperor said upon hearing of Ujitada. Taking a great interest in the child, he summoned him for an audience and presented him with a topic to see how well he composed. Undaunted in the least, Ujitada quickly produced a very fine poem.

He continued to excel in all things as he matured. When he took up musical instruments, whether strings or pipes, he rapidly moved beyond what his instructors could teach him, even in the most advanced of pieces. In the end he ceased to seek instruction from others and instead took to studying by himself, for it seemed he had an intuitive understanding that permitted him to master almost anything entirely on his own.

1. Historically, the location of the capital from 694 to 710, the period immediately preceding the move to Heijō (present day Nara). It was approximately twenty kilometers south of the later capital at Heijō.

   It is unusual for a fictional tale to begin with such a specific placement of the time setting, and we can be quite certain that a truly ancient tale would not have begun in this way: neither standard practice, nor the particular needs of this case, would have called for such specificity. In an era when "long ago" was likely to mean the mid-Heian period, however, Teika no doubt wished to ensure that the reader would immediately orient himself toward a much earlier time. The statement of a specific time setting is thus the first of the special devices he employs in his effort to create the impression of an ancient tale.

2. I introduce the boy's name here for convenience, though it does not actually appear until later in the text. As is customary in classical fiction, once Ujitada reaches adulthood he is referred to by title (*ben no shōshō*, "the controller-captain") rather than by name, but I have used his given name throughout.

3. Ages are given by the traditional Japanese count, indicating the number of calendar years in which an individual has lived.

At the age of twelve, Ujitada received the cap of an adult.[4] The ceremony was performed in the presence of the emperor, who took the occasion to make him a palace attendant. After this His Majesty kept Ujitada as a constant companion by his side. There seemed to be nothing Ujitada did not know, and before long he received both rank and office.[5] Then, in the year he turned sixteen, he was promoted to junior fifth rank upper grade, and appointed to serve as junior assistant minister of ceremonial, lesser controller of the right, and lesser captain of the Imperial Bodyguards.[6]

To Fuyuaki, Ujitada's rapid advancement at court seemed far beyond his due, and it filled him not only with awe but with apprehension—the more so, perhaps, because Ujitada was his only child. In any event, his feelings for his son could hardly have been shallow, for it was thanks to the boy's success that he could hold his own head high at the palace. He could take special pride, too, that even though Ujitada possessed all the advantages of countenance and intellect anyone could ever have wished for, he showed no inclination to indulge in amorous dalliance and frivolous pleasures as most young men did. Instead, he devoted himself single-mindedly to his duties at court and spent his time in scholarly pursuits. Everyone from the emperor on down considered him a most earnest and mature young man.

Inwardly, however, Ujitada had not all this time remained entirely free of those romantic sentiments so wont to torment a youthful heart. Since childhood he had held a special affection for Princess Kannabi, a very paragon of beauty

4. The bestowal of a man's cap was the central act in the coming-of-age ceremony for boys (here called *kōburi* but more frequently referred to as *genpuku* or *genbuku*), which a youth went through sometime between the ages of eleven and seventeen. With the performance of this rite of passage, a youth became eligible both for marriage and for court rank and office.

   The reader familiar with *Genji monogatari* will note certain parallels between the introduction of the hero in these opening paragraphs and the introduction of Prince Genji in the first chapter of that tale: e.g., his beauty and intelligence (along with fears, on the part of others, that a person of such beauty and talent is fated to die young—see Fuyuaki's apprehension below), his ability to compose Chinese poetry at the age of seven, and his coming-of-age ceremony at age twelve in the presence of the emperor. In choosing these particular details, the author of *Genji monogatari* was most likely drawing upon conventions established by still earlier tales for how a tale should begin or how a hero's childhood should be described. See, for example, the first section of the Toshikage story at the beginning of *Utsuho monogatari* ("The Tale of the Hollow Tree," ca. 983). Nakano (1981, 405–9) compares the first few paragraphs of *Matsura no miya monogatari* with those of *Utsuho monogatari*, and the direct correspondences he notes leave little room for doubt that Teika had the earlier tale spread open before him—or at least had it very fresh in his memory—when he committed his opening lines to paper. The two tales begin almost identically, both in pacing and in detail.

5. Entry rank for sons of senior nobles (third rank and above) was usually junior fifth rank lower grade.

6. It was not unusual for a nobleman to hold three separate offices concurrently, for many of the offices were not especially demanding of the officeholder's time. However, the first two offices named here both demanded a high level of scholarly knowledge, and for a youth of sixteen to hold these offices, especially on a concurrent basis, would have been quite extraordinary.

borne to the previous emperor by his empress,[7] and he had secretly vowed to himself that he would someday make her his own. Both he and the princess were young and inexperienced, however, and the time passed without his being able to reveal to her the feelings of his heart.

The Ninth Month came, and the Chrysanthemum Banquet took place as usual.[8] That evening, as the courtiers departed from the palace in their several directions, Ujitada decided to go to the former empress's apartments. Perhaps today he would have a chance to speak with the princess.

He found the former empress and her ladies sitting near the veranda, gazing out at the withered autumn garden. Since he was a frequent visitor with whom they were on familiar terms, they did not immediately withdraw to the inner rooms. The sound of a few casual notes from a lute sent a flutter of excitement through Ujitada's heart, for he recognized at once that they had come from the hand of the princess.

He seated himself on the veranda near the top of the steps leading up from the garden.

"Is the banquet over already?" Jōō no Kimi asked from behind a screen nearby. "We certainly did not expect a visit at this hour."

Ujitada's response, however, was for the princess:

1.	Ōmiya no	"I wonder if you know
	Niwa no shiragiku	How my heart has turned toward you—
	Aki o hete	As through the autumn
	Utsurou kokoro	In the garden of the Great Palace
	Hito shiran ka mo	The white chrysanthemums have turned pink."[9]

7. Though referred to here as *kisaki*, the princess's mother can be neither wife nor mother of the reigning emperor. She was presumably wife of the previous emperor, most likely deceased, who was either father (by another consort) or elder brother of the present sovereign.

8. The Chrysanthemum Banquet was held annually on the ninth day of the Ninth Month in the Shishinden at the imperial palace. The courtiers partook of food and wine, enjoyed various entertainments, viewed chrysanthemum displays, and composed Chinese poems on suitable topics. Chrysanthemums were associated with longevity and thought to have rejuvenative powers.

9. The final line of the poem (the first line of the translation) also means, "I wonder if people know." Along with his hope that Princess Kannabi has noticed how he feels, Ujitada expresses his fear or embarrassment that others besides the princess may have noticed as well because he shows his love so openly.

The first and fourth lines give the poem a distinctly archaic flavor, suitable to a tale set in the Man'yō age. At the same time the association of the phrase *utsurou kokoro* with chrysanthemums belongs to the Heian period and after, betraying a later date of composition for the tale. In *Man'yōshū* the verb *utsurou* (to change) was associated with *tsukikusa* (moonflower) rather than with the chrysanthemum. See following note.

Whichever the plant invoked, however, the verb conventionally carried a negative connotation suggesting the decline of love: the colors of fabrics dyed with moonflowers washed out quite easily, and so the flower was taken as a metaphor for fading feelings; chrysanthemums once turned pink could not be returned to their original pure white, and so became a metaphor for the irreversibility of feelings that have changed. The use of the color of the chrysanthemum as a metaphor for the glow of love at the beginning of a love affair would appear to be a novel one.

He had brought with him a spray of chrysanthemum that had caught his eye, and as he recited this poem, pushed it under the blind toward the princess. Her reply:

2. Aki o hete   "Whatever turns of color
    Utsuroinu tomo   May be brought by the passing autumn,
    Adabito no   Could you have thought
    Sode kakeme ya mo   The white chrysanthemum would easily submit
    Miya no shiragiku   To be plucked by a fickle sleeve?"[10]

She spoke as if to no one, her voice barely audible.

To sense her presence so close made Ujitada wish more than ever to be with her, and he could not bring himself to leave. He leaned against the railing of the veranda and began to play his flute. The picture he presented would have put even princes of the blood to shame: over a richly scented robe of figured silk he wore a cloak of pale purple lined with blue; his trousers were also of a figured material, and at his side was a sword.[11] A grander appearance could scarcely be imagined had he dressed for the most ceremonious of occasions at court.

As a gusting wind tore the last of the leaves from the trees, the moon rose into the sky beyond. The scent of dark incense[12] filled the air both inside and out, its matchless fragrance charming the hearts of everyone within its reach.

Though inexperienced in the ways of the world, the princess had not failed to notice, in the course of Ujitada's frequent visits to the former empress's

10. *Man'yōshū* 3058, Anonymous:

    Uchihi sasu   Though I may have come
    Miya ni wa aredo   To the palace of the bright sun
    Tsukikusa no   And of the finest men,
    Utsurou kokoro   The color of my heart will not change
    Waga omowanaku ni   Like the quick-fading color of the moonflower.

    Man'yōshū 3059, Anonymous:

    Momo ni chi ni   Though others may say
    Hito wa iu tomo   A hundred times, a thousand times
    Tsukikusa no   I am of faithless heart,
    Utsurou kokoro   How could my feelings for you change
    Ware motame ya mo   Quick as the moonflower fades?

    The princess questions Ujitada's sincerity and dependability. By introducing *adabito* (fickle person) in the third line, she recalls the conventional usage of the pun on *aki* ("autumn" and "to grow tired of" someone or something) and of *utsurou kokoro* to indicate a decline of love (as in the above poems from *Man'yōshū*). As a result, *utsurou* here carries both of its possible meanings, and serves ultimately to separate Ujitada from his metaphor: "Color may come to the flower with the passing of autumn, but will fade from your heart when you soon grow tired of me."
11. The precise nature of the colors and fabrics is uncertain.
12. *Kurobō*, a blend of six perfumes, including cloves, aloes, sandalwood, and musk, used to scent robes.

apartments, that he was far more handsome than other men. She had quite naturally come to regard him with some considerable affection, and so it was that today, while speaking only very softly and never at any length, she was not so reticent as to refuse to respond to Ujitada's inquiries altogether.

The night was growing late. Longing to hear more of the princess's music, Ujitada entreated her to play something for him on her zither, but the earnestness of his repeated appeals made her so self-conscious that she stopped playing after only a note or two.[13] Ujitada reached under the blind and seized her hand.

3. Koishinaba   "Feeling I would die—
   Koi mo shinubeki   Die of this unbearable yearning—
   Tsukihi hete   All these days and months,
   Ika ni mono omou   I have come to know how utterly
   Wa ga mi to ka shiru Helpless I am in this love."[14]

Tears overflowed his eyes, and he could do nothing to hold them back. Alarmed by Ujitada's outburst, the princess wished to withdraw to an inner room, but he had a firm hold on her hand, and any attempt to free herself was sure to attract attention.

13. Or it may be that she refuses to play at all.
14. Hagitani 1970, 128. Ujitada uses a common conceit in an attempt to prove the sincerity and depth of his feelings.
    Although this conceit, to die of yearning, cannot be considered to belong to any particular age, the distinctive phrasing of the first two lines echoes that in three poems from *Man'yōshū*:
    Man'yōshū 2370, Anonymous:

    Koishinaba   "Die!
    Koi mo shine to ka Die of yearning if you will!"—
    Tamahoko no   Is this what he would say?
    Michi yuku hito no Many pass along the highway
    Koto mo tsugenaku   But none brings word from my love.

    Man'yōshū 2401, Anonymous:

    Koishinaba   "Die!
    Koi mo shine to ka Die of yearning if you will!"—
    Wagimoko ga   Is this what she would say?
    Wagie no kado o   My beloved passes without a pause
    Sugite yukuran   Before the gate of my house.

    Man'yōshū 3780, Nakatomi Yakamori:

    Koishinaba   "Die!
    Koi mo shine to ya Die of yearning if you will!"—
    Hototogisu   Is this what it would say?
    Monomou toki ni   The cuckoo comes to sing its song
    Ki naki toyomuru   When I am deep in thoughts of love.

4. Nagaraete
   Sugusu tsukihi o
   Tare ka sono,
   Koishinu bakari
   Omou to wa min

   "To see you living on,
   Without change, through days and months,
   Who would have guessed
   Such torments seethed within your heart
   You felt you would die of yearning?"[15]

She was in a fluster of embarrassment and at her wit's end for what to do.

Her obvious distress so pained Ujitada he scarcely felt alive. Neither could he yield to his truest impulse and abandon all restraint, nor could he bear to tear himself away. Caught in a helpless tangle of feelings, he spent the night just as he was. Finally, near dawn, he said:

5. Itazura ni
   Akaseru yowa no
   Nagaki yo no
   Akatsuki tsuyu ni
   Nure ka yuku beki

   "Was it all in vain
   That I waited through the deepest hours
   Of this long autumn night?
   Must my homeward path be dampened
   Not only with dew but with tears?"[16]

After a moment of who can know what turbulent thoughts, he added, "I'll not tell your name."[17]

---

15. Princess Kannabi replies to the question posed in poem 1 as well as that in poem 3.
16. *Man'yōshū* 105, Princess Ōku:

   Wa ga seko o   In the deep of night,
   Yamato e yaru to   I stepped out, to wish him well,
   Sayo fukete   On his way to Yamato;
   Akatsuki tsuyu ni   Lingering in the darkness, I stood,
   Wa ga tachinureshi   Drenched with the dew before dawn.

   While the morning dew is one of the most commonplace images in classical Japanese poetry, the fourth line of poem 5 takes its particular phrasing from this well-known poem composed by Princess Ōku when her brother, Prince Ōtsu, left to return to the capital at Fujiwara after visiting her at Ise, where she was serving as vestal virgin.
17. *Man'yōshū* 2531, Anonymous:

   Wa ga seko ga   Do not forget—
   Sono na noraji to   Your lover has vowed upon his life
   Tama kiwaru   To guard your name;
   Inochi wa sutetsu   Never will he reveal it
   Wasuretamō na   Even should his soul expire.

   There are other instances in the literature where men vow not to reveal their lover's name (e.g., *Man'yōshū* 2407) or place of residence (e.g., *Man'yōshū* 854), or where ladies ask for such a promise from their lovers (e.g., *Kokinshū* 811; also, the wife of the governor of Iyo in chapter 2 ["Hahakigi"] of *Genji monogatari*—see n. 152, below). This was one of the conventional ways for lovers to pledge their faithfulness. Ujitada is making one last appeal for the princess to recognize his love before he takes his leave.

The tears seemed to come from the very depths of his soul, and the princess took pity on him.

6. Akatsuki no   "If you let not fall
    Tsuyu no sono na shi   So much as a hint of my name,
    Morasazuba   Fragile as the dew,
    Ware wasureme ya   Then how could I ever forget you
    Yorozuyo made ni   Even in a myriad generations?"[18]

The visit had served only to magnify his torments, and now, back at his father's mansion, Ujitada found himself unable to sleep. He rose much earlier than usual and wrote a note to Jōō no Kimi.[19]

"After yesterday, I thought I would finally be able to 'follow the changes of the months and years'[20] again, and I anticipated many days of joy to come. But now I find that my heart is in even greater turmoil than before. How painful it is to be reminded just how powerless we can be in this world, in spite of 'thoughts that swell up like waves on the open sea, a thousand times a day,'[21] to satisfy what our hearts truly desire. I hope you will understand my feelings.

7. Moe ni moete   "Surely she will see
    Koiba hito mite   The flaring flames of my passion
    Shirinubeki   Rise up higher and higher

18. The princess finally seems to offer Ujitada some encouragement in his suit.
19. Ujitada writes to, or in care of, one of the princess's serving women rather than directly to the princess herself because his relationship with her has not yet reached the stage where a "next-morning letter" (*kinuginu no fumi*) sent directly would be proper.
20. An allusion to *Man'yōshū* 2536, Anonymous:

    Iki no o ni   I think of her
    Imo o shi moeba   As constantly, endlessly as I breathe,
    Toshitsuki no   With no thought for my life;
    Yukuran waki mo   Is that why I can no longer follow
    Omōenu kamo   The changes of the months and years?

21. An allusion to *Man'yōshū* 409, Ōtomo Surugamaro:

    Hitohi ni wa   Thoughts of my love
    Chienamishiki ni   Swell up like waves on the open sea
    Omoedomo   A thousand times a day;
    Nazo sono tama no   Why can I still not make her mine,
    Te ni makigataki   A jewel to wrap around my wrist?

    It is the second line of the poem that has been taken for the present passage: *chienamishikite mo subenaki yo. Subenaki yo*, translated as "how powerless we can be in this world," may also be identified as distinctly Man'yō diction, though it is not possible to point to one particular poem as the source for its use here: it occurs fourteen times in *Man'yōshū* and only once in the entire poetic tradition thereafter (based on the search outlined in appendix B, section 5).

Nageki o sae ni	As the torments of new yearning are cast like firewood
Soete taku kana	Into the already blazing furnace of my heart."[22]

Jōō no Kimi showed the letter to the princess, who perhaps found it touching, for she wrote the following reply:

8.	Miteshikaba	"Were I to see you now,
	Ware koso kename	Surely I would be consumed
	Moe ni moete	In the rising flames
	Hito no nageki wa	Of a love that burns so furiously
	Takitsukusu ga ni	As even to consume itself."[23]

After this Ujitada was overcome with melancholy and spent most of his time gazing emptily into space.

Noticing how sunken in spirit his son was, Fuyuaki spoke to his wife.

"What could it be that has put him in such a dismal gloom? Even lesser men find ways enough to divert their minds without getting caught up in such needless brooding over themselves. Think of the honors he has received: high rank, important offices—so much more than any of us could normally have hoped for. What does he have to be so depressed about, to shut himself up like this? I'm beginning to be very concerned. Everybody speaks of him as though he were a special gift from heaven, but when I see him looking so despondent all the time I can't help but wonder if something terrible isn't going to happen. I want you to speak to him sometime when he seems to be in a relatively cheerful mood."

22. *Man'yōshū* 2566, Anonymous:

Iro ni idete	If I should allow
Koiba hito mite	The flaring flames of my passion
Shirinubeshi	To reflect on my face,
Kokoro no uchi no	Everyone will see and know of my love,
Komorizuma wa mo	O dearest one hidden in my heart.

Ujitada once again expresses his hope that the princess will recognize how much he loves her; at the same time, through an allusive variation on *Man'yōshū* 2566, he shows his fear that others might discover his love for her as well. Pivot words (*kakekotoba*) and word association (*engo*) play an important role in heightening the effect of the poem and emphasizing the point Ujitada wishes to make. *Kakekotoba*: *koi* (love), also read *kohi* (*hi*=fire); *nageki* ("torments" and "firewood"); *taku* ("to burn" and "to mount up"). *Engo*: *moe* (<*moyu*, burn), *hi*, *nageki*, and *taku*. Because some of the meanings stated separately and explicitly in the translation are derived from double meanings of single words or remain only implicit, the fire imagery is somewhat less overworked in the original than in the translation.

23. The pun on *nageki* is repeated (though it is missing from the translation), and *kename* (<*kiyu*) carries the two senses of the fire going out and one's life coming to an end. As in poem 7, word association—*kiyu*, *moyu*, *nageki*, and *taki* (<*taku*)—provides a strong unifying element.

The princess's poem acknowledges his love, but instead of showing that she is receptive to that love, or that she returns it, merely pokes fun at the extravagance of expression in Ujitada's poem.

His wife, however, was a mother who did nothing but dote on her son. "What could I possibly say to him?" she replied. "You know what they say about the child on your back showing you the way.[24] Now that he has grown up to be such a fine young man, I am counting on him more than ever."

Ujitada regretted causing his parents so much worry, but his longing somehow to make the princess his own grew ever greater, and his anguish remained unabated.

9.	Ashihiki no	"In the footsore hills,
	Yama no yamadori	The calls of the mountain pheasants
	Yamazu nomi	Never, never cease;
	Shigeki wa ga koi	So are my thoughts of you without pause
	Mashite kurushi mo	Ever deepening, more than ever tormenting."[25]

He longed to speak again with the princess, even if only as on the night of the Chrysanthemum Banquet—that he might then find some measure of relief for his aching heart. Before any such opportunity presented itself, however, he learned that the princess would soon be going to court.

The emperor had made it known on a number of occasions that he would like to receive Princess Kannabi into his household.[26] One did not go against the imperial wish even in matters of considerably less importance, and this was certainly not the sort of proposal to be refused. Her mother, the former empress, launched herself into an excited flutter of preparations for the princess's move to the palace.

Ujitada sank into an even deeper melancholy than before. Alone, on a night brilliant with moon, he gazed forlornly out into the open sky and composed:

| 10. | Yama no ha o | "The one I love, |
| | Idetsuru tsuki no | Like the moon from the mountain rim, |

---

24. I.e., "I am the one who should listen to him." From a saying that appears frequently in Edo period writings, and must already have been in use at the time this tale was written: "The child on your back shows you the way across the rapids."

25. *Ashihiki no* is a pillow word (*makura kotoba*), of uncertain origin, for *yama* ("hill" or "mountain"); the first two lines of the poem together form a preface (*jo*) introducing *yamazu* (does not end) in the third line.

The *yamadori* is more properly the copper pheasant. Because the male and female were said to spend the days together but the nights apart, on separate hills or peaks, the copper pheasant became a symbol of lovers who had to spend the night apart.

Hagitani suggests that the poem is an allusive variation on *Shūishū* 780, Anonymous:

Ashihiki no	Unable to see you,
Yama no yamasuge	I can but think of you without cease,
Yamazu nomi	O one that I love,
Mineba koishiki	With yearning as fruitless as the sedge
Kimi ni mo aru kana	That grows in the footsore hills.

Through the allusion, Ujitada expresses his deepest fear: his torments seem to be endless; will they also be ultimately fruitless?

26. The emperor is either her uncle or her half brother. See translation n. 7, above.

Sumu sora no   Rises high above,
Munashiku narinu   And I am filled with an emptiness
Wa ga kouraku wa   Vast as the moonlit sky."27

Even though he knew it was no use, he filled a letter with his most fervent appeals and sent it off. Jōō no Kimi wrote back that she could not arrange a meeting because the former empress was now constantly at the princess's side and nothing could escape her notice.

Ujitada lamented anew:

11. Aratama no   "A new fence,
    Sudo ga takegaki   Woven as tightly as a bamboo door,
    Hima mo naku   Bars the way, it seems,
    Hedate sourashi   With not even a crack for the winds
    Kaze mo morikozu   To bring me word of my love."28

27. A pun on *sumu* ("to be clear" and "to live") establishes the rising of the moon as a metaphor for the princess's going to live "high above," at the imperial palace.

There is possibly an allusion to *Man'yōshū* 2461, Anonymous, of which there are several variant readings. Hagitani (1970, 240, n. 42) gives the following:

Yama no ha ni   Ever so briefly,
Sashiizuru tsuki no   As the moon that rises from the mountain rim
Hatsuhatsu ni   I saw my love—
Imo o zo mitsuru   Enough only to increase manyfold
Koishiki made ni   The yearning that fills my heart.

This allusion would bring to Ujitada's poem a sense of how short-lived his hopes for union with the princess had been.

28. Probably an allusion to *Man'yōshū* 2530, Anonymous:

Aratama no   Had you let me see you,
Kihe ga takagaki   Even if only through the tiny spaces
Amime yu mo   In the bamboo fence of Kihe,
Imo shi mienaba   Do you think I would still be suffering
Ware koime ya mo   From such endless, hopeless yearning?

The original reading as well as meaning of *kihe* remains uncertain. Here I have treated it as a place name, as one theory posits. To judge from line two of poem 11, as well as from other occurrences of the same line, however, medieval poets appear to have read *sudo* for *kihe* and glossed the word as "woven bamboo door." Some manuscripts of *Matsura no miya monogatari* read *suko*, a reading that did not become current for *Man'yōshu* 2530 until after 1246, when Man'yō scholar Sengaku (or Senkaku, b. 1203) completed the first of his three editions of *Man'yōshū*.

Theories about the meaning of the pillow word, *aratama no*, are numerous, varying according to the word or words to which it is thought to have originally been attached. It, too, may have been a place name. I have ignored it in translating *Man'yōshū* 2530; in poem 11 I have taken the sense of "newness" that is attributed to the word by one theory, since the particular "fence" that Ujitada speaks of here is indeed a new one.

For details on both questions, see Hagitani 1970, 240, n. 43; on the pillow word, Fukui 1960, 168–71.

As Ujitada thus passed the days in unrelieved grieving over his sorry plight, an imperial order came down appointing him deputy ambassador of the embassy scheduled to depart for China the following year. It came as a severe blow to his parents,[29] but they knew that only the best men were chosen for such missions, and could think of nothing they could do to prevent their son's departure.

Ujitada wept tears of blood over his redoubled woes,[30] knowing all too well that in neither matter could his own wishes have any bearing on the outcome. Indeed, Princess Kannabi's move to the palace took place as scheduled, and Ujitada could soon see for himself that she had become the favorite among the emperor's ladies. Whenever he heard others talking about the attentions His Majesty lavished upon her he sank into an even deeper state of despondency.

12. Ōkata wa   "Oh, how I wish
    Uki me o mizute   I were going to far Cathay,
    Morokoshi no   Even to the clouds beyond,
    Kumo no hate ni mo   Without the painful memories
    Iramashi mono o   Of these heartrending days."

Going to the palace to carry out his court duties became increasingly unbearable to Ujitada, and he found himself actually taking comfort in the thought that he would soon be sailing far away: it would be much easier to forget everything once he had left the capital behind. But he was also overcome with regrets that he would be unable to look after his parents or to witness the heights to which the princess was sure to rise at court.

The months passed and the day of departure neared. Imperial Advisor and Senior Assistant Minister of Ceremonial Abe no Sekimaro had been named ambassador.[31] Learned men of all the important disciplines and specialties gathered to test the knowledge of those who were to go on the mission, and challenged them to further advance their studies before the trip. Ujitada displayed his brilliance in every subject, outshining all the others. So impressed was the emperor by his performance that he ordered him promoted a step to senior fifth rank lower grade in the New Year's lists.[32]

On the day of departure, crowds of well-wishers high and low accompanied the embassy party to its first stop. There a grand farewell banquet was held and the courtiers spent the entire night composing poems in Chinese.

29. The ocean crossing to China involved a great deal of danger, so they feared for the safety of their only child.
30. The hyperbolic evocation of "tears of blood" to express the extent of one's grief was frequent in poetry. In this case it is possible that Teika was still following the opening paragraphs of *Utsuho monogatari*. See translation n. 4, above.
31. The positions Abe held indicate that he was a man of considerable learning.
32. Of Ujitada's seventeenth year.

As the party was about to resume its journey the next morning, Ujitada received a letter. It was from Princess Kannabi, and had been delivered in the utmost secrecy.

13. Morokoshi no   "My heart journeys with you
    Chie no namima ni   Across the thousand waves that lead
    Tagueyaru   To far Cathay—
    Kokoro mo tomo ni   Earnestly praying for your safe return,
    Tachikaeri miyo   And the day we can meet again."[33]

Not once since going to court had the princess spoken or written to him, and Ujitada had resentfully begun to think that she had lost all care for him. But now there was this, and Ujitada rejoiced with tears of blood to see that she had not forgotten him—that she had not missed this final opportunity to write to him.

Since the messenger had disappeared into the crowd, Ujitada asked an acquaintance who would be remaining behind to take his reply to Jōō no Kimi:

14. Iki no o ni   "With your heart beside me,
    Kimi ga kokoro shi   I would gladly throw my own self

33. Teika has drawn deftly on three different farewell poems to add dimension to the princess's poem. Episode 6 of *Yamato monogatari* provides the only precedent for line three, in a poem Fujiwara Asatada writes to a lady he has secretly been seeing, but who is now about to go off to the provinces with her husband (Takahashi 1972, 274; translated in Tahara 1980, 7):

    Tagueyaru   I send my spirit
    Wa ga tamashii o   To accompany you;
    Ika ni shite   How can you abandon it
    Hakanaki sora ni   And forget me
    Mote hanaruran.   On your forlorn journey?

When Taira Yorisuke left the capital to take up his post as governor of Michinoku in the north (parts of present day Miyagi and Iwate prefectures), Ki no Tsurayuki wrote (*Fūgashū* 889 [*Shinpen kokka taikan* I.17.899]; *Tsurayuki shū* [*Shinpen kokka taikan* III.19.748]):

    Tōku yuku   Warmest regards,
    Kimi o okuru to   I send to you, as you leave
    Omoiyaru   For far away;
    Kokoro mo tomo ni   My heart journeys with you
    Tabine o ya sen.   To share your traveler's bed.

Neither of the two other precedents for line four of Princess Kannabi's poem is a travel poem, so it seems quite clear that Teika was alluding to Tsurayuki's poem for its similar conception.

Finally, in chapter 12 ("Suma") of *Genji monogatari*, as Prince Genji is about to depart for exile, Ōmyōbu writes a poem that provides the only precedent for line five (Abe et al. 1970–76, vol. 2, 175; translated in Seidensticker 1976, 229):

    Sakite toku   Quickly the blossoms fall. Though spring departs,
    Chiru wa ukeredo   You will come again, I know, to a city of flowers.
    Yuku haru wa
    Hana no miyako o
    Tachikaeri miyo.

The reasons for travel and the relationships between the authors and the addressees of the poems are quite different, but each adds overtones to the princess's poem.

Taguinaba	Upon the vast waters;
Chie no nami wake	Calm the thousand waves are sure to be,
Mio mo nagu gani	Calmed by your gentle heart."[34]

"Let us see him off as far as the Bay of Naniwa,"[35] said Major Captain Fuyuaki.

"This separation is no doubt the will of the gods," his wife replied, "and I can do nothing to prevent it. But at least I can go to the farthest boundary of our land, where I will be a little closer to the son so dear to me."[36]

The previous year she had arranged for a small palace to be built for her on a mountainside in Matsura.[37]

"Until the day our son returns, I will wait on Scarf-Waving Peak in Matsura gazing out at the western sky. Young and old alike, our lives are so uncertain— even without the perils of a voyage to China. Once Ujitada has set out to sea, he is entirely at the mercy of the winds and waves. My waiting may be in vain; we may never see each other again, my son and I. But I will follow the example of Princess Sayo, who gave the mountain its name."[38]

34. There are puns on *nagu* ("throw" and "to become calm") and *mi o* (myself) and *mio* ("waterway" or "channel"). *Iki no o ni* is distinctly Man'yō diction (see, for example, translation n. 20, above), as is *gani*.

35. The port of departure for embassies to Korea and China was at Mitsu on Naniwa Bay (present day Osaka Bay).

36. Or, perhaps, "The length of our brief time in this world is determined by the gods, and none of us can hope to remain together with our children beyond this present life. As long as I am in this world, I want to remain as close as possible to my beloved son. If he is to go to a foreign land, how can I be anywhere but at the farthest boundary of this land?" (Hagitani 1970, 18, n. 4; 134.) The text is garbled, but even so Hagitani's rendering seems to supply more than is necessary to construct a coherent reading.

37. Matsura included present-day Saga and Nagasaki prefectures on the island of Kyushu, together with the Gotō Islands. The name is most frequently written with characters that mean "Bay of Pines," but, following the usual pun on the word *matsu*, is also intended to suggest "Bay of Waiting." In poems 15, 16, and 17, below, this name is used as a pivot to refer both to the place and to the act of waiting. Since no further thematic use is made of this play on words in the rest of the tale—Ujitada several times thinks of his parents waiting for him, but without reference to Matsura—it would appear that the tale takes its title solely from this passage. See chapter one, pp. 5–6, and nn. 3 and 4.

38. The name Hirefuru-yama (Scarf-Waving Peak) remains in use today as one of the names of a mountain located a short distance east of the present city of Karatsu. The headnote to *Man'yōshū* 871 offers the following account of how the mountain got this name (translated in Levy 1981, 379):

> The youth Ōtomo Sadehiko received the favor of a special imperial command ordering him to serve as messenger to the outer provinces. He readied his ship, then set out into the rising waves. His lover, Princess Sayo of Matsura, sighed over the ease with which fate had taken him away, and lamented the difficulty of ever seeing him again. She climbed to the summit of a tall mountain and watched his ship fade into the distance. Her heart was broken with sorrow, and her soul was choked with darkness. At last she removed the scarf from around her neck and waved it at him. None of those who stood beside her watching could keep from crying. Therefore this mountain is named *Hirefuru-mine*, Scarf Waving Peak.

With these words, she set out to accompany Ujitada on his westward journey.

Though his responsibilities at court hardly permitted him to do so, Fuyuaki decided to go along as well.

"I want at least to see how you will live there, in such a remote place," he said to his wife.

The journey went entirely without incident. Favorable winds carried the ship swiftly on its way, and it arrived at Dazaifu around the twentieth day of the Third Month.[39] The governor-general of Dazaifu ordered up an even more lavish welcome when he saw that Fuyuaki had come with the embassy party. They passed the days in concerts, and composing Chinese poems.[40]

The party remained in Dazaifu until after the tenth of the Fourth Month. Finally the ship was ready and the day of departure was at hand. Ujitada's mother gazed out over the sea stretching endlessly into the distance. She thought she had prepared herself for this parting, and yet now, when the time was actually before her, tears flowed anew as all her worst fears for her son pressed upon her mind:

15. Kyō yori ya   "From this day forth
    Tsuki hi no iru o   I shall be the more attached
    Shitaubeki   To the setting sun and moon
    Matsura no miya ni   As I prayerfully await my son's safe return
    Wa ga ko matsu tote   In my palace on a mountain in Matsura."

Her husband also composed a poem:

16. Morokoshi o   "Alone in the capital,
    Matsura no yama mo   With even the mountains of Matsura
    Haruka nite   So far, far away,
    Hitori miyako ni   Must I abide in solitary anguish,
    Ware ya nagamen   My gaze ever cast toward China?"

He longed to remain with his wife so that they could wait for their son's homecoming together, but he had been ordered in no uncertain terms to return to court immediately. He knew he could not stay.

39. Dazaifu was located to the southeast of the present city of Fukuoka. It was the seat of the governor-general of a territory that included the nine provinces of Tsukushi (Kyushu) and the islands of Iki and Tsushima. The nearby port of Ōtsu was the official international port during the Heian period.

    All but the earliest of the embassies to China involved two or more ships, and the time of this tale—around the beginning of the eighth century—corresponds to the period when the number of vessels sent was increased from two ships to four (Mori 1966, 25–27). However, since nothing in the text indicates that more than one ship went on the mission of which Ujitada was a member, I have translated in the singular.

40. Although the relative status of the offices involved here went through a number of changes over the centuries, the normal assumption would be that the governor-general ranks higher than the ambassador but lower than Fuyuaki, who is a major counselor. This would explain why the governor-general goes to such lengths when he sees that Fuyuaki is in the party.

Ujitada's parting poem:

17. Namiji yuku   "I sail across the sea
    Ikue no kumo no   To the distant land that lies beyond
    Hoka ni shite   Numberless banks of clouds;
    Matsura no yama o   But my heart will be turning ever homeward
    Omoi okosen   With thoughts of the mountain in Matsura."

The majestic ship released its moorings and moved away from shore. Before long it looked like no more than a fragile fallen leaf tossed helplessly upon the waves. Ujitada's mother raised her blind and gazed sadly after the vessel until it disappeared among the clouds and haze on the horizon.

Fuyuaki, too, was deeply saddened by their son's departure, and when he saw just how profoundly stricken his wife was, he could hardly bear to think that he would soon be separated from her as well. He worried about how she would pass the coming days and months in this place so far from the capital, and he earnestly wished he could remain with her. But a strongly worded message from court reminded him that it had been only under a special and unprecedented dispensation that he was permitted to be away even this long, and to extend his absence further was simply out of the question. His departure for the capital seven days later became an occasion for many more tears.

Fuyuaki's poem:

18. Shirazarishi   "Never did I expect
    Wakare ni soeru   To be parted from my son like this,
    Wakare kana   Nor, then, from you;
    Kore mo ya yoyo no   Is this, too, a mournful legacy
    Chigiri naruran   From our former lives?"

His wife's reply:

19. Ikanarishi   "What could they have been?—
    Yoyo no wakare no   The partings of a former life
    Mukui nite   For which I now must pay
    Inochi ni masaru   By bearing the sorrow of twin separations
    Mono omouran   More painful even than death."

She covered her face with her sleeve and wept.

Fuyuaki tried to comfort her as best he could, even as he fought back tears of his own. It was time to go, and the ship set sail. One after another, memories of all the joys and honors his wife had brought him flooded through his mind,[41] and with the memories came a new wave of grief over their parting. His tears now flowed without restraint.

This was Fuyuaki's forty-sixth year. He was in the prime of his life and exceedingly handsome. Today he wore a lined cloak of yellow-green over a robe of pale purple and crimson, and figured trousers of a slightly different shade of

---

41. Joys and honors that had been his because he had received a princess of the blood for his wife.

purple—a subdued combination that for its very lack of ostentation made him look all the more magnificent. His wife, Princess Asuka, had turned thirty-four this year. On this day she had thrown a fine white cloak over robes of pale purple and yellow-green. The combination was not particularly striking, but on her it seemed to heighten her natural nobility and elegance.[42]

Aboard ship, Ujitada's thoughts were filled with bittersweet memories of all that had happened to him, his grief over his separation from his parents and Princess Kannabi, and all the countless uncertainties awaiting him in the days ahead. His only comfort was the princess's last letter, which he carried close to his heart.

20. Taguekeru   "Is it perhaps because
    Hito no kokoro ya   Her heart does journey with me,
    Kayouran   Just as she promised?—
    Omokage saranu   Even here upon the waves
    Nami no ue kana   I see her image before me.[43]

21. Wata no hara   "My drifting boat:
    Oki tsu shioai ni   I know not where it takes me
    Ukabu awa o   Upon this vast sea,
    Tomonau fune no   Tossed among the mingling currents
    Yukue shirazu mo   Like foam from the surging waves."[44]

As for the ambassador, he had left behind a young wife and child whom he missed dearly, and the sentimentalism that comes with old age further multiplied his tears.

22. Kasuga naru   "From beloved Kasuga,
    Mikasa no yama no   Where it cast its light on Mikasa Hill,
    Tsukikage wa   The moon has come
    Wa ga funanori ni   Joining me in my shipboard journey
    Okurikurashi mo   To see me on my lonely way."[45]

---

42. Hagitani (1970, 245, n. 62) wonders if "crimson" (*kurenai*) in the description of Fuyuaki's clothing, and "yellow-green" (*moegi*) in the description of his wife's, have perhaps been inadvertently transposed by a copyist. The presence of crimson seems to contradict the description of Fuyuaki's clothing as *wazatonaranu* ("casual"—not looking as though he had devoted special attention to it), while yellow-green would fit that description quite naturally; on the other hand, since women more commonly wore crimson, his wife's clothing would remain "not particularly striking" (or "unusual," "original"—*kotonaru iroai naranedo*) even if it included a garment of that color.

43. The poem echoes the princess's parting words in poem 13.

44. *Kokinshū* 910, Anonymous:

        Watatsumi no   Like the white foam,
        Oki tsu shioai ni   Tossed up by the mingling currents,
        Ukabu awa no   Upon the vast sea—
        Kienu mono kara   Neither can I fade quietly away,
        Yoru kata mo nashi   Nor can I find place to moor.

45. The ambassador's name, Abe no Sekimaro, is clearly modeled on that of Abe no Nakamaro (698–770), a member of the embassy sent to China in 717. Appropriately enough, the poem

Their ship was troubled less by storms and unfavorable winds than anyone could have hoped, and on the seventh day after setting sail the call went round that they were approaching land. Indeed, far ahead a thin line of coast had appeared on the horizon, and, as their vessel drew nearer, the rocky shoreline proved to be more glorious than any they had ever seen before.

The ship docked at the port of Ming-chou that night.[46] A messenger was immediately dispatched to inform the Chinese emperor of their arrival and their purpose. The governor of the province welcomed the envoys warmly and entertained them with poetry exchanges and music.

All of the sounds of this country were new and marvelous, from the manner of the people's speech to the songs of the birds in the trees. With everything so delightfully different from what he had been accustomed to in Japan, Ujitada was for a time distracted from his endless brooding over not knowing where the future would lead. Before long, however, all his memories and uncertainties pressed back in upon his mind, and he found himself gazing longingly out across the vast plain of sea over which he and his countrymen had so lately come. Beyond the blue waves rising and falling on and on into the distance, layer upon layer of clouds stretched across the horizon, as if heartlessly to block

Sekimaro composes here is an allusive variation on a famous poem said to have been composed by Nakamaro when he was in China. *Kokinshū* 406:

Ama no hara	When I turn my eyes
Furisakemireba	To gaze out across the heavenly plain,
Kasuga naru	Behold, the brilliant moon—
Mikasa no yama ni	Just so did it cast its light
Ideshi tsuki ka mo	On Mikasa Hill, in beloved Kasuga.

Long ago, Nakamaro was sent with an embassy to study in China, and remained there a great many years without being able to come home. He was at long last able to leave the Chinese capital when another embassy sent from this country was ready to return. His Chinese friends gave him a farewell banquet on the coast of Ming-chou, and on the night of the banquet, as a flawlessly brilliant moon rose into the sky, Nakamaro composed this poem. Such is the account given of this poem.

Although Nakamaro departed, in this way, with the returning embassy party, he failed to reach home. His ship was blown off course to the far south of China and he returned to the Chinese capital where he served the T'ang court for the rest of his life. Mori 1966, 135.

The year in which Abe attempted to return home was 753, about half a century after the time in which this tale is set.

46. The story of Abe no Nakamaro's famous poem (see previous note) makes Ming-chou the obvious choice as a port of landing for an embassy in a work of fiction. The port was located near present day Ningpo in Chekiang province, about 150 kilometers south of Shanghai, and was the port of arrival or departure for many Japanese embassies to China.

Crossings of under ten days did not become possible until the Japanese adopted the direct route across the sea to China in place of the northern route, which skirted the Korean peninsula, or the southern route, which descended along the chain of islands south of Kyushu before setting out across the sea. Although records are not complete for all of the embassies known to have gone to T'ang China, the best indications are that the direct route was not attempted until late in the eighth century. Mori 1966, 39ff.

from sight the land of all his memories. One after another the images of those he yearned to be with came before him, and his eyes quickly filled with tears.

The others in the party, too, were thinking of home, and a heavy somberness filled the air. Even so, their Chinese hosts could see that Ujitada's distress was greater than any of the others', and they did one thing and another to try to cheer him so that his grass pillow might be spared the dampness of dew.[47]

Thanks to these attentions, Ujitada finally managed to regain sufficient composure to join in the poetry exchanges alongside the ambassador. Both of them acquitted themselves most impressively, and the Chinese marveled that men of such remarkable learning could come from overseas. It was enough to convince them that Japan must indeed be a land of high cultural achievements.[48]

Before long the embassy received permission to proceed to the capital and set out on the long overland journey that would take them through great mountain ranges and across countless rivers and plains. As they proceeded along their rugged route, over many a treacherous mountain path, they were slowed by the interminable Fifth-Month rains that forced them time and again to halt their progress and seek shelter. In due course, however, they arrived safely in Ch'ang-an.[49]

The Chinese emperor was a man in his thirties, who had shown great wisdom in ruling over his empire.[50] He summoned the Japanese emissaries for an audience in the Outer Hall of the Wei-yang Palace.

47. A conventional poetic figure for the loneliness and sadness of a traveller who must spend the night away from home. The dew is of course associated with tears.

48. Or "Meanwhile the ambassador was busy composing poems in turn with his hosts. Inwardly he could but exclaim over the number of learned men who came forward, even in a city so far away from the capital, to compose the most accomplished of poetry. China was indeed a land of high culture." Hagitani 1970, 23, n. 10. Hagitani's handling of the conjunctive particle *ba* seems awkward, however.

  Not surprisingly, Japan and the Japanese are portrayed favorably elsewhere in the tale, both through the brilliant accomplishments and heroic feats of Ujitada, and through direct statements crediting the Japanese with a reputation for courage and wisdom. My reading of the present passage would place it in the same category as other such self-laudations of Japan. It also better reflects the broad pattern of resemblances observed between this tale and *Hamamatsu Chūnagon monogatari*, which Hagitani himself notes in several other places, including the passage just below where the arrival of the embassy in the Chinese capital is described. Chūnagon's remarkable performances are twice the occasion for observations about how remarkable and splendid a land Japan must be. See n. 50, below.

49. The capital of China during the T'ang Dynasty (618–907). It is not specifically mentioned by name here in the original text.

50. Hagitani (1970, 23, n. 13) notes a resemblance here and in the following paragraphs with the passage in *Hamamatsu Chūnagon monogatari* where Chūnagon, the central character of that tale, first meets the Chinese emperor (Matsuo 1964, 155; translated in Rohlich 1983, 56–57):

  An Imperial messenger came with an invitation for Chūnagon to meet the Emperor at the Ch'eng Yüan Hall within the Inner Palace. The Emperor was a young man just over thirty, very handsome and dignified, but even he thought Chūnagon magnificent beyond compare. With men such as Chūnagon, the ministers and counselors mused, Japan must indeed be a remarkable place. They were certain that even P'an Yüeh of the Hoyang District could not have been as charming as this counselor from Japan. And when they

The members of the embassy arrived at the palace and proceeded to the Outer Hall to present themselves before the emperor. Ranked on either side of the approach to the throne were the imperial bodyguards, in full splendor and looking most forbidding. The audience began with performances of music, and, since their party was made up of men of accomplishment, the Japanese were able to join in without disgrace. Next came poetry. The emperor asked each of his visitors to compose a poem, and immediately recognized in Ujitada a man of superior talents. He noticed, too, that his brilliance of mind was matched by a no less dazzling countenance.

"How old is this young man?" he asked the ambassador.

"Seventeen, Your Majesty."

"Then he is practically still a child! And he has already learned so much! Can it be possible?" the emperor exclaimed in amazement.

Because Ujitada was both young and so magnificently handsome, the emperor took a great liking to him and wanted to keep him nearby. He ordered one of the grand ministers[51] who lived near the palace to arrange apartments for Ujitada and see that he would find nothing wanting.

Each morning he summoned Ujitada to court at dawn, to have him demonstrate his many talents and great knowledge, as well as to have him instructed in new areas of learning. In everything Ujitada did, he quickly surpassed the accomplishments of even the native courtiers and scholars. This gave rise to a certain amount of resentment in some quarters, but no one dared to treat him with anything but the most indulgent kindness, for it was clear that he enjoyed the imperial favor.

When the emperor continued to single Ujitada out for his attention and to keep him constantly at his side, however, the ministers and counselors began to submit written remonstrances, admonishing His Majesty at considerable length:

"From the time Your Majesty first came to reign over all under heaven, you have heeded the advice of your humble subjects, and your rule has been as placid and smooth as the progress of a boat poled downstream with the current. You have never failed to listen to the concerns even of lowly haymakers and woodcutters. Yet, now you consult only with a youthful visitor from a far-off land, whom you keep by your side at all times. It concerns us deeply that this may come to leave an ugly blemish upon your otherwise flawless reign."

> tested him at writing poems and playing musical instruments, they discovered no one could excel him. "We should learn from this man. What could we possibly teach him, even of the arts of our own land?" thought the Emperor in amazement. The courtiers found that his constant company assuaged their grief and worry.

> The following lines, found only a few paragraphs later, may also be noted (Matsuo 1964, 158; translated in Rohlich 1983, 59):

> No one among the princes and nobles could equal Chūnagon in composing Chinese verse. Everyone, including the Emperor, was amazed at his talents; they thought he must be from an unusually splendid land.

51. *Daijin*, a title not actually used in China during the T'ang dynasty.

To everyone's great dismay, however, the emperor showed no inclination to take such admonishments to heart.

"Did not Emperor Wu of the Han employ Chin Mi-ti, even though he was not of our race?"[52] he said. "A ruler's choice of advisors must be based solely on the individual's character and merit."

The ministers could but watch with growing alarm as the emperor took their youthful visitor from Japan even more fully into his confidence than before.

His Majesty, for his part, was convinced that Ujitada was a paragon of beauty and intellect such as the Chinese court was never likely to see again, and he had developed a special fondness for him. He treated him with the greatest of favor, instructing him personally in the finer subtleties of Chinese poetry and discussing with him other matters of taste and learning, so that in the course of only a few days Ujitada's knowledge of these things increased immeasurably.

52. The Go-Kōgon manuscript gives a *katakana* gloss of "Kin Jichi-tei." Chin Mi-ti was born the son of a king of one of the Hsiung-nu ("barbarian") tribes to the north of China. He became a slave of the Chinese court at the age of fourteen, but later drew the attention of the emperor and became one of his confidants. He is credited with having saved the emperor from an assassin at one point. His biography is included in book 68 of *Han-shu* ("History of the Former Han") by Pan Ku, of which an English translation can be found in Watson 1974, 151–57. The following excerpt from the translation is of some interest in light of the way Ujitada's character is described below, as well as of the alarm that high ranking courtiers show over the emperor's generosity toward Ujitada. Hagitani (1941, 18) notes several phrases in *Matsura no miya monogatari* that are virtually direct translations of phrases in this passage of *Han-shu*.

> Because Chin Mi-ti's father had not surrendered but had been killed, he, his mother the consort of the late king, and his younger brother Lun all became government slaves. Chin Mi-ti was assigned as a keeper of the horses of the Yellow Gate. He was fourteen at the time.
>
> After a considerable time had passed, the emperor one day decided to hold a banquet and review his horses. The ladies of the palace were grouped about him in large numbers as Chin Mi-ti and the other grooms, thirty or forty men in all, led their horses past the hall where the emperor was sitting. None of the other grooms failed to steal a glance at the women; Mi-ti alone did not dare to look up when his turn came to pass in review. He was eight feet two inches [a little over six English feet] in height and had a very stern face and manner, and in addition his horses were sleek and well cared for. The emperor, impressed, asked him who he was and he replied with the full story of his origin. The emperor, judging him to be a man of unusual worth, on the same day ordered him to bathe, wash his hair, and put on a robe and cap, and appointed him superintendent of horses. In time he advanced to the posts of attendant in the inner palace, commandant of the imperial horses, and counselor to the keeper of the palace gate.
>
> After Chin Mi-ti had become a favorite of the emperor he was never guilty of error or oversight. The emperor loved and trusted him greatly, presenting him with a thousand catties of gold on several occasions. Abroad he rode by the emperor's side; within the palace he was constantly in attendance. Many of the emperor's relatives and other persons in high position were secretly resentful, saying, "His Majesty by some quirk of circumstance gets himself a barbarian boy and what does he do but treat him with honor and respect!" When the emperor heard of their remarks, he only treated Chin Mi-ti more generously than ever.

Also see n. 80, below.

The emperor took special pleasure in having the young crown prince with him, and at such times he always called on Ujitada to attend him. He seemed intent on having Ujitada become as familiar with the crown prince as with himself. This, too, was cause for alarm in the eyes of the ministers and counselors. They began to fear that the presence of this remarkable foreigner at court might upset both the stability and the continuity of the emperor's sage reign.

His Majesty summoned countless lovely dancing girls, all decked out as colorfully as flowers, to perform to the sounds of enchanting melodies, and he had beguiling beauties gathered from throughout the land to charm Ujitada with entertainments that might well have stopped his heart from beating. Ujitada, however, had always been of a retiring and sober nature, and he continued always to conduct himself with his characteristic restraint.

"Perhaps the people of Japan are more serious-minded than I thought," the emperor noted with approval. He continued to be exceedingly generous toward Ujitada.

Ujitada, for his part, knew how formal and particular the Chinese were about matters of decorum, and how heavy the penalty could be if he were guilty of even the slightest breach. Adding restraint to restraint, he spent his nights alone. Before long it was autumn.

On the thirteenth night of the Eighth Month the moon rose clear and bright and cast its light into every corner of the Thirty-Six Pavilions.[53] Ujitada had received no special summons requiring his attendance, and with the guards at their stations looking their most forbidding, carefully questioning all who entered, he was not inclined to go of his own accord. Feeling for once free to do entirely as he chose, he lay down and let his mind roam. Almost immediately his thoughts drifted homeward, and his heart was filled with an uncontrollable yearning for the ones he loved, "three thousand leagues away."[54]

Unable to divert his thoughts, Ujitada decided to go for a turn in the night air. He took with him only a token guard of one or two men, and set out aimlessly, to go wherever the path might lead. Presently he emerged from the city into open country, where fields and meadows filled with autumn flowers, some familiar and some not, stretched on and on towards the horizon. Far off to

---

53. I.e., the palace compound.
54. The phrase "three thousand leagues away" (*san-ch'ien li wai*) appears quite a number of times in poems by Po Chü-i, but the time of year, scene, and particular wording of the text here suggest rather an allusion to the one instance when the figure was *two* thousand leagues (perhaps to avoid redundancy with "thrice"). *Haku Raku-ten shishū*, book 14, "On the Night of the Fifteenth of the Eighth Month, On Duty Alone in the Forbidden City, Gazing at the Full Moon and Thinking of Yüan Chen," lines 3 and 4:

On this thrice-fifth night, as the moon rises bright,
I think of an old friend two thousand leagues away.

one side he could see a great endless sea, the bright light of the moon dancing upon its waves as they rolled one after the other to shore.[55]

Gazing off into the distance, Ujitada spurred his horse forward along the path to see where it might take him. After some time—the position of the moon indicated it must now be close to midnight—he came to the foot of a tall, pine-covered mountain, on the top of which stood a small cottage. The sound of a zither[56] issued from this cottage to mingle its tones with the soughing of the wind in the pines.

Ujitada turned his horse up the mountainside toward the cottage, his interest aroused by the strains of music coming from within.[57] He arrived at the bottom of a flight of stone stairs, dismounted, and began climbing; it remained some distance to the top.

On the mountaintop was a clearing where the ground was covered with pure white sand. The cottage, small and rustic, stood on the southern edge of this clearing, looking out over the sea far away. Except for the music of the zither, there were no other signs of anyone about.

Never had Ujitada heard such beautiful strains as these, rising so transparently clear into the nighttime sky, and nothing could suppress the desire that now filled his heart, to learn to play this music himself. In a state of increasing excitement, he ascended the steps leading up into the building, brushing aside all caution the remoteness of the place urged upon him.

Inside, not a single speck of dust clouded the rays of moonlight that shone on the figure of an old man leaning over a zither. He went on playing, oblivious to the intrusion. White-haired and frail, he looked perhaps eighty, but he had a noble and dignified bearing. On his head he wore a simple, hoodlike cap; by his side lay an inkstone and writing brush.

Ujitada seated himself on a small bench near the top of the stairs to listen. As the music enveloped him, a wondrous serenity seemed to come over his soul, and tears fell from his eyes.

The old man began to sing, apparently still unaware of Ujitada's presence. His seasoned voice blended in inimitable harmony with the music from the zither to create an effect unlike any Ujitada had ever heard.

55. There is no sea, of course, in the vicinity of Ch'ang-an. Hagitani speculates that Teika may have been misled by certain phrases in Chinese poems he had read. For example, *Monzen* (Chinese *Wen-hsüan*), book 1, "*Fu* on the Western Capital":

> East of the City there is a great canal, connecting with the Wei and Yellow Rivers; the waters carry boats to the east of the mountain, and, flowing down the Huai and across the lake, join with the waves of the sea.

Likewise, *Haku Raku-ten shishū*, book 9, "Moon over the Forbidden City," lines 1 and 2:

> The bright moon rises over the face of the sea,
> To light the Forbidden City on this clear autumn night.

56. *Kin* (Chinese *ch'in*), the seven-stringed Chinese koto. See chapter one, n.1.
57. It should be remembered that Ujitada has been represented as a peerless musician.

After some time, the old man looked up from his zither. He showed no surprise to see Ujitada, said nothing, and continued to play as if in a trance. Ujitada could but continue to listen in silence.

As the moon started to fall behind the western mountains, the old man returned the zither to its case, which had been lying nearby, and set it aside. He then retrieved his cane from where it rested against the railing of the veranda, and started down the steps.

Under his breath, as if only to himself, Ujitada recited a poem. It expressed the sentiments of a traveler far from home, arrested by the sound of a zither and held captive to its music all night long.

The old man heard him and halted his steps before reaching the bottom of the short stairway. After a brief pause he responded with a poem that explained his own circumstances: he was but an old man, retired from office and no longer serving at court, given to gazing at the moon from this cottage; it was a special joy to meet such a magnificent young man from the Land of the Rising Sun.[58]

Ujitada still wished, no less than before, to learn the secret of playing the zither as the old man had played. He quickly followed the old man's reply with another poem. After several more exchanges, the old man began a lengthy discourse.

"It is not by mere accident that we have met here tonight," he said. "Long before I heard you speak, long before I ever learned your name, I knew of you, and knew that you would come here this night. You have been brought here by a special bond—a bond that has destined you to learn the secrets of this zither music and transmit them to your own country. That is why you were called upon to leave your parents behind and travel to an alien land.

"For all of my many years, I have lived in this country, and for seventy-three of them I have played the zither. In the course of those years, my skill on the zither brought me high rank, far above my due, and many other honors I could never have hoped to receive; at times it also brought me undeserved hardships and grief too great for a single heart to bear. In the last of my years at court I received the Order of Merit and was appointed governor of Honan and grand tutor to the crown prince. But it was clear that the end of my time was approaching: I had more and more difficulty making my way about, and found myself troubled with illness. I decided to resign my offices in order to seek rest for my aging body. This is already the fourth year of my retirement, my fourth year of viewing the moon from this cottage. Now, when I look at the moon of autumn

58. The designation for Japan in early Chinese sources was *Wokuo* (Japanese *Wakoku* or *Wa no kuni*), possibly meaning "land of the dwarfs." By the time of the T'ang dynasty the name *Jih-pen kuo* (Japanese *Hi no moto no kuni*), or "Land of the Rising Sun," was also in use. By the end of the twelfth century, when this tale is believed to have been written, the latter of these seems to have been the standard name used for Japan in Chinese sources. Hagitani 1970, 251, n. 85.

or the blossoms of spring, I have nothing but the sound of my zither from which to take comfort for my soul and sustenance for my body.

"Regardless of my past accomplishments, however, I cannot now compare with Princess Hua-yang in my skill on the zither. She, more than I, understands the most profound secrets of the instrument. It is from her that you must learn. Every year, on the nights of the full moon in the Eighth and Ninth Months, she goes into retreat on Mount Shang[59] to practice her zither.

"She is but a woman, and only in her twentieth year—sixty-three years younger than myself. But she came to this world with an inborn understanding of the zither from having mastered the instrument in a former life, and in this life she has received further instruction in its deepest secrets from an immortal sage.

"Return now to the capital. Do not fail to seek out Princess Hua-yang on Mount Shang. However, if you truly wish to learn the secrets of the zither, you must not allow any frivolous thoughts to enter your mind. You must remain sober and serious at all times. Tell no one about this. The ways of our people may appear tolerant, but in fact are narrow; they may seem flexible, but in fact are rigidly set. Our rulers have expressly forbidden the teaching of such deep secrets to those from other lands.

"I speak to you openly in this way because many years have passed since I resigned my offices; also because I have received and adhere to the teachings of Buddhism and I do not wish to break the precept against falsehood. But remember this: once you have learned this music, you must never, never allow anyone of this country to hear you play it. And remember this too: when you are receiving instruction from the princess, you must not permit any untoward thoughts to enter your heart, or to distract you from your purpose.[60]

59. Southeast of the capital.
60. Ujitada's foreordained destiny, its revelation, the instructions to seek the teaching of another, and the proscription against playing the music he learns while still in China, all parallel details in the story of Toshikage, in the first chapter of *Utsuho monogatari*. Toshikage, sent on an embassy to China, is shipwrecked on the shores of Hashi (generally identified by scholars as a name for Persia, though, clearly, the author used it without any real knowledge of the geography of continental Asia). He remains in Hashi some twenty-three years, and almost every experience he has during this time in some way involves the *kin*, the same kind of zither that plays such a major role in *Matsura no miya monogatari*. Out of wood cut for him by an asura (see n. 186, below), thirty of these instruments are constructed, lacquered, and strung for him by a number of celestial figures who descend from above. When he tests the instruments, Toshikage discovers that two of them have magical powers. Some time later, when Toshikage is rehearsing upon a zither, a celestial lady comes to him and tells him (Harada 1969, vol. 1, 18; Kōno Tama 1959–62, vol. 1, 44),

> By the will of heaven, you are destined to found a house here on earth that will prosper by the music of the zither. I once committed a sin for which I was required to do penance for a period of seven years in a land west of here but east of the land of the Buddha. While there I gave birth to seven sons. These sons remain there today, playing their zithers in harmony with the music from the Pure Land Paradise. Before you return to the Land of the Rising Sun, you must go to them and learn from them the music that they play. Of the

"Eighty years I have been allotted in this life, and my remaining days are few.[61] Even were it not so, our paths would not likely cross again, for this country is destined to experience a time of great turmoil. Still, with this meeting here tonight as a bond, we will surely meet again in another life. Do not forget any of the things I have told you."

With these words the old man once again ascended the stairs into the cottage, to fetch the zither he had played that night. He returned and gave it to Ujitada.

"Take this with you and seek out Princess Hua-yang on Mount Shang," he said. "Once you have learned the secret music, you must never play it again while you remain in this country."

The pale colors of dawn were spreading across the sky. Ujitada parted with the old man after repeating his promise to do exactly as he had been instructed. As he retraced his steps over the path he had followed the night before, a vague sadness came over him, and he remained lost in abstraction the entire way home.

Even before the sun had gone down that evening, Ujitada set out for Mount Shang according to the directions he had received, spurring his swift steed onward as fast as its legs would carry him. As on the night before, the time had advanced to around midnight when he heard some strains of zither music coming from high atop a tall mountain. He began to climb in pursuit of the still distant music, and as he made his way up the long path he passed one magnificent estate after another, with countless roofs shining like mirrors in the moonlight. The music, however, seemed to be coming from a much smaller establishment of a distinctly humbler appearance—a cottage with an outbuilding or two, and nothing more. This, no doubt, was where he would find the lady he sought.

He approached the cottage through the trees, where he could remain hidden in the shadows, then ascended the steps and entered the building. Inside, just as the old man had said, was a supremely beautiful lady, alone, gently plying her hands upon the strings of a zither. Indeed, she was as brilliantly beautiful as a polished jewel. In spite of the old man's repeated warnings that

thirty zithers you have received, I have chosen names for the two that are superior to the others. One shall be called Nanfu, the other Hashifu. You must never play these two zithers before anyone other than my seven sons.

61. The age figures the old man gives do not add up consistently. The best explanation would seem to be that *hachijū-nen* is used here in the loose sense of "eighty-odd years," or perhaps simply "very old." Alternatively, it is possible that the figure of sixty-three years given as the difference between the old man's age and the princess's age (twenty) is in error. Hagitani (1970, 30, n.9) notes that if the old man has been playing the zither for seventy-three years and he began playing on the sixth day of the Sixth Month of his sixth year, the customary time for a child to begin such training, then he would now be in his seventy-ninth year and would indeed have only "a few days remaining" until he reaches the eighty years he claims to have been allotted.

he must maintain his composure at all times, Ujitada was as if struck dumb from the moment he first set his eyes upon the princess. He had thought the dancing girls at the palace as lovely as the loveliest of flowers; suddenly they were like the dirt beneath his feet. Back home he had thought no one could match the beauty of Princess Kannabi, who had so stirred his heart; now he could see that next to this lady she would be like the unkempt daughter of a provincial rustic.

Her hair was gathered on the top of her head and held in place with a profusion of ornamental pins that might have seemed excessive and in poor taste on anyone else, but on this lady it had quite the opposite effect.[62] Indeed, to look upon her enchanting elegance and serene beauty was like gazing at the flawlessly clear harvest moon illumining the soft autumn night.

He struggled to control the turbulent feelings in his heart, reminding himself over and over of the true purpose of his having come here. When finally he had managed to regain his composure enough to listen to the music, it became instantly apparent that the princess was a far more accomplished player than the old man of the night before. Her music blended in absolute harmony with the myriad sounds of nature and echoed across the heavens with a perfection of tone even the old man had not been able to attain. Ujitada could but wonder if he had wandered into a dream.

As if in a trance, and with no special prompting from the princess, Ujitada took out the zither the old man had given him and began to play. At this the princess interrupted the piece she had been rehearsing and started playing instead a simpler piece—one more suitable for Ujitada to begin on. He listened as she played the piece through to the end without stopping, then joined in when she started at the beginning again. He followed with ease from the first, not missing a single note, and as the music gradually cleared his heart of all other thoughts and concerns he found that he was able, quite naturally, to match the subtlest tones of the princess's playing; before long their performances had become indistinguishable. Playing together in this way they moved from one piece to another, and by the time the night was over Ujitada had mastered a great many pieces perfectly.

62. The description of Princess Hua-yang's beauty and Ujitada's response to it parallels the description in the following scene from *Hamamatsu Chūnagon monogatari*, where Chūnagon sees the Hoyang Consort for the first time (Matsuo 1964, 159):

> Court ladies in Japan left their long straight hair free to fall loosely over their shoulders and cheeks, and Chūnagon had always thought this style most to his liking: it held a certain unaffected elegance that he found especially attractive. But there was something different about this lady. On her, nothing could have done more to bring out the full beauty of her features than the way she had arranged her hair on the top of her head with dazzling ornamental pins.

There are many parallels between Chūnagon's subsequent relationship with the Consort and Ujitada's relationship with Princess Hua-yang (as well as with another lady later in the tale). Just in the scene where the above passage appears, for example, the following additional points might be noted: when Chūnagon first sees the Consort, he is hiding in the shade of a tree or shrub in the garden of her mansion, having heard some music from a short distance

With the first signs of the approaching dawn,[63] the princess pushed her instrument aside and prepared to leave. The sorrow that came over Ujitada now was unlike any he had ever known, and he was helpless to stop the tears that poured from his eyes. The princess, too, was overcome with emotion. The incomparable beauty of her profile as she gazed up dolefully, plaintively at the face of the moon stirred Ujitada's heart anew.

They exchanged poems in the customary manner before parting.

"I will teach you the remaining pieces next month," the princess said, "on the five nights beginning with the thirteenth."[64] Her poem:

23. Kumo ni fuku   "Somehow I knew,
    Kaze mo oyobanu   Though no one had ever told me,
    Namiji yori   A visitor would come—
    Toikon hito wa   Traveling farther across the sea
    Sora ni shiriniki   Than even the wind in the clouds."

    Ujitada's reply:

24. Kumo no hoka   "Many were the dear ones
    Tōtsu sakai no   I left behind in my beloved homeland
    Kunibito mo   Far beyond the clouds;
    Mata kabakari no   Unhappy though those partings were,
    Wakare ya wa seshi   None were so painful as this."

Before he had finished, the approach of the princess's escort could be heard. Following her instructions, Ujitada departed by way of a side door, where he could slip away unseen behind the ridge of the mountain.

Although he hastened homeward with great speed, hoping to arrive before the light of day was completely upon him, it was midmorning by the time he reached his quarters and retired directly to bed. Feeling quite as though his soul had deserted his body, he lay awake in a state of feverish agitation over the beautiful princess he had met the night before. He knew his agitation could do nothing but increase, and he brooded on and on over what he was to do.

Since the princess had indicated he should not return that night, he knew it would do him no good to go, yet he longed to do so if only to catch a fleeting

away and taken care not to be seen as he approached; she is playing a zither; she appears to be about twenty years of age; and the music she is playing is lovelier than any Chūnagon has ever heard.

    For another translation of the above passage and a translation of the scene as a whole, see Rohlich 1983, 59ff.; for further parallels, see n. 65, below.

63. All manuscripts read *Tsuki no akeyukeba*. Hagitani emends the phrase to read *Yo no akeyukeba*.
64. In Japan the moon of the thirteenth night of the Ninth Month was called *nochi no meigetsu* ("the latter harvest moon," perhaps—two days prior to our "hunter's moon"). The custom of regarding the moon on this night as special did not exist in China; in Japan it was begun by Retired Emperor Uda in the year Engi 19 (919), more than half a century after the colophon would have us believe the tale was written.

glimpse of her from the distance.[65] The emperor, however, had planned a banquet in celebration of the full moon, and Ujitada's attendance was commanded. The entire night was spent in various amusements and Ujitada had no chance to slip away. The following day, too, he was required to wait upon the emperor and unable to obtain leave.

That night heavy rains made his solitary traveler's bed feel even more forsaken than usual, and with a second image now added to the one that had so long come before him whenever he closed his eyes, he began truly to pity himself for all the anguished yearning he had been fated to suffer.

25.	Shirazarishi	"To a traveler's tears
	Omoi o tabi no	Are added these unexpected tears
	Mi ni soete	Of a forbidden love;
	Itodo tsuyukeki	Damper still it has become—
	Yoru no ame kana	This night of heavy rains."

Although they could be no different from anywhere else, the days and months had seemed somehow longer since he came to this alien land, and now this lonely autumn night seemed long enough to exhaust all his torments. If

---

65. This would be the night of the fifteenth of the Eighth Month, the night of the harvest moon. The text reads *koyoi wa binnage ni notamaitsuredo*, literally, "Although she had said tonight would not be good." When Ujitada left the princess on Mount Shang, her instructions were in terms of when he *should* return—on the thirteenth of the Ninth Month—and she said nothing about her convenience at any other time. The locution here thus strikes the reader as a bit strong, though it might simply be explained that Ujitada is drawing an inference from what the princess said.

There is another possible explanation, however, which requires a brief summary of a fortuitous meeting between Chūnagon and the Hoyang Consort in the first chapter of *Hamamatsu Chūnagon monogatari*:

One night while he is visiting Shan Yin, a place about a day's journey from the capital, Chūnagon is drawn by the sound of a *biwa* (a kind of lute) to an elegant, though unfinished, dwelling. When he seeks out the source of the music, he finds several ladies seated near the veranda of the main building. One of them bears a remarkable resemblance to the Hoyang Consort, who had left a deep impression on Chūnagon on the night he secretly witnessed her playing the zither (see translation n. 62, above). Chūnagon impulsively approaches this lady, and before the night is over they have exchanged vows of love.

The reader knows that the lady is in fact the Hoyang Consort herself, in retreat at this place because a diviner warned her that she must observe a period of abstention. Chūnagon does not know this, however, and the Consort and her ladies take care to keep her true identity concealed. As dawn approaches and the Consort tells him he must leave, Chūnagon insists on another meeting that evening. The Consort replies, "Today and tomorrow I am in a period of strict taboo so you must not come here. Two or three days from now come late at night to my mansion in Ting Li. I am to be here for only a few days and the period of taboo must be strictly observed." (See Matsuo 1964, 176–80; Rohlich 1983, 74–76.)

The many similarities between circumstances and developments in the relationship of Chūnagon and the Consort on the one hand and those in the relationship of Ujitada and Princess Hua-yang on the other strongly suggest that Teika referred frequently to the earlier tale as he wrote. It seems possible that he inadvertently confused the two stories, and was in fact thinking of the Hoyang Consort's words quoted above when he had Ujitada recall that Princess Hua-yang "said tonight would not be good."

only he could take up his zither and play the melodies the princess had taught
him!—he could at least feel a little closer to her then. But he knew this was
forbidden, for he had not forgotten what the old man had said. Lacking any
other means to vent his feelings, he composed another poem.

26. Wasureji to   "Could I only
    Tsutaeshi koto no   Play aloud the notes I learned
    Ne ni tatete   Never to forget,
    Koi dani miba ya   How it would ease the yearning in my heart
    Aki no nagaki yo   And the passing of this autumn night."[66]

Although the night seemed interminable, the drum that announced the
break of day finally sounded. Messengers from the palace rushed about sum-
moning Ujitada and all the other courtiers to another day of entertainments, and
by the time the sun was fully risen everybody had assembled. Ujitada joined in
as best he could, but his mind strayed elsewhere. As before, he was not permitted to leave until the following morning.

On this day Princess Hua-yang returned to the capital.[67] Long ago, when
she was still very young, the princess had gone to Mount Shang in order to
observe a period of abstinence.[68] While she was there, on the night of the

66. The first two lines carry a second meaning, deriving from a pun on the word *koto* ("zither" and
    "words"), that does not come through in the translation: "The words of admonition I received
    and promised never to forget"—namely, the admonition from the old zither player that
    Ujitada must not play the music he learned from Princess Hua-yang so long as he remained in
    China, which is the reason why he cannot play music here.
67. It is now the eighteenth of the Eighth Month.
68. Or, "in order to avoid a directional taboo," according to Hagitani 1970, 35, n. 13. My reading
    provides not only a more direct translation of the word *monoimi* in the text, but also reflects the
    pattern of parallels that can be noted between this tale and *Hamamatsu Chūnagon monogatari*:
    the Hoyang Consort went into retreat at the place where Chūnagon found her (see translation
    n. 65, above) because a diviner had told her, "You must go away from here and observe a
    period of strict abstinence" (*tokoro o sarite imijiu kataki mono o imasetamae*; Matsuo 1964, 176).
    Hagitani interprets *monoimi* in this case to mean *kataimi*, referring to the elaborate system of
    directional taboos that was followed to one degree or another both in Japan and China. On a
    given day or for a given period certain directions in relation to (or, in some cases, certain
    locations within) one's place of residence or point of departure would be "closed" owing to the
    position of the stars, the individual's horoscope, and a variety of other permanent or temporary
    factors. One was required to avoid moving, spending the night, or conducting other specified
    activities in these directions and locations as long as they remained closed. Some directional
    proscriptions applied to everyone at the same time, depending on the current position of
    various gods who traveled from one place or section of the compass to another following a fixed
    calendar; others applied only to individuals according to the year of their birth.
    It can be imagined that the potential of such a system for disrupting necessary activities and
    business would have been considerable, and so it is not surprising that a corresponding system
    of maneuvers for circumventing or disarming the taboos came into practice. Hagitani appears
    to believe that it was such a maneuver, or *katatagae*, that first took Princess Hua-yang to Mount
    Shang. It should be noted, however, that although the princess could certainly have chosen to
    travel such a distance on her own volition, the rules for *katatagae* would not have required her
    to remove herself so far away as Mount Shang. For details regarding *kataimi* and *katatagae*, see
    Frank 1958.

harvest moon, a divine sage descended from above and transmitted to her the secrets of the zither. Every year since then she had made it her custom to go to Mount Shang around the times of the full moon in the Eighth and Ninth Months, to rehearse the secret music she had been taught.

The princess and the emperor were born of the same mother, a former empress, and everyone at court knew of the unequaled solicitude with which His Majesty looked after her. She was always treated with the greatest of deference by all, and it was not surprising that her return to the palace was greeted with a considerable commotion. Ujitada heard the clamor from a different part of the palace and was filled with a deep melancholy. He could do nothing now but wait for the thirteenth night of the Ninth Month to come.

One empty day followed another, and the appointed day arrived. The emperor had been indisposed since the previous day, and there was no summons, so Ujitada was free to make his planned excursion to Mount Shang. Without even waiting for the sun to complete its descent, he set out as if in a dream.

Everything about the cottage was exactly as it had been the time before. Princess Hua-yang played through all of the remaining pieces for Ujitada and finished shortly before dawn, as the moon was about to disappear beyond the mountains.

"You must go now," she said.

Ujitada could not bring himself to move, caught in a spell cast over him by the stunning beauty of her face and figure, by the enchanting sound of her voice as she spoke this single fleeting phrase, by the marvelous perfume of her robes. She was in every way so far beyond compare that Ujitada found it difficult to believe he was not in fact dreaming.

"When you return tonight we will play the pieces together," the princess finally added.

With this reassurance, Ujitada prepared to go. Even so there were tears in his eyes as he recited a parting poem.

27. Yoshi koko ni   "May it be broken,
    Wa ga tama no o wa   The jeweled cord of my life,
    Tsukinanan   On this very spot:
    Tsuki no yukue o   That my soul need not be forced to part
    Hanarezarubeku   From the moon when it leaves at dawn."[69]

69. *Tama no o* means both "jeweled cord" and "cord of one's soul." In the latter sense it is often used independently, as it is here, in place of the word *inochi* (life). As a pillow word (*Tama no o no*—see poem 30 and n. 74, below) it is used to modify such words as *nagashi* (long), *mijikashi* (short), *tayu* ("to end" or "to break off"), *midaru* (to become tangled, disordered, confused), and others; it is mainly associated with poetry of the Man'yō period.

The moon represents the princess, much as it represents the Hoyang Consort in a poem by Chūnagon in *Hamamatsu Chūnagon monogatari* (Matsuo 1964, 185; translated in Rohlich 1983, 80):

The princess was deeply moved.[70]

28. Tenarenuru   "Because we are bound
    Tama no o-goto no   By the jeweled cords of the zither,
    Chigiri yue   So dear to my hands,
    Aware to omoi   I think of you with tenderness,
    Kanashi to mo miru   And look on you with love."[71]

But even as she replied she was hurrying him on his way.

This time, too, Ujitada took care not to be seen as he departed. The grief of the parting affected him so much more profoundly than before that he could not bear to leave the vicinity of Mount Shang. He found lodging near the foot of the mountain and passed the day there.

29. Ōzora no   "While I wait for nightfall,
    Tsuki ni tanomeshi   To meet again the brilliant moon
    Kure matsu to   Shining in the sky,

    Haru no yo no   The spring moon is gone,
    Tsuki no yukue o   I know not where.
    Shirazushite   Now in misery
    Munashiki sora o   I watch the empty sky.
    Nagamewabinuru

Chūnagon composes this poem in the midst of a prolonged depression following the disappearance of a lady with whom he has spent a fleeting night, and who reminds him of the peerless Hoyang Consort. Chūnagon later learns the lady was in fact the Consort herself, but he is never able to meet her in private again. See translation n. 65, above.

In chapter 8 ("Hana no en") of *Genji monogatari*, the same image is used by Prince Genji after Kokiden's sister Oborozukiyo ("the lady of the misty moon"), with whom Genji has spent a night, leaves the palace for home (Abe et al. 1970–76, vol. 1, 430–31; translated in Seidensticker 1976, 154):

    Yo ni shiranu   I had not known the sudden loneliness
    Kokochi koso sure   Of having it vanish, the moon in the sky of dawn.
    Ariake no
    Tsuki no yukue o
    Sora ni magaete

70. Poem 27 and this line are missing from the Go-Kōgon manuscript. Hagitani emends the text from the Fushimi manuscript.
71. The first lines of the Hoyang Consort's parting poem in the scene from *Hamamatsu Chūnagon monogatari* described in translation n. 65, above, resembles the lower verse of Princess Hua-yang's poem (Matsuo 1964, 180; translated in Rohlich 1983, 76.):

    Ushi to omou   Wretched and yet tender
    Aware to omou   Is the fate which ties me to one
    Shirazarishi   From the unknown land far beyond the clouds.
    Kumoi no hoka no
    Hito no chigiri o

Yama no shizuku ni   In the dew of the mountain
Sode wa nuretsutsu   I dampen the sleeves of my robe."[72]

That night and the following nights[73] Ujitada returned to the cottage to receive instructions in the deepest secrets of the zither, and each morning he departed dutifully at dawn. As long as there was more music to be learned, which demanded his total concentration, he could keep his mind from the turbulent feelings that raged in his heart. But on the final night, the knowledge that this would be his last meeting with the princess filled him with such sadness that he burst into tears the moment they finished rehearsing the last of the secret pieces.

The princess could see how distraught Ujitada was, and felt exceedingly sorry for him. Her eyes, too, overflowed with tears as she gazed sadly at the moon, now low in the sky with the approach of dawn. She recited a poem.

30. Tama no o no   "The cord of jewels
    Tayuru hodo naki   Holding my soul to this earthly life
    Yo no naka o   Is destined soon to break,
    Nao midarubeki   Yet, still the bonds of former lives
    Mi no chigiri kana   Entangle my heart in deepest passion."[74]

    Ujitada responded:

31. Tama kiwaru   "Should my soul expire
    Inochi o kyō ni   And my life suddenly come to an end

72. *Man'yōshū* 107, Prince Ōtsu:

    Ashihiki no   In the footsore hills,
    Yama no shizuku ni   Amidst the dew of the mountain,
    Imo matsu to   Waiting for my love,
    Ware tachinurenu   I stood alone, forsaken and drenched,
    Yama no shizuku ni   In the dew of the mountain.

    Man'yōshū 108, Lady Ishikawa's reply:

    A o matsu to   In the footsore hills,
    Kimi ga nureken   Amidst the dew of the mountain,
    Ashihiki no   You waited for me, you say,
    Yama no shizuku ni   Oh, that I could have been the dew
    Naramashi mono o   That drenched you through and through.

73. *Amata yo o suginu*. The phrase clearly indicates the continuation, for several more nights, of Ujitada's musical training. Hagitani (1970, 37, nn. 6 and 7) interprets the phrase as a reference to the "many nights" that have passed since Ujitada's meeting with the princess the month before, rather than to the "several-night" duration of his current training, and is therefore troubled by the fact that Ujitada's training seems to last only one more night even though the princess had said she would teach him the remaining pieces over a period of five nights. Although *amata* does indeed signify very large numbers in many cases, *Daijiten* (1980, vol. 1, 407) confirms that it often means simply a number greater than one or two—i.e., "a few" or "several."

74. For *tama no o no*, see translation n. 69, above. Here the phrase is both a conventional epithet for "life" and an image to introduce *tayu* (to break) and *midaru* ("to become tangled, disordered, confused"—in this case with passion). The princess wonders why her heart should be so filled with passion when she knows she is destined soon to die.

Kagiru tomo   On this very day:
Mi o ba oshimaji   Even so I would have no regrets;
Kimi o shi zo omou   Even so I could love you no less."[75]

Clasping the princess's hand, he broke into tears again. It tore at her heart to see him in such distress.

"From the time a devout sage built this cottage so long ago," she said, "it has been a place of inviolate purity, watched over from above by the sun and the moon, guarded from below by the gods of the earth. Because the contours of the mountain on which it stands are so especially suited to the tones of the zither, I have for the last seven years made it my custom to practice the secret music here in this cottage. Over the years divine sages have come down from above many times, to repair my zither or to put the cottage in order. My time in this life will soon come to an end, but, like these sages, even in my next life I will return here, to this place, to hear music played by others. If I now did anything to violate the purity of this place, I would regret it forever, throughout all of my future existences; whether I lived or died would make no difference, for never again could I face anyone, either on earth or in heaven, without shame. I would not have taught you the secrets of the zither nor have become so intimate with you if it were not for a bond from a former life. You were led to find me here because I was destined to experience the trials of love and face the censure of the world.[76]

"My allotted time in this world is short, and I will not be permitted to live out even that brief span if I should surrender to the impulses of my heart. But if your affection for me is so great that you would give your life for my sake, then come to the Pavilion of the Five Phoenixes[77] in the Forbidden City on the third night of next month, when the moon is about to set. I will be there without fail."[78]

The princess then hurried Ujitada on his way with even more urgency than she had on the previous occasions. There was nothing he could say. He

75. The origin of the pillow word *tama kiwaru* is unknown. Because it can be interpreted to mean one's soul (*tama*) reaching its limit (*kiwaru*), it was frequently used in association with the word *inochi* (life) to signify the end of a person's life. Fukui Kyūzō 1960, 408–12; *Daijiten* 1980, vol. 7, 178. See *Man'yōshū* 2531 in translation n. 17, above.

76. The text for this line is probably garbled. Hagitani's attempt to make sense of it would seem to turn it into a logical circle: "Because I succumbed to the ways of love (with you), I was condemned to face the censure of the world, and that is why you were brought to me here."

77. Po Chü-i makes reference to such a pavilion in one of his poems (*Haku Raku-ten shishū*, book 26, "A Night in the Pavilion of the Five Phoenixes"), but it seems to have been located in Lo-yang rather than Ch'ang-an. It is not surprising, however, that Teika confused the two cities, for Lo-yang had been the capital of the Eastern Chou (770–256 B.C.E.), the Latter Han (25–221 C.E.), and several other shorter-lived dynasties, and was considered the "Eastern Capital" of the T'ang dynasty. The author of *Hamamatsu Chūnagon monogatari* appears to have been the victim of a similar confusion. See Rohlich 1983, 57, n. 9.

78. What Princess Hua-yang tells Ujitada in this long speech is in its essential elements similar to what the Hoyang Consort tells Chūnagon in the scene referred to in translation nn. 65, 68, 69, and 71, above. In each case the lady claims a strict proscription that prevents her from submitting to the man's wishes; she suggests another meeting at a different location and on a later date; and she anxiously hurries the man on his way.

departed in tears, overwhelmed by grief that seemed to have multiplied many-fold since their last parting. The image of the princess remained vividly before his eyes all the way home.

32.	Mineba ushi	"Unbearable though it is,
	Chigiru sono hi wa	I cannot see my love again
	Haruka nari	Until a distant day;
	Nani ni inochi o	In what will I gain the strength to live
	Kakete sugusan	Through days of such wretched longing?"

Back at the palace, what had seemed to be but a mild indisposition failed to respond to any of the medicines prescribed, and His Majesty's condition took a turn for the worse. Everyone at court became increasingly concerned as day after day went by bringing no sign of improvement.

Ujitada thought it best to remain away unless he was expressly summoned. Even so, he spent a great deal of time at the emperor's bedside, as the emperor sent for him whenever he was feeling the least bit better. Ujitada felt honored beyond his due to be so taken into His Majesty's confidence.

"You came to us from a distant land, and we have not known each other for very long," he said one day. "But yours is the face of one who is destined to bring peace and tranquility to this land. This illness will be my last, I know, and a time of violent upheaval is sure to follow after I have gone.[79] When this happens, you must not fear for your life; you must not attempt to run away. Stay always with the crown prince. If you do this, I can assure you, your life will be preserved, and you will be able to return safely to your homeland. I tell you this now for a special reason—you must never speak of it to anyone in this country. There is a bond between us from another life, which will keep us together even after you have returned to your distant country. Do not forget what I have told you, and do not fail to do as I have said."[80]

79. Or, reading a hypothetical *ba* instead of the *wa* that Hagitani prefers, "If this illness proves to be my last, a time of violent upheaval is sure to follow after I have gone." As a reason for his preference, Hagitani states his belief that Teika was using an archaic locution in order to lend more dignity to the emperor's speech. Such a device is not used elsewhere, however, and a more straightforward reason for preferring the nonhypothetical form of the statement might be that it is consistent with the prophetic nature of the latter half of the emperor's speech: as with what he says about Ujitada, the emperor is not merely speculating about his own fate—he has reason to know. Such supernatural foresight on the part of the emperor is both implicitly and explicitly corroborated later in the tale.

80. Ujitada's role vis-à-vis the Chinese court is modeled on a composite of the figures of Chin Mi-ti (see translation n. 52, above) and Ho Kuang as portrayed in book 68 of *Han-shu* (Hagitani 1941, 20 and 1970, 257–58, n. 116; translated in Watson 1974, 123):

In the spring of the second year of *hou-yüan* (87 B.C.), the emperor went on an outing to the Palace of Five Oaks, where he fell gravely ill. Ho Kuang, in tears, said, "If that which I dare not speak about should occur, who ought to be appointed as successor?"

The emperor replied, "Have you not yet perceived the meaning of the picture I gave you [of the Duke of Chou bearing on his back the infant King Ch'eng and receiving the

The emperor's words saddened Ujitada immeasurably. He began to protest that he could not even tell one end of a bow or arrow from the other, and so could hardly be of use in quelling violent disturbances. Some others entered the room, however, and the emperor broke off the conversation. Ujitada saw that he had been taken more fully into His Majesty's confidence than courtiers who had served the court for many years, and it redoubled his feelings both of affection and of pity for the emperor.

At long last, the third night of the Tenth Month came. Ujitada's heart quivered with excitement as he recalled the princess's promise and turned his steps toward the palace to keep their appointment. A state of increased vigilance had been ordered at the time the emperor first became ill, and tonight the palace seemed to be swarming with guards. Even so, Ujitada managed to steal past watchful eyes and find his way to the Pavilion of the Five Phoenixes with little difficulty.

Princess Hua-yang did not keep him waiting: she emerged from the pavilion as soon as the moon had gone from the sky.[81] Under the dim glow of the stars she appeared even more beautiful than she had in the full light of the moon, and a flood of tears quickly choked off Ujitada's every attempt to speak.

They lingered on the stone terrace that circled the building for scarcely a moment before passing through the vermilion doors into the darkness within. The fragrance of her robes filled the room—it was no ordinary perfume she had used to scent them. No joy could have been greater for Ujitada than to be once again in the presence of the princess's infinite beauty. He could never tire of gazing upon her. Yet now that they were together, they were both so helplessly overcome with tears that for a time neither of them could speak.

feudal lords in audience]? I want my youngest son set up, with you to act the part of the Duke of Chou."

Ho Kuang bowed his head and begged to be excused, saying, "I would not be as good as Chin Mi-ti," but Chin Mi-ti in turn said, "I am a foreigner—Ho Kuang would be better!"

The emperor thereupon appointed Ho Kuang grand marshal general in chief, and appointed Chin Mi-ti general of carriage and cavalry. . . .

The following day (March 29), Emperor Wu passed away and his heir succeeded to the position of highest honor, being known posthumously as Emperor Chao the Filial.

The following passage also bears noting (Watson 1974, 154):

When the emperor fell ill, he asked Ho Kuang to assist his youthful successor. Ho Kuang deferred in favor of Chin Mi-ti, but Mi-ti said, "I am a foreigner. Moreover, if I were to accept the task, it would cause the Hsiung-nu to look upon the Han with disrespect." As a result he ended by acting as Ho Kuang's assistant.

Since Chin Mi-ti died the following year, it was Ho Kuang who remained to protect the interests of the new child emperor.

81. Under the lunar calendar, the almost-new moon of the third of the month would disappear from the sky around 6 P.M.

Seeing the obvious depth of Ujitada's feelings for her, the princess felt herself losing all care for this world. She had not personally been guilty of any wrong, she told herself. Events in her former lives had ordained that she would have to face the anguish of an impossible love, and there was nothing she could have done to forestall such a fate. This must have been what the sage had meant when he told her, years before, that the secrets of the zither would one day lead her to her death. Now that day had come.

To have perceived this brought no relief, however, for affairs of the human heart are seldom so easily resolved. Indeed, she felt more helpless than ever to contain her swelling passion, and there seemed nothing left but to abandon herself to it completely.

"If you truly love me," she said, "and can promise never to forget me even after you have returned to your homeland, then I will tonight give up my hold on this transient life, and pledge myself to you so that we can meet again in our lives to come."

From the sash of her underrobe she took a crystal jewel nearly large enough to fill the palm of her hand, and gave it to Ujitada.

"If your feelings are as you say they are," she continued, "and if you would truly be faithful to the vows we have made to each other, then carry this jewel with you always. Even in the face of the most violent of storms, even if you are about to be swallowed up by towering waves at sea, never let it be separated from you or lost. I have heard that in the Land of the Rising Sun there is an image of Kannon[82] enshrined at a place called Hatsuse.[83] When you have returned safely to your homeland, take this jewel with you to Hatsuse. Go to worship at the temple there, and perform the prescribed twenty-one-day rituals.[84] Only if you do this will we be able to meet again without fearing the censure of others in this world."

Princess Hua-yang withdrew while the night was still young,[85] and no words could describe the regret with which Ujitada watched her go. Wave after

82. Avalokiteśvara (Chinese Kuan-yin), the bodhisattva of compassion and mercy.
83. Or Hase, about ten kilometers northeast of the Fujiwara capital or twenty kilometers southeast of Heijō (present-day Nara). A temple dedicated to Kannon was built there in 727 (the image itself was dedicated in 733) and became one of the three most important centers of Kannon worship during the Heian period. It should be noted that, according to the time set at the beginning of book one, the events of this tale are supposed to have taken place two or three decades before these dates.
84. *San'nanuka sono hō*: a prescribed series of rites and services that took three times seven, or twenty-one, days to complete in full.
85. More literally, "Saying this, Princess Hua-yang withdrew. . . ." This would leave no time for lovemaking, even though the location from which she has taken the crystal jewel—the sash of her underrobe—would suggest that she was preparing for just that. Because the conventional invocation of unspecified "vows of love" as a figure for lovemaking is replaced in this instance by relatively detailed statements of the princess's pledge and the conditions under which she and Ujitada are to meet again in Japan, and because these statements so fill the scene as to leave no time for lovemaking, it is possible that the princess once again draws back from the

wave of new tears poured from his eyes as he made his way from the palace, a sleeve pressed to his face and the precious token of his beloved clutched tightly in his hand. The devastating grief he felt tonight surpassed even that of the last time he had parted with the princess on Mount Shang.

33.	Samenu yo no	"The way to my love—
	Yume no tadaji o	Oh, that it were so straight in life
	Utsutsu nite	As in an unending dream;
	Itsu o kagiri no	But when can I hope to see her again
	Wakare naruran	After this parting tonight?"[86]

The princess returned to her own apartments in the palace and reflected on her fate with quiet resignation. Perhaps it was for the best that she had not been destined to remain long in this world. Were she to go on living beyond this, with the burden of this entanglement weighing so heavily upon her mind and her feelings so utterly out of control, it would be merely to become the talk of the gossips and gain an ill reputation for herself.

Alone, she gazed up into the moonless sky and left her fingers to find their own notes on the zither at her knees. The melody rose soft and clear to meet the soughing of the pines surrounding the palace enclosure, creating a tone more plaintive than words can describe.

complete consummation of their love. In spite of the lack of any explicit indication of lovemaking, however, it must surely be assumed to have taken place, both from the circumstances under which the meeting was originally arranged (p. 89) and from the manner in which it is referred to later (p. 116). The express purpose of meeting at the Pavilion of the Five Phoenixes was to allow the princess and Ujitada to "yield to [their] deepest desires" without violating the sanctity of the cottage on Mount Shang. Further, at the time she promised this meeting, the princess indicated that to "surrender to the impulses of [her] heart" would be to shorten her allotted time in this world, and it is because she knows this that she speaks, in the present passage, of giving up her hold on this transient life: if she intended to defer the consummation of their love further, she would have no need to relinquish her attachment to this life.

The later reference appears in book two, where the crystal jewel is referred to as *kokoro midareshi koromo no ura no tama* ("the jewel from beneath her rumpled robe in her moment of abandon"), with *midaru* (disordered) acting as a pivot word to describe the state both of the princess's heart and of her robe. Since it is the same verb that is used just before the princess speaks in the present scene, to indicate that she is *about to* lose control of her passions (*tsui ni midare ide kon to su*), the locution in book two would seem to confirm that the meeting at the Pavilion of the Five Phoenixes did indeed lead to its originally intended outcome.

86. An allusive variation on *Kokinshū* 558, Fujiwara Toshiyuki:

Koiwabite	Helpless with yearning,
Uchinuru naka ni	I drifted off to sleep, and then
Yukikayou	Suddenly I was with her;
Yume no tadaji wa	Oh, that the path so straight in dreams
Utsutsu naranan	Could be as straight in reality.

Suddenly the sky was filled with flashes of lightning, and mysterious clouds began to form.[87] The princess murmured a poem:

34. Inazuma no   "Above the clouds
     Sayaka ni terasu   Lightning flashes across the sky
     Kumo no ue ni   In violent confusion;

87. The text gives no indication of how much time has passed since Ujitada arrived at the palace under what we must infer were clear skies (p. 91, above: the princess appeared "as soon as the moon had gone from the sky"), and in any case weather conditions can change in a matter of minutes quite naturally. However, the supernatural power of music to affect meteorological phenomena appears to have been a convention of tales in which a certain character's extraordinary musical skill is used as an important plot element, such as *Utsuho monogatari* and *Sagoromo monogatari*.

In the former of these tales, for example, sudden meteorological changes and other supernatural phenomena frequently accompany the musical performances of Toshikage and his descendants (and in one case of another musical master):

Toshikage accepted the zither and began to play. When the tones of the first piece rose to echo among the rafters, the roof tiles began to crumble and scatter like cherry blossoms before the wind. When he began another piece, snow like large balls of cotton began to fall from the mid-Sixth Month sky.

"This is extraordinary," His Majesty said in amazement. "Surely few have ever heard such marvelous music. . . . It is said that the emperor of China once caused rooftiles to crumble and snow to fall with his playing, but such virtuosity has never been known in this country. . . ." (Harada 1969, vol. 1, 25; Kōno Tama 1959–62, vol. 1, 52–53)

[The sound of the zithers] echoed above the clouds and shook the earth below. The wind and the clouds were stirred, and the moon and stars danced in the sky. Hail as large as stones fell as thunder and lightning filled the sky. Then came huge puffs of snow, like balls of cotton. (Harada 1969, vol. 1, 327; Kōno Tama 1959–62, vol. 1, 379)

When next she played the Hosoo zither, all sizes of hail began to fall, the stars danced, and clouds suddenly began to appear in the sky. They were most marvelous clouds, not threatening in the least. (Harada 1969, vol. 3, 381; Kōno Tama 1959–62, vol. 3, 514)

When she began to play one of the pieces originally transmitted to her father by the Seven Lords of the Mountains, the tones echoed still more sublimely across the heavens, thunder and lightning filled the sky, and the earth shook as in an earthquake. (Harada 1969, vol. 3, 385; Kōno Tama 1959–62, vol. 3, 519)

A few other passages could be cited as well. As indicated in the first example, the convention appears to have had its origins in Chinese sources. See Harada 1969, vol. 1, 26, n. 11.

Whatever the origins of this convention, however, the immediate source of reference for Teika was probably an early scene in *Sagoromo monogatari*. The hero of that tale, Captain Sagoromo, is a peerless flutist who plays so marvelously that at one point a heavenly page boy appears and attempts to steal him away. Earlier in the scene where this occurs, "the sky was filled with flashes of lightning, and mysterious clouds began to form" in response to the sounds of his flute. The close resemblance between these lines from *Sagoromo monogatari* and the lines of the present passage in *Matsura no miya monogatari* seems unlikely to be mere coincidence:

(*Sagoromo monogatari*)
. . . fue no ne itodo suminoborite, sora no hate made no kotogoto ayashiku, suzuro samuku *monokanashige ni, inazuma no tabitabi shite, kumo no tatazumai reinaranu o* . . . (Mitani and Sekine 1965, 45)

Wa ga omou koto wa   The turbulence in my heart, it seems,
Sora ni miyurashi   Is known even on high.[88]

"Even should my mortal life end this night," she said, "if the special bond that brought me first to learn and then to teach your deepest secrets beneath the brilliant moon of Mount Shang is not to be broken, then, when I am reborn far away across the sea and beyond the clouds, in heaven or on earth, do not fail, O my beloved zither, to come to me again."

She raised a section of her elegant blinds and pushed the zither out, then took up and waved a white fan that had been lying at her side. The zither rose into the air and flew off into the nighttime sky.[89] The princess sadly followed it

(*Matsura no miya monogatari*)
    . . . hikisumashitamaeru koto no ne, mi-kaki no matsukaze ni kayoiaite, iu yoshi naku *monoganashiki ni, inazuma shikiri ni shite, kumo no tatazumai tadanaraneba* . . . (Hagitani 1970, 42)

88. *Kumo no ue*, can be read both literally ("above the clouds") and metaphorically ("the emperor"); *sora ni miyu* means "to be vaguely, instinctively, or indirectly aware of something." Thus, in addition to the surface sense ("the heavens seem to know just how I feel"), Hagitani (1970, 42, n. 5) gives the poem two further meanings: "His Majesty has somehow sensed all that I have been going through," and "all the turbulence in my heart has come from having sensed instinctively that the end of my allotted time has come." The latter of these perhaps comes through more clearly when the poem is read together with what the princess utters following the poem.

    The former, however, seems somewhat problematical, for Hagitani fails to relate it to any other action or event in the story. It is certainly in keeping with the conventional use of "above the clouds" to refer to the imperial palace or to the emperor himself, and we have seen, above, that the emperor is endowed with prophetic insights. But nothing in the narrative, either earlier or later, requires the princess to realize at this point that the emperor knows, nor does anything require the emperor to know in the first place. In the one instance further on in the tale where the emperor's prophetic insight is mentioned, it is his knowledge of Ujitada's background that is significant, and whether or not he knew anything about Princess Hua-yang is of no consequence. If the reading Hagitani provides was intended, it stands in total isolation and adds nothing to the interest of the narrative (though see n. 90, below). It seems more likely in this case that "above the clouds" was meant to be taken only literally, and not metaphorically.

89. The zithers in the first chapter of *Utsuho monogatari* are also transported by air:

    Having received the thirty zithers, Toshikage determined to go to the margosa forest, located west of this forest, to try them out. As he prepared to go, a great whirlwind arose and carried the thirty zithers away. (Harada 1969, vol. 1, 17; Kōno Tama 1959–62, vol. 1, 42)

    Following the instructions he had been given, Toshikage proceeded westward from the garden of flowers, and came to a great river. A peacock appeared from the river and carried him across. The zithers were again carried by the whirlwind. Farther west he came to a canyon. A dragon appeared from the canyon and carried him across. The zithers were carried by the whirlwind. (Kōno Tama 1959–62, vol. 1, 44)

    A whirlwind arose as before and swept the zithers up into the sky. . . . Toshikage returned to the mountain where he had stayed for three years. As he was telling the three men there all that had happened to him in the intervening days and months, the whirlwind arrived and deposited the zithers at their feet. (Kōno Tama 1959–62, vol. 1, 50)

with her eyes until it was no longer visible, shielding her face with the fan to hide the tears that spilled from her eyes.

After a short while she lay down on her side. Never could she have been more beautiful than she was now with the soft light of a lantern falling across her face. As the moments passed, however, the life began to fade from her face like dew vanishing from the grasses in the morning. Her ladies cried out in alarm and raced about in utter confusion trying to think what to do. So great was the clamor, it reached even the ears of the emperor in his sickbed. He grieved bitterly when he learned what the commotion was about.[90] As the dawn approached, it became clear that the end was near and there was nothing more anyone could do to save the princess. Great haste was made to have her removed from the palace.[91]

It would be folly to attempt to describe how Ujitada felt when reports of the princess's sudden demise finally reached beyond the palace walls under the first light of dawn.

Before Ujitada could recover from the shock of the princess's death, the emperor too passed away, and the entire nation went into deep mourning. Then, as if this were not enough cause for distress, the late emperor's younger brother, the King of Yen, rose in armed rebellion against the emperor's son, who, as crown prince, was the rightful successor to the throne, but who remained still a small child.[92] Of the nobles at court, those who had served closest to the late emperor rallied around his son, though without any notion of how to go about alleviating the crisis. Others feared the power of the rebel forces and

90. Or perhaps more directly, "He grieved bitterly over the loss"—if one accepts Hagitani's reading of poem 34 and assumes the emperor would have known immediately, without being told, what the cause of the commotion was. See translation n. 88, above. It should be stressed that the wording here remains entirely ambiguous and provides no grounds for argument one way or the other regarding Hagitani's interpretation of poem 34. Hagitani's characteristically literal modern Japanese translation is itself ambiguous, and one cannot tell whether or not he intended the reader to make a connection with poem 34.

91. Hagitani (1970, 157) translates, *Toriaezu (go-itai o) kyūchū kara o-utsushi mōshiageyō to sawaide iru*, or "They were in a great hurry to have her (*corpse*) removed from the palace" (parentheses his, emphasis added). She has not yet been declared dead, however, and the word *mazu* ("first," "to begin with," "before anything else") suggests that the concern is to remove her from the palace *before* she dies: *mazu kokonoe o idashitatematsuran to sawagu*. This certainly would have been the concern in Japan, where it was customary for anyone (other than the emperor himself) judged near death to be removed from the palace in order to prevent defilement of its sacred precincts.

92. The King of Yen in this tale may have been partly modeled on Liu Tan, third son of Emperor Wu of the Han Dynasty, who was enfeoffed as ruler of the northern Chinese kingdom of Yen by his father. An account is found in *Han-shu*, book 63, and is included in Watson 1974, 54–65, which see for details. In brief, upon the death of Emperor Wu (see translation n. 80, above), Liu Tan refused to acknowledge the accession of his half brother, aged eight or nine, to the

chose to join them rather than risk their disfavor. Still others gathered their own armies in independent attempts to overthrow the new emperor and his mother, the empress dowager. Next door neighbors who had always come and gone through adjoining gates suddenly became bitter enemies. In some cases plots were uncovered and the conspirators executed;[93] in other cases plotters escaped to join the rebel forces after assassinating one or another of the new emperor's most trusted counselors or generals—men who in normal times would have been in full charge of the affairs of state and commanded the absolute loyalty of all military men. Indeed, one outrage followed another, and there seemed no end in sight.

As members of an official foreign delegation to the Chinese court, Ujitada and his colleagues continued their intercourse with the loyalists, and so, however unwillingly, became a party to the strife. Ujitada, for his part, had little to do but faithfully guard the crystal jewel he had received from Princess Hua-yang. Nothing would have suited him better than to leave the country and thereby remove himself from the turmoil, but, with the two sides so bitterly faced off against each other and maintaining the sternest of vigilance, this was impossible. It was all too obvious that any attempt at escape would end in failure, even if he should initially manage to evade enemy eyes for a time. He could but watch with increasing despair as the upheavals continued.

The fighting forced the court to postpone the services that ought to have been performed in behalf of the deceased emperor and princess, while attention was given to the more pressing matters of recruiting men and laying battle plans. The rebels were fierce fighters, and they were led by the King of Yen himself, who not only had a considerable advantage in age over his youthful nephew, but was also a master tactician; they seemed to grow more powerful by the day as they advanced toward the capital.

When the rebels broke through the T"ung-kuan Pass,[94] the defending imperial troops took to their heels.

"It is useless to try to fight head to head with such powerful bowmen and warriors," they said, as they beat a thundering retreat. The sound of their panic-stricken footsteps enveloped the Wei-yang Palace like a sudden squall of rain and brought terror to the hearts of everyone within.

throne, and began planning his overthrow. Two separate plots ended in failure when fellow conspirators were exposed and executed; in both cases the plots were uncovered before reaching the stage of decisive action. After the second failure, Liu Tan hanged himself. Ho Kuang (again, see translation n. 80) was the loyal defender of the throne during these disturbances.

In this tale, the King of Yen is the new emperor's uncle rather than his half brother, but many of the other details are similar to the historical circumstances.

93. Teika may have been thinking of the men who went in league with Liu Tan but were exposed and executed (see previous note).

94. In present-day Shensi, about two hundred kilometers east of Ch'ang-an, near where the Yellow River turns from its southward path to flow eastward to the sea.

The new emperor and his mother abandoned the palace immediately and fled to the west, traveling together in the same palanquin.[95] Accompanying them, of course, were the civil and military officials loyal to the court, and they did not neglect to take with them the most important of the national treasures; but the imperial retinue presented a pathetic sight indeed as terrified noblemen stumbled over one another in their haste to put as great a distance as possible between themselves and the capital. Having been forced by circumstances to cast their lot with the new emperor, Ujitada and his fellow countrymen now had no other route of escape; they, too, found themselves dashing night and day along the westward road.

95. In having the emperor flee from the capital as soon as the rebel troops break through the T''ung-kuan Pass, Teika was probably following accounts of An Lu-shan's rebellion. An Lu-shan, a powerful general who controlled a great many troops on the northern frontier, revolted in the year 755, first capturing Lo-yang, then advancing on Ch'ang-an. Emperor Hsüan-tsung fled westward to Szechwan when An Lu-shan overran the loyalist army attempting to hold the T''ung-kuan Pass. The rebel general established his government at Lo-yang and made himself the emperor of "Greater Yen," as he styled the empire he had won (this may be another reason for choosing "the King of Yen" as leader of the rebel army—see translation n. 92, above). An Lu-shan was killed by his own son in 757, and Hsüan-tsung's son eventually returned to the throne, with the help of "barbarian" forces, to carry on the T''ang dynasty. Reischauer and Fairbank 1958, 191–92.

As Ishida (1940, 82–83) notes, some of the details given in this passage also suggest that Teika was influenced in shaping the scene by what he had witnessed, either directly or indirectly, of the events surrounding the flight of the Heike from the Japanese capital in 1183, in the middle of the Genpei War. *Heike monogatari*, book 7, chapter 13, which provides an account of the events, describes the departure of the child emperor Antoku and his mother Kenreimon'in as follows (Ichiko 1973–75, vol. II, 85–86; translated in Kitagawa and Tsuchida 1975, 430):

[T]hey made the imperial palanquin ready for the august departure. The emperor was only six years of age, and so, without knowing anything of what lay before him, he was seated in the palanquin. His mother, Kenreimon-In, rode with him. The three imperial treasures were carried out of the palace to go in the imperial procession.

The disorder and panic at the time of departure and the pathetically reduced size of the Heike armies are other images that are prominent in the *Heike monogatari* passages describing the flight from the capital.

Heike monogatari probably was not committed to paper in anything close to its present form until after the turn of the thirteenth century—which is to say, after the composition of *Matsura no miya monogatari*—and even though the oral tradition from which *Heike monogatari* grew would have sprung up immediately after the events described (spanning mainly from the Shishigatani Incident in 1177 to the Battle of Dannoura in 1185), there is no way to know how or when the individual episodes in the narrative began to take on their present form. However, the important details of a scene such as that described in the above excerpt would most likely have remained essentially the same from the very first accounts to circulate after the events actually took place: the scene contained a special poignancy owing to the involvement of a child emperor, and would have quickly captured the imagination of the court and populace as well as the storytellers of the time. Readers of *Matsura no miya monogatari* would no doubt have instantly recognized the resemblance of the events in the tale to those they themselves had witnessed or experienced only a few years earlier. Was the child emperor of the tale destined to meet the same end as Emperor Antoku? they would have wondered—and anxiously read on, held by the narrative suspense the historical similarity created for them.

The ranks of the pursuing armies were filled with men of great might who flinched at nothing in pressing the attack. The retreating imperial troops, on the other hand, were hampered in their flight by the needs of the child emperor and his mother. Their progress through the same rugged mountains and across the same deep rivers was slower than that of their pursuers, and each new report indicated that the enemy was rapidly closing the gap. Before long the weak of heart began to desert the imperial train, slipping off one after another under cover of the mountain forests. The imperial army quickly dwindled to less than half the size it had been when the emperor first fled the capital.

Late one afternoon, as evening approached, the bedraggled retinue stumbled into the precincts of a ruined temple to set up camp for the night. There seemed no escape from the rebels, and a pall of hopelessness hung heavily in the air.

Book Two

The Tenth Month had already advanced past its twentieth day, and cold winds stormed across the mountains. The many-colored leaves of the trees seemed to vie with one another in their flight to the ground. Between intermittent squalls of a chilling rain, the sun managed now and then to break through the heavy clouds, but even its light seemed to carry a funereal gloom. The colorful blinds of the imperial palanquin alone stood out with incongruous brightness in an otherwise dismal scene.

The emperor's banners still fluttered in the wind as a symbol of his authority, but they had long since become faded and soiled from repeated exposure to the dew and the rain.[96] In such a state they could hardly have inspired those in the retinue with hope, nor fired in them renewed determination to place their fate with the emperor and defend him to the end. Were there any chance at all of still preserving themselves by deserting, some might have done so, but the time for such recourse had passed. They were doomed, they knew, and this so paralyzed them with fear that not a man among them was capable of rationally assessing their predicament and deliberating upon a course of deliverance.

The empress dowager summoned her most trusted advisors to an audience at her palanquin and besought them once again to devise a plan.

"In fear of the arrows loosed by the King of Yen's troops, we have shamelessly fled the capital," she said, "hoping to find refuge in the distant mountains of Shu, protected by the narrow and precipitous Chien-ko Path.[97] There, we

---

96. Much of the imagery of this opening passage to book two, including the reference to the imperial banners, is reminiscent of Po Chü-i's "Ch'ang-hen ko" (Japanese "Chōgonka," "Song of Unending Sorrow"), which describes Emperor Hsüan-tsung's westward flight from the armies of An Lu-shan (see translation n. 95, above). Lines 43–48 (*Haku Raku-ten shishū*, book 12) read:

> As the yellow dust swirled up before a desolate wind,
> They climbed the winding Chien-ko Path over bridges among the clouds.
> Few were the number remaining at the foot of the O-mei mountain;
> Colorless were the imperial banners and faded the light of the sun.
> In Shu the rivers shone the brightest blue, the mountains a most verdant green;
> But they served only to deepen the grief that consumed him from dawn to dusk.

For another translation, including the entire poem, see Birch 1965, 266–69. Also see following note.

97. The mountains of Shu (present-day Szechwan) provided a place of refuge for embattled governments of China on a number of occasions because its terrain, most notably the Chien-ko Path through the mountains that separate Szechwan from Shensi, provided considerable advantages for defensive action. When Emperor Hsüan-tsung fled before the forces of An Lu-shan (see translation n. 95, above), it was to Shu that he went.

thought, our faithful followers might at least be saved from certain death. But the way remains long, our people are already beyond exhaustion, and the enemy troops press close on our heels. To be cut down here, at the side of this forsaken road, as helplessly as deer driven into the open hunting ground, would be a shame greater than any other that could befall us. Can anyone here bear to think what future generations would say about us? If we are to die, let us at least die in the fight to throw back this treacherous insurgency. What shall be our plan?"

Her appeal was met with silence. All color had gone from her advisors' faces, and none among them could find either the words or the voice to speak. Their terror over the extremity of their circumstances clearly had reached new heights.

After several moments, the empress dowager spoke again. "The rebels' general, Yü-wen Hui,[98] is a man in form but a tiger in spirit. His mighty blows would dislodge the very mountains; his arrows would pierce through solid rock.[99] Even were our army equal to his, he is not a man to be brought down with ordinary human strength. But, alas, many of our men have left us, and our forces now number less than one tenth the rebel army: we are in no condition to engage them in the open field. Our only hope is to return at once to the mountains we passed through today, and lie there in ambush. We will wait until the rebels have all gone by, and then fall on them from behind, raising battle cries from both front and rear and fighting until we are but dust and ashes in a common grave. Yü-wen Hui may be of such heart as to betray his country, and of such strength as to crush to nothing whatever may stand in his way, but he knows little about strategy in battle and he is reckless in his command of men. If we attack his troops as I have said, they are sure to lose the will to fight."

In spite of her redoubled appeal, few seemed ready to turn back to meet the enemy.

The empress dowager asked Ujitada to approach her palanquin so that she could speak to him in private.

"It has not been long since you came to us from an unknown land beyond our borders, and too few days and months have passed for us to form the kind of bond of loyalty that is proper between ruler and subject. The faithfulness you have shown us in this time of great trial goes far beyond the call of duty. I can but think it is for a cause. There must be a reason why His Late Majesty

---

98. The Yü-wen surname came originally from one of the northern tribes, the Hsien-pei, who were gradually assimilated into the Chinese population from around the time of the Sui and T'ang dynasties.

99. *Han-shu*, book 54 (translated in Watson 1974, 17):

> Li Kuang was out hunting one time when he spied a rock in the grass which he mistook for a tiger. He shot an arrow at the rock and hit it with such force that the tip of the arrow embedded itself in the rock.

concerned himself so personally with your welfare, and why you have continued to this day to walk with us our path of woe.[100]

"The enemy may overtake us and attack us this very night. If you have not forgotten all that His Majesty did for you in his lifetime, then lay now a plan for our defense and lead us in the battle. Among the lands of mighty warriors, Japan may be small,[101] but I have heard that she enjoys the most resolute protection of the gods, and that her people are of great wisdom. Can you not show us, then, a better plan? Tell us what we must do, and fight with us as we fight for our lives."

Tears streamed down her face as she spoke.

Ujitada was not of a rank or position to be offering opinions about the empress dowager's plan, but one thing was clear: there could no longer be any hope of survival in abandoning the imperial retinue and seeking refuge on his own. Whichever path he chose to take, this day was certain to be his last. Just to have been summoned into the presence of such a paragon of beauty as the empress dowager, and to have heard, in such close proximity, the wondrous timbre of her voice—this alone was enough to choke Ujitada's heart with emotion and make him vow never to abandon her side. For her then to have spoken to him personally in this way, pleading for his help—it was simply out of the question that he should refuse anything she asked of him.

"At home, in my country, I never even learned to tell which way an arrow should fly. Even so, I can at least throw my own self at the enemy and give my life in your defense. Perhaps it is the only way I can repay you and your court for all that you have given me."

Ujitada withdrew and began making ready to march for the mountains they had come through that day.

In the course of recent events, many of the ablest ministers and generals relied upon by the late emperor had died at the hands of treasonous plotters or had been cut down by the rebels, and there remained only a handful of men capable of directing the imperial troops in their final stand. Four men were now commanded to lead the forces that would join Ujitada in the counterattack: the empress dowager's brother, Teng Li-ch'eng, who was minister of military affairs and general of the Imperial Bodyguards; Ch'ang Sun-ch'ing, minister of works and marquis of Chi-yin; Yang Chü-yüan, cavalry general with the Order of Merit; and Tu Ku-yung, the dragon general. Two others were to remain behind to defend the imperial palanquin: Wang Yu, the assistant minister of state, and

100. The empress dowager refers to her late husband as Ta-hsing Huang-ti, the customary name used after an emperor's death but before the bestowal of a posthumous name as part of the memorial rites. There was no time to conduct the proper rites before the rebellion broke out.

101. Japan is here called "Wakoku," but with its pejorative sense erased by the use of the homonymous (in Japanese) character signifying "land of peace and harmony." See translation n. 58, above.

Ch'en Hsüan-ying, the general of the left. As they went among their men to offer them wine and rally their spirits for battle, they could but despair anew to see how drastically their number had dwindled.

Fewer still in number were the men Ujitada managed to gather from among his Japanese compatriots—some fifty or sixty men in all, many of them un-armed and unlikely to be of any genuine use in battle. But whatever the odds, Ujitada felt a deep pity for the empress dowager and could not bring himself to turn his back on her. Prepared to fight to the death, he and his men took up their positions in the vanguard and led the column off to meet the enemy.

Ujitada prayed to the gods and buddhas of his homeland for protection as they went. The last light was already fading from the sky when they set out, and the full darkness of night had closed in on them by the time they reached the mountains. Undaunted, they pressed on, climbing over great boulders and stumbling over tree roots that lay invisibly in their path, proceeding into ever wilder terrain. More than a few fell from the treacherous path to their deaths in the blackness below without ever seeing the enemy.

Their path took them between a series of tall peaks on one side and a great lake on the other and it was clear that there was no other route through the mountains. Taking advantage of this terrain, Ujitada stationed his men in ones and twos on the mountainside along the way, choosing places where they would themselves be concealed by the dense foliage but yet would have an unob-structed view of the enemy troops as they advanced. At each of these places his men gathered a large pile of dead branches and leaves. Ujitada himself con-tinued farther along the path and positioned himself atop one of the towering peaks to wait for the enemy's arrival.

As dawn approached, the pursuers, nearly thirty-thousand strong, reached the lake and proceeded along the path where Ujitada's men lay in wait. As the last of the rebels passed beneath where Ujitada stood, fires suddenly leaped up from everywhere along a stretch of steep, forested mountains some twenty to thirty *li* across,[102] sending thick clouds of smoke billowing into the still black sky. At once Ujitada raised a piercing battle cry and swooped down upon the rear of the enemy column.

The rebels were caught completely off their guard by this attack from behind, and were too dazed to fight. When next the loyalist army cried out in unison from both the front and the rear, the rebels believed they were about to be engulfed by a mass of enemy troops far greater than their own, and they stumbled over each other in panic and confusion as they tried to escape in the direction of the lake. Powerless to return the attack, they fell like hunted deer beneath a shower of loyalist arrows.

General Yü-wen Hui was a warrior unequaled under heaven, and his great stature and prowess were not those of an ordinary mortal. There was no one in all

---

102. The length of a *li* did not remain constant over time, but during the T'ang period it was a little more than 650 meters, or about 720 yards.

the land who did not tremble in fear at the mere mention of his name. Now neither the suddenness nor the direction of the ambush daunted him in the least, and he took fearlessly to the fight from where he stood at the vanguard of his army. Catching sight of Tu Ku-yung, he descended upon him in a flying gallop, drew him close, and cut off his head before the loyalist general could so much as utter a challenge. None who had witnessed this dared face Yü-wen in combat.

As Yü-wen Hui proceeded to cut down every loyalist warrior within his reach, word came forward that an expert bowman was decimating the rear ranks. Without a moment's pause, he abandoned his position and galloped off to meet this new challenge.

The first pale streaks of daylight were coming into the sky when Yü-wen found his man, and he flew toward him like the wind, heedless of the arrow loosed from Ujitada's full-drawn bow. Unfaltering even when the arrow pierced a seam in his armor, the rebel general unsheathed his mighty sword and pressed his attack, joined by seven or eight of his best horsemen who surrounded Ujitada and rushed down upon him from every direction.[103] There was nothing for Ujitada to do but draw his own sword to meet the onslaught.

Yü-wen was certain of victory and sped toward his rival as though his trophy were already in hand. Suddenly, Ujitada was not alone: to his left and right stood four new figures, four warriors identical in every way, from armor to saddle to mount. At this, even the formidable Yü-wen Hui, so fearless of heart, seemed to waver.

Instantly recovering his fierce courage, however, he fixed his eyes on his foes with renewed determination and raised his blade for the kill. At that moment five more identical warriors descended upon Yü-wen and his men from behind, cutting all eight of them down as though they were but bamboo stakes, slashing each of them with a single stroke from raised sword arm through saddle and horse. Having witnessed what happened to their great general, no longer did any of the insurgents have the courage to draw a bow or lift a sword against Ujitada.

From the outset, Yü-wen had relied solely upon his own prowess. He knew nothing about enlisting or commanding others in his cause, and his rebel force, gathered without care, was made up of shameless men who had no concern for the honor of their names. Now, in utter panic, they threw down their armor and weapons, and fled into the hills or took to the water; few escaped the reach of the loyalists, however, who cut them down on sight. By the time the day had fully dawned, not one of the thirty thousand retained the will to fight.

Since the rebels had come prepared for a protracted campaign, with supplies to last for many days and months, the tired loyalist troops were able to replenish their strength and celebrate their victory with all the food they could eat.

103. The number of warriors on Yü-wen's side is not entirely clear. Here the text states "seven or eight"; below, the figure is always given as eight, but the ambiguity remains unresolved because the figure appears sometimes to include Yü-wen, other times not.

The ten identical warriors who had appeared in battle had vanished, no one knew where.[104] Even the erstwhile detractors, who had spoken ill of Ujitada because he was a foreigner, now rejoiced over what he had done. They knew they owed their lives to Ujitada's heroism, and they were inwardly ashamed of the way they had treated him before. As for Ujitada himself, he modestly praised the sagacity of the empress dowager's plan, and thought nothing of his own part in the victory.

Other than the twenty or so men who had been cut down by Yü-wen, there were no casualties among the thousand and some troops on the loyalist side.

Even as the loyalists were resting and celebrating with greater joy than can be described, however, another army of untold numbers marched into sight along the road Yü-wen's army had come only a short time before. The sight of this second force advancing around the lake struck fear anew into the loyalists' hearts; a wave of panic swept through their ranks, and many turned to flee, for the briefest glance told them that their own forces would be no match for this new army, either in size or might.

Ujitada called out to those who fled, exhorting them to take hold of their courage once again. "Will you still turn tail at first sight of the enemy? Do you still not see that we can have no hope in flight? If it is our fate to die, let us at least die fighting the enemy to the end."

They returned to their previous positions on the mountainside and once again waited in ambush. It seemed the enemy had spied their movements, however, for a messenger came forth from their ranks and approached the loyalist troops.

"This is the army of Wei-ch'ih Hsien-te, deputy to the minister of state for the Honan circuit, general of the Imperial Guard, and governor of Hsü-chou, one who enjoyed the particular favor of His Majesty the late emperor, but who, owing to duties in the distant borderlands, was absent from the capital at the time of national tragedy. Alarmed by subsequent reports of an armed rebellion against the rightful heir to the throne, we made all possible haste to join the imperial train and army. The army of Yü-wen Hui stood in our way, however, and impeded our progress. Having now learned that the rebel and imperial armies clashed during the night, we have rushed to join you."

Those who had fled the capital with the new emperor rejoiced once again, each and every one of them shedding tears of gladness and relief as they waited for Hsien-te's army to join them. They had known of Hsien-te's loyalty and had prayed night and day that he would arrive in time to come to their aid.

The combined armies marched off together toward the place where the remainder of the imperial forces had encamped for the final defense. The

104. Actually only nine of the warriors have disappeared, since Ujitada himself is the tenth.

column stretched out so far back along the trail that the rear of the column could not be seen. Even so the army was not of a size that could normally have hoped to overcome the force of thirty thousand led by Yü-wen and defeated during the night; it numbered only some three thousand horses.[105]

Hsien-te had taken this road fully believing it would mean certain death at the hands of the rebels. To his great surprise, however, when he finally came upon the enemy, they were in desperate retreat, attempting to take to the water or escape into the mountains. His troops easily took them captive—many of them well-known men of rank and position. He and his troops were still exulting in their unexpected good fortune when they passed the gruesome scene of the eight rebels cut to pieces next to each other. None remained unshaken by the sight.

From there they all proceeded together to the encampment where the new emperor and his mother were waiting.

The empress dowager shed endless tears of joy when she heard how the thirty thousand rebels had been so quickly routed, and saw also that Wei-ch'ih Hsien-te had finally arrived.

"My most loyal subjects, who have accompanied us on this grim journey," she began. "Beneath the skies of this forsaken territory we have seen an army of thirty thousand men crumble to nothing before our very eyes. What need have we now to continue on toward the treacherous Chien-ko Path? Let us return to the capital. What have we to fear?"

Many of her advisors were alarmed by the empress dowager's words and were quick to express their opposition.

"The King of Yen has only recently taken power: his troops are fresh from victory, and the horses of his barbarian collaborators are well fed. Our men, however, are weary and exhausted from the hardships of this bitter journey; they are in no condition to face the defenders of the capital with any hope of success."

The empress dowager addressed Hsien-te. "From the beginning of the present war until today, the King of Yen's troops seemed truly invincible. To stand in their way was as surely to fall at their feet. But why was this so? Was it because of the commanding authority of the King of Yen? Or was it because of Yü-wen Hui's fearsome might?"

Everyone agreed it was because of Yü-wen's fearsome might.

"And yet," the empress dowager continued, "Yü-wen and eight of his ablest warriors, men who were known far and wide for their valor in battle, now lie dead in a single spot on the battlefield, cut down by heaven. So confident

---

105. As with other references to the sizes of armies, there is an inconsistency between the first impression given of the great size of Wei-ch'ih Hsien-te's army above, and the indication here that even the combined forces were of inadequate size to have hoped to overcome the rebel army.

was Yü-wen of his own prowess, he gave no thought to seeking strong allies. Relying on close relatives and old friends, and using the influence of his general's title, he gathered an army of bounty seekers. When these men saw him go to his death, not one of them chose to fight to uphold the honor of his name. They all fled shamelessly, and were taken prisoner by Hsien-te. In the same way, the men the King of Yen has gathered about him are but grasping merchants and drunken and dissipated youths. What could they know about military strategy? Indeed, is there a single man among them we have ever heard spoken of before?"

None of her listeners had any names to offer.

She went on: "Humble and unworthy woman though I am, His Late Majesty, by his bountiful grace, granted me the privilege of serving his august person from the time I was but a small child. In the ten springs and autumns I have passed in this rank far above my due, I have heeded without fail the admonition regarding hens that crow,[106] and, even in strictly personal matters that had no bearing beyond the women's quarters of the imperial palace, I refrained from speaking out except at His Majesty's command. Now, at this time of shocking tragedy for our nation, my only regrets are that I did not follow the example of Princess Yüeh,[107] and that, by my failure to do so, I have lived to see the shame of a land convulsed in turmoil.

"Normally, the proper course for me to follow would be to select capable men from among His Majesty's loyal subjects to carry out the affairs of state. But the men the late emperor summoned to his bedside for special instructions, the men to whom he entrusted the fate of the new reign, have been murdered by treasonous conspirators, while those who came with us in our flight from the capital are self-effacing men of strict decorum, concerned only with keeping to their proper places. Thus, even though I am an ignorant and useless woman with no special abilities, I have made bold to take the reins of government in my own hands, to risk following in the example of those empresses of the past who

---

106. "When the hen crows the dawn, the house is destined to fall." An old saying expressing metaphorically what was perceived, through historical experience, to be one of the greatest threats to the survival of a dynasty in China: "When a woman rules the land, taking a role that should properly be filled by a man, the dynasty is destined to fall." See n. 108, below.

107. When King Chao of Wu fell seriously ill, his consort Yüeh gave her own life in an attempt to save him.

Hagitani (1941, 22–23) demonstrates that the character of the empress dowager, whose surname we have learned is Teng (her brother is named on p. 103), is at least in part modeled on the Ho Hsi Empress Teng whose biography appears in *Hou Han-shu* ("History of the Latter Han Dynasty"), book 10, section 10, part 1. After the death of her husband, Empress Teng took charge of the affairs of state during the reigns of two child emperors. Several close parallels may be noted between the description of circumstances and events in the life of the empress dowager in the tale and the biography of the historical Empress Teng, as recorded in *Hou Han-shu*. One is this exclamation of wishing to follow the example of Princess Yüeh.

led the empire into confusion and disorder.[108] The swiftness with which this calamity overtook the nation allowed no time for careful pondering. Since I had in the past faithfully followed the admonition not to speak out of turn, I reassured myself, I surely would not be accused now of attempting to usurp the throne.

"I am a person of but little ability, and my ambition to achieve great ends goes no further than today. I believe there will come no better time than now. With Yü-wen dead, the King of Yen is like a man who has lost his four limbs. If we advance on the capital now, who will there be to stand in our way? If, on the other hand, we continue in our retreat to Mount Shu and allow the King of Yen to fully establish his rule, gain the support of the people, and bring his own peace to the empire, when could we ever hope to return from the wilderness? This is why I say that we must turn back today, and make all speed for Chang-an."

"Indeed, it is as Your Majesty has said," the advisors replied. "We feared that our ignorance of military strategy and the exhaustion of our men could result only in disaster, but Your Majesty's wise words leave no doubt about the course we must take. Let us return to the capital at once."

"However," they added, "let us at least rest our troops for the remainder of today. We can march at dawn tomorrow."

Thus it was determined that they would stay one more night in their wilderness encampment.

Never had Ujitada imagined he would find such strength on the battlefield, nor had he thought he would be hailed as a hero. It all seemed no more real than walking on air, and, since he was quite exhausted from the exertions of mortal combat, he sat down to rest in the shade of a tree a short distance removed from the main part of the camp, and closed his eyes.

All at once, a figure exactly like yesterday's phantom knights stood before him, saying,

35. Nami no hoka   "This is a land
    Ki shimo sezaran   To which I do not often come,
    Sato nagara   Far across the waves;

108. There are numerous instances in Chinese history where the rule of an empress dowager in place of her young son led to political struggles that threatened the longevity of the ruling dynasty. Empress Lü of the Former Han (206 B.C.E.–8 C.E.) ruled in place of her young son after the death of Emperor Kao-tsu (r. 206–195 B.C.E.) and had all but succeeded in usurping the throne for her own family before she died and her entire clan was massacred by men loyal to Kao-tsu's line; another of Kao-tsu's sons was placed on the throne, and the dynasty continued for nearly two more centuries. The kin of an empress of the Wang family gained influence following her son's accession in 33 B.C.E. leading eventually to the usurpation of the throne by Wang Mang and the end of the Former Han dynasty in 8 C.E. See also n. 144, below.

> Wa ga kunibito ni   But wheresoever my countrymen go,
> Tachi wa hanarezu   There, at their side, go I."[109]

The knight presented Ujitada with a suit of armor, a bow and arrows and spear, and a fully appointed mount.

Ujitada opened his eyes to discover it had not been merely a dream, for there in front of him stood a horse, and at his feet lay the arms and armor. No ordinary words can describe the triumph and jubilation that filled his heart at this sight. He bathed and cleansed himself in a nearby spring, and offered a prayer to the god who had appeared in his vision. Then, thoroughly refreshed and ready to face any challenge, he hurried through the approaching dawn to attend the emperor and his mother.

The empress dowager summoned Hsien-te and Li-ch'eng and showed them a note the late emperor had given her before he died. It instructed that considerations of humble origins or youthfulness should not prevent her from bestowing high rank and office upon anyone who might render distinguished service to the throne. Clearly, the late emperor had foreseen the events of the day before. The empress dowager proposed to appoint Ujitada the new dragon general, and, hearing no dissent, did so immediately.

Ujitada readied himself to march. He rode at the head of the column, sitting astride a magnificent horse and carrying a great longbow such as none in this country had ever seen. The men at his side brandished stout spears from which dangled the severed heads of those eight rebel warriors who had instilled so much terror in everyone's heart. Though many of the insurgents remained armed and at large, a single glimpse of these trophies was enough to extinguish any will they might have had to fight, and they took instantly to their heels.

Everywhere along the way, people flocked to the roadside. Elderly monks from the monasteries they passed, laymen too old to have been impressed into the rebel army, the women of the small country towns and villages—all came to see the imperial procession and cheer the loyalist forces in their triumphal return to the capital.

Men who had dropped out of the imperial retinue on its outward journey now rushed to rejoin the ranks, making various excuses about being taken ill, or needing to care for their bedridden parents. Before long the loyalist army had swollen to more than ten thousand strong.

The column marched on and on over many a mountain and across many a moor. Nightfall left them still far from the capital, and so the emperor and his

---

109. *Shūishū* 587, Anonymous:

> Sumiyoshi no   They say
> Ki shimo sezaran   The god of Sumiyoshi
> Mono yue ni   Does not often come,
> Netaku ya hito no   And it is for this reason
> Matsu to iwaren   The lady waits so bitterly.

Poem 35 in any case identifies the phantom figure as a protective deity from Japan, but to readers who recognize that a line has been quoted from this *Shūishū* poem, it suggests that the mother once again passed the night in a temporary shelter at the roadside. Men of proven capacity were chosen to stand watch during the night. It was on the third day that they finally reached the gate of the capital.

In the early days of his insurgency, the King of Yen had persuaded some northern barbarians to join his army. When Yü-wen Hui set out in pursuit of the imperial train, these men had remained behind to guard the gates of the capital, and in the interim they had strengthened the fortifications of the city by building new emplacements and digging new trenches. Now, as the imperial troops approached, they were so sure of their own unassailable might that they did not even don helmets or armor, and, indeed, the sight of them brandishing their spears and readying their poison-tipped arrows to throw back the imperial attack brought new fear to the hearts of the loyalist troops.

While the others halted their steps, however, Ujitada advanced with undaunted courage. Standing out of range of the barbarians' smaller weapons, he raised his great bow and loosed a long and mighty arrow such as none had ever seen. The arrow pierced through the heavy plank wall of the newly built parapet as though it were nothing more than a withered leaf, and struck down one of the defenders. The sight sent a shudder of fear through the barbarian ranks, and touched off a wild scramble to escape.

Now the nine knights of identical color and form who had rescued Ujitada in the previous battle appeared from the opposite direction, and began cutting down the fleeing barbarians as fiercely as they had felled Yü-wen and his men. None was allowed to get away, and the entire force of defenders was soon reduced to nothing. The knights broke open the city gates for the emperor and empress dowager to enter, and then disappeared into the confusion.

To those inside the walls, the nine knights had seemed to come in over the gates, while members of the imperial train had found their view of the battle obscured by a heavy fog: no one saw or understood what had really happened.

The troops entered the city through the newly opened gates. Bodies lay strewn everywhere, covering the road so thickly that there was scarcely room to place one's feet. Horses deprived of their masters raced about wildly. Bows, arrows, swords, and daggers littered the ground like fallen leaves. Cries of astonishment and horror rose one after another as the troops made their way slowly through the aftermath of carnage, spread before them seemingly without end.

The King of Yen had fled the palace, hoping to escape from the city. Hsien-te was sent after him, to capture him and his three sons. Taking them alive, he imprisoned them in Chin-yung Ch'eng;[110] later he had them executed with poisoned wine.

protector is the god of Sumiyoshi. The protector is not explicitly identified until much later (p. 152).
110. An old city near Lo-yang, and the place of demise of many individuals who ended on the losing side of palace intrigue. Hagitani (1970, 270–71, n. 179) cites a sequence of events described in *Chin-shu* ("History of the Western Chin"), book 4, in which several persons were sent to Chin Yung Ch'eng and executed between the years 291 and 304; he notes one particular entry for the year 299, in which "the crown prince and his three sons" were made commoners and sent to Chin Yung Ch'eng, as a probable source for the similar details in the present passage.

The child emperor and the empress dowager were at long last able to return to the imperial palace.

During the uprising, Ujitada had single-handedly taken on the eight stalwarts of Yü-wen's army and more than seventy of the finest barbarian warriors, and he had reduced them all to dust and ashes on the battlefield. No one had lent him a hand. Yet never once did Ujitada boast of these feats; he conducted himself with the utmost modesty and restraint, and asked permission to resign the high rank and office that had been conferred upon him.

"In the midst of war, when we faced a fearsome enemy," he explained, "such a title could give me the authority I needed to effectively command my men, and so I did not insist on refusing it. But it is in fact far beyond the capacity of a wandering youth like myself, with no special accomplishments, to discharge the duties of such an important office."

The empress dowager would not hear of it. "By the great mercy of heaven, the villainous rebel armies have come to a quick end. But many others who betrayed the state have yet to be apprehended."

She commanded Ujitada to keep a vigilant guard over the gates of the palace.

All those who had been forced to pay obeisance to the King of Yen against their will were pardoned, while those who had of their own accord turned their backs on the court and joined the rebellion were sought out and executed, together with their entire lineage. In this way, peace and order were restored before many days had passed.

Once the new emperor had been formally installed upon the throne, arrangements were made to conduct a proper funeral for his father the late emperor. All of the appropriate rites and services were performed with unsparing attention to detail.

Quite apart from the restraint that would be in order at any time of national mourning, the empress dowager was one who believed in exercising economy in all matters, and she did everything within her power to lighten the burdens of the people. In order to help her subjects recover from the ravages of war, she relieved them of corvée duties. There was no one who did not rejoice in the respite.[111]

Each day the empress dowager held audience in the early morning, handing down instructions from within her gossamer curtains in the Hall of State. When official business was finished for the day, she withdrew to the inner chamber and summoned erudite men to instruct the emperor in increasingly advanced levels of learning. From morning to night they explicated the classics and expounded upon the principles of virtue, showing His Majesty how to bring

111. The empress dowager's views and actions here parallel those of the Ho Hsi Empress Teng, described in *Hou Han-shu*. See translation n. 107, above.

prosperity to the nation and peace and comfort to the people. Although the emperor was still a small child, he understood, perhaps even more fully than his mother or father, the great virtues of the ancient sage emperors. Seeing this, everyone at court strove to rectify his thoughts and deeds and to refrain from any manner of excess. In this way the young emperor already inspired the deepest respect and loyalty among his subjects. Within twenty or thirty days, peace and tranquility had spread even beyond the borders of the empire.

Though Ujitada continued to serve the court as before in the midst of such events and developments, his private thoughts strayed elsewhere, for he longed more than anything to return to his homeland. The custom established by prior missions to China, however, required that Ujitada remain for a period of three years. Furthermore, some of the courtiers declared that no precedent existed for a visitor who had received court appointment, however low in rank, to return to his homeland,[112] and they began to cast slurs upon Ujitada for wishing to leave the court. The entire matter threatened to become quite troublesome for him.

Fortunately, the empress dowager was in sympathy with Ujitada and continued to treat him with the utmost of solicitude.

"For this man," she said, "precedents are of no concern. We must not contradict his wishes."

She did urge him, however, to delay his departure until spring, for rough seas prevented safe crossing during the winter. Ujitada passed the days and months waiting anxiously for the arrival of spring.

Owing to an illness, the ambassador who headed Ujitada's mission had failed to accompany the imperial retinue when it fled to the West; he had slipped away instead to convalesce at a temple deep in the mountains. Because of this he was open to the charge of having cast his lot with the King of Yen, and he might well have faced punishment. He appealed his innocence to the court, however, and was absolved of any wrongdoing. He was granted a stipend as before, and it was determined that he would complete the customary term of three years before returning to Japan.[113]

The new year came. A fine spring haze hung in the air, suffused with the fragrance of plum blossoms, and the song of the bush warbler rang out in every

112. This is not historically accurate. Abe no Nakamaro (see translation n. 45, above), for example, was given permission to return to Japan after being appointed to office in the Chinese court. Also, even for those who did not remain in China as long as Abe, the granting of titular offices was a standard part of the Chinese reception of Japanese emissaries. See Borgen 1982, 4; Reischauer 1955, 79.

    Neither is it historically true that custom required envoys to remain in China for three years, whether for three full years or for parts of three calendar years.

113. It was indeed customary for the Chinese government to provide for the basic daily needs of the members of official foreign embassies, and in at least one case on record some or all of the members were provided with stipends as well. See, for example, Reischauer 1955, 80.

direction; each passing day brought new beauty to the colors of spring. As the time of his departure neared, Ujitada's mind was filled constantly with thoughts of home, and he passed the nights in restless longing.

Each day the morning drum summoned a continuous stream of courtiers to the palace, but the evenings were quiet and offered more time for reflection, whether on public matters or private, as those who had come to lecture on the essentials of the classics took their leave. One evening, the empress dowager was speaking at length about one thing and another, and Ujitada saw no reason to hurry away even though most of the others had gone. As night fell, bringing an uncommonly bright and beautiful moon from behind the mountain rim, the empress dowager abandoned her usual reserve to speak with him more freely.

"So often when we try to put our innermost thoughts and feelings into words they suddenly seem hardly worth uttering. Thus it is that I have busied myself with the affairs of state, submerging myself in all my ignorance of such things, while I have continued to delay speaking frankly to you of my many thoughts and concerns.

"The recent rebellion drove this nation to the very brink of disaster. In sheer physical strength, Yü-wen Hui had no equal under heaven; in heart he was as fierce as a tiger or wolf. The late emperor knew of his ambition for power, and so gave him no rank or office and refused to take him into his confidence. Perhaps he should have simply had him executed, but, with the barbarians a constant menace on the northern borders of our empire and disturbances of one sort or another so frequent, he thought he could not afford to lose such a valiant fighter. He simply left Yü-wen without title or means, and kept him at a distance. Unfortunately, this only served to deepen the man's resentment. In the end he persuaded that grasping blunderer, the King of Yen, to join him, and succeeded in placing the King on the throne. As long as there was a loyalist resistance to be fought, he made a pretense of subservience, but it is obvious that once his hold on the throne was secure, he would have quickly done away with the King; he would have overthrown the dynasty altogether, and installed himself as the new sovereign.[114]

"Although I was from a young age permitted to serve the emperor in a rank far above my due, I am but a lowborn woman of little resource. I could have done nothing to resist capture or physical violation. To die thus, 'the fate of my life beyond the power of my own heart to decide,'[115] would have been the shame of all shames: I could not bear the thought of it, and so I chose the lesser

114. It will be remembered that the rebellion was a succession struggle between two members of the same dynasty—the late emperor's brother and son—and not, at least on the surface, an attempt to overthrow the dynasty altogether.

115. *Shikashū* 180, Priest Genhan:

Mata kon to	Not even with you
Tare ni mo e koso	Can I leave a solemn promise
Iiokane	That I will come again—
Kokoro ni kanō	The fate of my life is beyond the power
Inochi naraneba	Of my own heart to decide.

shame of a corpse abandoned at the side of an unknown path in the wilderness. Never did I dream that I would be saved even from this shame by the miraculous strength of a single man—nor that I would be able to return once again to pray at the dynastic temple and worship the gods of the soil and grain.[116]

"My debt to you is greater than can be expressed in words either spoken or written. According to the standards that have been followed through the ages, even should I turn all the affairs of state over to your charge and grant you half the empire as your own, it would still be insufficient to repay the great service you have done this court. Should I now leave a precedent for failing to repay such service with due reward, it will lead to suspicion and loss of faith among the loyal subjects of the court. In the past, no one has ever left this court and returned to his homeland after being awarded even an insignificant office far lower in rank than that bestowed on you. Thus, though I know it is contrary to your deepest desire, if I recognize my great debt to you as well as the burden of the precedents that have come down from the past, it is my duty to spare no word or kindness that might persuade you to remain with us.

"Yet it is clear that His Majesty the late emperor knew you were no ordinary man, and, meager though my understanding is, I have reason to believe he was not mistaken. If I stood in the way of your departure, heedless of your most resolute desire to return to your homeland, not only would I be betraying the true spirit of my gratitude to you—it seems I would be acting against the very will of the gods. The divine protection you received, and the ferocious gods[117] who appeared at your side to join in the battle—these are beyond the experience of any ordinary man. They show that some guardian god of your country is with you, watching over you, and that a safe return to your native shores is divinely willed.

"Thus, in the end, I know I cannot hope to detain you, regardless of means. It is beyond regretting, yet I cannot help but regret the bonds from other lives that have ordained such a fate—a fate that, at a word from your sovereign, led you to brave violent storms in a perilous voyage to an unfamiliar land, and yet prevents me, for the very reason that you did so, from adequately repaying the great debt I owe you. My gratitude swells higher than a mountain, it is deeper than the sea, and yet I am grieved that the day of your departure approaches so rapidly and there is nothing within my power to delay it even for a short while.

"Quite apart from the deeper designs of fate, the simple truth is that you came forward to help at our time of greatest need. When we were about to be struck down helplessly upon an unknown field, there were many in our retinue whose devotion and loyalty had been a constant source of strength to us for as long as memory serves. Yet, even when it became clear that certain doom awaited us all no matter how far we might flee, these men so feared for their

---

116. I.e., that I (or, more accurately, the emperor) would return to rule.
117. *Onigami*, used in this tale as the name for supernatural spirits that appear in human form, without distinction between whether the spirit is perceived to be evil or benevolent.

lives that they would not turn round to face the enemy. But you, an unknown traveler from a distant land, a youth of but tender years—you willingly stood in the vanguard and instilled new spirit in our weary fighting men. That day, as I watched you march off to meet the enemy, I realized you had vowed in your heart not to begrudge your life no matter how uncertain your prospects for rebirth in the future,[118] and I wished I might at least show you how profoundly grateful I am for what you have done. 'If only my color could reflect the sentiments held deep in my heart . . .'"[119]

The charming elegance of her every expression and movement as she spoke, tears streaming down her face, was more exquisite than pear blossoms freshly moistened with rain, more marvelous than cherry blossoms bursting forth upon a willow branch and effusing the scent of plum.[120] To gaze so closely upon such supreme beauty filled Ujitada with an awe greater than he had ever known before.

Lest he give offense to his hosts, Ujitada had from the time of his arrival taken the greatest of care to refrain from any kind of immodest behavior, and ever since Princess Hua-yang had, in their moment of abandon, given him that special jewel from the sash of her underrobe, he had not allowed thoughts of any other woman to stir his heart. From his first glimpse of the empress dowager, however, he had come under her spell, and was powerless to do anything that might be against her wishes. Until now, whenever he was reminded of home and of his beloved parents who so anxiously awaited his return, he had been quite convinced he would die were his time away from home extended for so much as the briefest moment. But how could he compare his own feelings to those Her Majesty had expressed to him today? Tears of tenderest pity and affection overflowed his eyes, and he could think of no words adequate for a reply.

The emperor was nearby and had heard his mother's words. He, too, pressed a sleeve to his eyes to catch the tears that would not be stayed. A remarkably handsome child, he bore a strong resemblance to his mother.

The empress dowager seemed to know a great deal about Ujitada and his past, including his former lives, and he did not know whether to feel honored or embarrassed. For the moment, such thoughts drove from his heart all the

---

118. Or perhaps, "I realized that you had vowed not to begrudge your life even if it meant you would be born again into this uncertain world."

119. An allusion to *Kin'yōshū* 479, Saneyoshi:

Wa ga koi no	If only my color
Omou bakari no	Could reflect the tender sentiments
Iro ni ideba	Held deep in my heart,
Iwade mo hito ni	Then you would know just how I feel
Miemashi mono o	Without need for me to say.

120. The line would seem to allude to two different sources: Po Chü-i's "Ch'ang-hen ko," lines 99–100 (*Haku Raku-ten shishū*, book 12; translated by Witter Bynner, in Birch 1965, 269):

And the tear-drops drifting down her sad white face
Were like a rain in spring on the blossom of the pear.

And *Goshūishū* 82, Nakahara Munetoki:

longings that had so occupied him of late. Uncertain how to respond, however, he remained as he was, in respectful silence.

"What I did was of no extraordinary merit," he finally said. "I merely attended Your Majesties on your unexpected journey, and did as you commanded. Though I had no experience in battle, what else could I do but give up my life and turn to meet the rebel attack? Having abandoned the capital, none of us could hope to escape alive before the arrows of the enemy. If only as a desperate attempt to save myself, I had no choice but to fight. Even so, every one of us would most surely have been reduced to dust and ashes on the battlefield if it had not been for your own wise instructions. We escaped with our lives for no reason but that we followed your plan.

"As for my desire to return home, from the time I first arrived in this land I have been haunted by the memory of my parents' immense grief and anxiety at having to see their young, inexperienced son sail off across the vast sea. It has weighed heavily on my mind that if I should fail to see them again in this life I will surely pay for my neglect in future lives. This is why I sought your gracious leave to embark without delay, that I might see my parents again in this life and be able to experience the true joy of returning home.[121]

"But it is a life I once gave up, when I turned to face the mighty arrows of the enemy: just to be here before you now is a blessing beyond any I could have hoped for then. At least so long as we remain in this same world together, I can continue to hope that I will one day be reunited with my parents, and I am grateful for this. As Your Majesty's humble servant, it is not for me to express my wishes regarding how much sooner or later that day may be."

They were noble words, evenly spoken, but his inner thoughts could hardly have been so assured.

"Alas! How could I possibly set anything in the way of one who speaks so dutifully," the empress dowager exclaimed.

Touched by the sadness of it all, she turned to look at the moon, one night less than full, climbing higher among the scattered clouds to cast its pure, clear light across the darkened sky. The matchless beauty of her profile as she sat gazing so plaintively at the moon moved Ujitada to verse:

36. Hate mo naku	"The brilliant moon
Yukue mo shirazu	Of boundless light, destined
Teru tsuki no	I know not where—

Ume ga ka o	Oh, that I could
Sakura no hana ni	Make the lovely cherry flower
Niowasete	Effuse the scent of plum
Yanagi no eda ni	And blossom forth upon a willow branch:
Sakasete shi gana	What a wondrous sight it would be!

Through the allusion to Po Chü-i's famous poem, the narrator evokes the legendary beauty of Yang Kuei-fei as a comparison for the empress dowager, and suggests the latter is the more lovely; through the allusion to Munetoki's poem he suggests that the empress dowager is a paragon of every ideal of beauty imaginable.

121. I.e., the joy that will be his if he reaches home before his parents die, but not if he fails to arrive until after.

Oyobanu sora ni   Crosses the heavens far beyond reach,
Madou kokoro wa   And leaves me in helpless turmoil.

"Alas, what can I be saying?"[122]

The words were spoken only in his heart, however, and no one could have heard them. Was it, then, the tear she saw Ujitada brushing away that moved Her Majesty to pity?

37. Ama tsu sora   "Across the entire sky
     Yoso naru kumo mo   Let the other clouds be seized
     Midarenan   In feverish turbulence,
     Yuku kata saranu   So long as you can see that the moon
     Tsuki to dani miba   Does not depart its appointed course.[123]

"What is it the poet said about the color of her heart?"[124]

However wise and knowledgeable the empress dowager was, how could she have been familiar with such poems from ancient Japan? Surely we must conclude that Ujitada misheard what she said.[125]

---

122. The moon in the poem is a metaphor for the empress dowager. All too sensible of his own humble station, Ujitada is in essence recoiling from the boldness of his unspoken poem, lest he be guilty, even if only in his heart, of an insult upon the empress dowager's exalted position.

123. I.e., "I do not care what others may think or say, so long as you realize I have a special bond with you."

   Hagitani (1970, 180) offers a different reading: "The other clouds, too/ Would be seized in feverish turbulence/ Across the entire sky,/ If the moon were seen always to remain/ With a single favored cloud." That is, the empress dowager is saying she must be careful not to show favoritism, which, true as it may be, is a strange way for her to show her pity.

124. An allusion to *Man'yōshū* 3058 and 3059 (see translation n. 10, above), serving, in effect, to reiterate what she has said in her poem.

   If we take Hagitani's reading of poem 37 (see previous note), the allusion stands in contrast to the poem, and provides the missing element of pity: "I have to be careful not to show favoritism, but let me assure you I have special feelings for you." However, one would normally expect the main sentiment to be expressed in the poem, with excuses or explanations following after.

125. The narrator has from time to time stepped back from his characters and used conjectural locutions when describing their inner thoughts or motivations. Here, however, he seems to step back farther than in any other instance, and to address the reader openly and directly. The line stands out in sharp relief, and begs to be explained.

   Hagitani suggests that the narrator is attempting to head off the reader's disbelief of the empress dowager's clairvoyance by, in essence, having the narrator deny the reality of the event he has just described. This seems a rather unlikely explanation, however, when one considers that the narrator is never at pains to explain away any of the other supernatural or miraculous events in the tale. It is more probable that he is deliberately calling the reader's attention to the supernatural character of the exchange, as a kind of foreshadowing, even as he rather coyly and playfully brushes it aside for the moment by saying that Ujitada must have misheard.

   There was a previous hint that the empress dowager may know more than either Ujitada or the reader has been told, when she says that she has reason to believe the late emperor was correct in seeing Ujitada as more than an ordinary man (p. 115). There and here Teika is building toward the revelation that the empress dowager, too, is no ordinary mortal. Since, as

When the empress dowager withdrew to her own apartments, the marvelous scent of her perfume lingered behind. She was indeed the very moon, whose brilliance defied description.[126] Ujitada rose to go, and emerged from the palace in utter distraction, his heart helplessly adrift. Back in his quarters he left his shutters open and passed the night in reverie, gazing endlessly at the moon.

38. Miru goto ni   "My grief is multiplied
      Obasuteyama no   With each glance at this brilliant moon,
      Kazu soite   So far from my home—
      Shiranu sakai no   Like the reflected moons of Mount Obasute
      Tsuki zo kanashiki   Where parent was abandoned by child."[127]

Yet, in truth, it was the empress dowager's perfume, seeming still to cling to him, that kept him from sleep.

39. Omou tomo   "She does not even know
      Kou tomo shiranu   That I love her or think of her;

Hagitani notes, the poem by itself stands as sufficient hint of the empress dowager's superhuman nature, there is in fact no need to draw the reader's attention to it by addressing him directly in this way; there are, however, other indications of the somewhat playful attitude Teika held toward his tale, such as in his fictitious colophon, and just such a playfulness may well be the most important aspect to note in the brief narrative aside found here.

One might add, incidentally, that this is not the first time the empress dowager has shown a familiarity with Japanese poetry. See above, pp. 114–16 and nn. 115 and 119.

126. She is both as wondrous and as unreachable as the moon.

127. *Yamato monogatari* ("Tales of Yamato," ca. 951), episode 156, tells the story of a man who has lived with his aunt ever since losing his parents at a young age. His wife hates the aunt, and tells him to take her into the mountains and abandon her. At length he yields to his wife's insistence and takes his aunt away. Upon returning home, however, he remembers that his aunt has been like a mother to him, and he is unable to sleep. He recites a poem (Takahashi 1972, 406; translated in Tahara 1980, 110):

      Wa ga kokoro   As I gaze at the moon
      Nagusamekanetsu   Shining on Mount Obasute
      Sarashina ya   In Sarashina,
      Obasuteyama ni   My heart cannot be consoled.
      Teru tsuki o mite

He then goes to bring his aunt home, and the story concludes with the note that the mountain has ever since been known as Obasuteyama ("Aunt-discarding Mountain") and is frequently cited as a symbol of inconsolable grief.

In the later poetic tradition surrounding Mount Obasute, one of the important images has been that of *tagoto no tsuki* ("moon in every paddy"). A linked-verse dictionary from the Muromachi period (1336–1573), *Moshiogusa*, states that *tagoto no tsuki* refers to the forty-eight levels of terraced paddies on the side of Mount Obasute, each of which reflects a separate moon when viewed from the mountain. It is to this "multiplication of moons" that Ujitada compares his increasing grief in poem 38—a grief that multiplies each time he sees the empress dowager, so like the brilliant moon in her enchanting beauty, because at every sight of her his resolve to hurry home to his parents weakens, and he feels as though he is abandoning his parents much as described in the Obasute legend.

See Keene (1971, 124–28) for a discussion of a few other aspects of the Obasute legend, including its possible origins in a Buddhist sutra, as well as modern writers' use of the legend.

Omokage no	But when I close my eyes
Mi ni sou toko wa	Her phantom figure lies with me
Yume mo musubazu	And keeps me even from dreams."[128]

Thoughts of Her Majesty continued to push all else from his mind.

40.
Ware nagara	"Oh, how have I become
Oku to wa nageku	So possessed by a forbidden love
To bakari mo	That to wake is to weep?—
Yurusanu sode zo	Crimson tears stain my sleeve,
Iro ni idenuru	And show the color of my heart."[129]

As always, Ujitada hurried to the palace at daybreak, but he spent the morning in a most uncommon state of abstraction. Afterwards there were the usual lectures on the classics for the emperor. Today, however, the empress dowager withdrew almost immediately with no further remarks or inquiries. Ujitada was free to go, and so he returned to his apartments to rest.

A strong wind had risen since yesterday and had brought with it masses of heavy clouds and flurries of snow. It was melancholy weather for a melancholy heart. The events of the night when he had received the zither from T'ao Hung-ying[130] came back to him as if they were even then taking place, and he was overcome with painful feelings of nostalgia and longing. He had lost track of T'ao's whereabouts, however, when the old man had fled deep into the mountains to escape the harsh rule of the King of Yen. He had retreated beyond where others came and went, and now Ujitada could but lament that they probably would never meet again.

128. Even a dream would be more substantial than the visions he has in his one-sided and impossible love.

129. *Kokinshū* 486, Anonymous:

Tsure mo naki	How maddening it is
Hito o ya netaku	To meet a heartless man, and fall
Shiratsuyu no	So utterly in love,
Oku to wa nageki	That to wake is to weep anguished tears,
Nu to wa shinoban	While sleep brings helpless yearning.

Oku means both "to wake" and "to settle." In its former meaning it is associated with and set off against *nu* (sleep); in its latter it is associated with the "white dew" of the third line (missing from the translation), which is its pillow word, and which in turn suggests tears, especially in association with *nageki* ("anguish" or "torments").

Poem 40 builds on these same conventional associations, and by quoting the fourth line of the *Kokinshū* poem evokes the same torturous mixture of anguish and tenderness; but through the image of crimson tears (if the sleeve is stained, convention says it must be with crimson tears) it further intensifies the degree of misery, and with the word *yurusanu* (meaning both "unrequited" and "forbidden") it changes the implied situation of the poem to reflect Ujitada's own. Thus, because his love is unrequited and forbidden, he weeps, and his sleeves become stained with his tears; the stained sleeves are in turn cause for added grief, for they will reveal to one and all that he is in the throes of a forbidden love.

130. We are here given the octogenarian zither player's name for the first time.

As daylight gave way to evening shadows, the dreariness of his interminable reverie grew greater than Ujitada could bear. Restlessly, aimlessly, he set out for a walk, and before long had wandered out of the city into hill country, where the scent of flowering plums came to him from every direction. Proceeding in the direction of the most alluringly scented breath of wind, he arrived at a cluster of dwellings nestled against the side of a small mountain. In the distance he could hear the wind sighing in the pines, and as the last light of the evening faded into darkness the moon rose above the ridge of the mountain to cast its cool, clear brightness across a sky now emptied of clouds. Entranced by the serene beauty of the night, Ujitada pressed on through a large grove of trees.

To his ear came several strains of music. Could it be a *hichiriki*? he wondered. He had never found the tones of the instrument especially to his liking back home in Japan, but it sounded so different here, more beautiful than anything he had ever heard. It was, no doubt, an effect of this place he had come to. The *hichiriki* was known as a *shō* here in China.[131]

Now I can believe the ancient legend, thought Ujitada, about the princess who was carried away to the realm of the immortals for her playing of the *shō*.[132] Tears of wonder welled in his eyes.

The nation was still in mourning for the deceased emperor, and the sound of strings and pipes had not been heard elsewhere for quite some time. Perhaps it owed to the remoteness of this mountain region that music was being played here. But what kind of person would it be who lived in a place like this?

Still searching for the source of the music, Ujitada came upon a lady dressed most elegantly, standing alone before a simple pinewood gate. Her face was hidden behind a fan and Ujitada could not see clearly what manner of woman she might be.

"Who are you, and why do you stand here before this gate?" he asked.

Without answering, she turned to go inside. Ujitada followed. Although the grounds were in need of care, the building itself stood tall and elegant, not at all like the rustic structure at the desolate estate he had visited on Mount Shang. The pillars seemed new, their color fresh and unweathered. The bamboo

131. The two instruments are in fact quite different, though both are wind instruments. The *hichiriki* resembles the Western flageolet; the *shō* is a kind of mouth organ, made of bamboo pipes cut to different lengths and arranged in a cylindrical pattern above a mouthpiece. No explanation has been given for why Teika might have thought these names designated the same instrument; and nothing in the text reveals which of the instruments he thought he was naming, though clearly it was necessary to introduce the name of the *shō* in order to facilitate, immediately following, Ujitada's association of the music with the legend of Princess Lung-yü.

132. The story appears in the Chinese *Lieh-hsien ch'uan* ("Biographies of the Immortals," ca. 6 B.C.E.) as well as in the extant version of the Japanese *Kara monogatari* ("Tales from China," ca. 1170): Duke Mu gives his daughter, Princess Lung-yü, in marriage to Hsiao Shih, a virtuoso on the *shō*. The princess also learns to play the *shō*, with such mastery that when she imitates the cry of a phoenix, a phoenix descends upon their house. In the end, after a night of playing the *shō* together beneath the moon, the phoenix (accompanied by a dragon in the Chinese version) flies off carrying husband and wife up to heaven.

blinds, still green, stood out all the more vividly because it was a time when the blinds at the palace had been dulled in observance of the national mourning.

The fragrance of plum blossoms filled the air, and from within this building came the music Ujitada had heard. He started to follow the woman up the steps into the building, but paused to listen before reaching the top. The place was completely quiet, with no sounds to indicate that anyone else was about. He peeked through a crack in the blinds: the musician was apparently a lady. The wonderful perfume that came from within seemed somehow familiar to him, and Ujitada marveled that it was a remarkable land indeed where there could be another lady like the empress dowager in such a remote place.

Still curious about just what sort of place he had come to, Ujitada circled around the veranda to the right. He found no signs of people about; no one stopped him to challenge his intrusion. Returning to the front of the building, he entered the main room, but even now there was no indication that anyone would come forward to speak to him.[133]

The tones of the music seemed to rise clearer and purer as the night deepened. Breathing deeply the intoxicating fragrance of plum, Ujitada listened in rapture. Nothing could have induced him to leave; instead, he slid farther into the room.

The lady with the *shō* indicated no surprise at his movement, and played on without interruption. Since the room was deep and she was seated near the back, Ujitada still could not see her clearly. The strangeness of it all brought, for a moment, a twinge of fear, but enticed by the scent that so thickly filled the air, he moved yet closer. Even then the lady seemed not to notice him.

"I came in search of your wondrous music, under the bewitching spell of the moon," he said, but his words were to no avail, for the lady remained silent. Charmed by the uncanny familiarity of her perfume, Ujitada tugged at her sleeve, then took her hand. She showed no alarm, nor did she shrink from his touch. The absence of the slightest indication of shock or rebuff aroused Ujitada to further boldness; he drew her to him. She pliantly yielded to his embrace, and he could no longer restrain himself. He was more helplessly captive to his worldly passions now than he had ever been before.

His meeting with Princess Hua-yang had been like a meeting with the moon that courses the heavens: it had not seemed to be of this world. But the experienced and welcoming manner in which this lady responded to his advances suggested that she was most certainly of this world. Her alluring charm and beauty were beyond compare. Ujitada thought how unbearable it would be to be parted even for a moment from such a lady, but no amount of begging or imploring could bring her to speak. She remained silent, and merely added her own endless flow of tears to Ujitada's.

Had the night been as long as a thousand nights,[134] it would not have been long enough, and yet already the cock was crowing. Neither Ujitada nor the

133. Or, "but the lady made no move to speak to him."
134. A hyperbolic figure commonly used by lovers to lament the brevity of the night and their time together. The following exchange of poems between lovers reunited after a period of

lady stirred. Ujitada could think of no place to go even if he should rise. He wished instead that his life might come to an end on that very spot.

The waiting woman—the lady who had been standing by the gate the night before—began noisily clearing her throat to call their attention to the hour, but the lady in Ujitada's arms, perhaps because she, too, was still overcome with emotion, did not try to hurry him away. She went on weeping and said nothing.

The waiting woman came nearer. "It is beginning to grow light," she said. "This is a most disagreeable place in the daytime." She seemed exceedingly anxious that he be on his way.

As they gathered up their garments and began to dress, Ujitada hardly felt alive. In vain would one attempt to describe how bereft of soul he felt by the time he actually departed. He could see from the lady's expression that the parting was as painful to her as it was to him, but even now she did not speak.

Over and over Ujitada repeated his vow to come back again, both to the lady and to the serving woman, and then finally took his leave.

He emerged from the building feeling no more certain of what had taken place than if he had been walking on air, and irrepressible doubts quickly arose in his heart. He called one of his close attendants to his side.

"Stay here and watch this building," he said. "If anyone comes out, follow her and find out where she goes."

Leaving him behind, Ujitada made all haste for the city. It would be unseemly to be seen like this in full daylight.

It was not long before his man returned with a report. "I watched carefully to see if anyone would come out of the building, but though I waited no one emerged. Nor did I hear any sounds of people inside. It all seemed so strange, I decided to go in and take a look around. Finding no one at all in the main house, I finally came upon an old, white-haired woman in an outbuilding some distance away. I asked her who lived in the main house, and she told me no one did. Apparently travelers sometimes spend the night there, she said, but she never troubles herself to check on them."

A strange mystery—indeed, too strange to let pass. But Ujitada was not at liberty to excuse himself from the day's proceedings at court. Quickly he changed into court dress and hurried to the palace.

separation appears in *Ise monogatari* ("Tales of Ise," ca. 935), episode 22 (translated in Helen McCullough 1968, 87):

Aki no yo no	Would I be satisfied
Chiyo o hitoyo ni	If I might count
Nazuraete	A thousand autumn nights as one,
Yachiyo shi neba ya	And sleep with you
Aku toki no aran	Eight thousand nights?

Aki no yo no	Were we to make
Chiyo o hitoyo ni	A thousand autumn nights
Naseri to mo	Into one,
Kotoba nokorite	There would still be things to say
Tori ya nakinan	At cockcrow.

When the day's audience was over, Ujitada was summoned as usual to attend the emperor during his lessons. As he had become more and more familiar with the empress dowager, and had had numerous opportunities to observe her close at hand, it was quite natural that he should become increasingly taken by her unparalleled beauty. Today, however, being near Her Majesty seemed to do nothing but bring back to him the indescribable touch, the matchless charm, of the lady with whom he had passed the night. The almost startling vividness with which the sensations of the night before came back to him made Ujitada wonder if he had fallen into the clutches of a demonic spirit bent upon driving him to distraction. Preoccupied with questions about the lady, Ujitada forgot all concern for where he was and quite openly stared on and on at the empress dowager.

Her Majesty today was having the scholars read from the *Ch'ün-shu chih-yao*,[135] and she took it upon herself to explain the most important points to the emperor. The depth of her understanding and wisdom seemed to know no bounds. Indeed, for one so young and beautiful to be called mother of a nation seemed wholly incongruous, and yet here she was discussing for the emperor the ways in which the lives of the people could be made easier and the nation made to flourish and prosper. The courtiers and scholars attended their majesties until the sun began to sink low in the sky, then departed in their separate directions.

Ujitada's tears of longing for home had not once dried since the new year, but now, with this new concern on his mind, his distress reached unprecedented proportions. This evening he was too impatient even to wait for the sky to darken into night before setting out for the soughing pines of the night before. When he reached the place, however, he found no trace of any visitors. Even so, the otherworldly fragrance that had surrounded the lady seemed still to linger in the air, and Ujitada passed a sleepless night grieving over the loneliness of his solitary bed. Should he wait, there might be a sign, he told himself hopefully, but he waited in vain.

Knowing that others might look askance upon his being abroad at such an early hour for no apparent reason, Ujitada hurried home as quickly as he could. Back in his apartments, his turbulent thoughts raced first one way and then another, and he could do nothing to damp the fire that burned so furiously in his heart.

Night after night he returned to the place, unable to relinquish the hope that one night he might find her there again. Before long, the plum blossoms that had been at their height when he first went were all but gone, scattered in the wind. Still there was no sign of anyone else having come there.

135. "Extracts from the Great Books on the Essentials of Government," a document, in fifty volumes, commanded by the T'ang emperor T'ai-tsung and compiled by Wei Cheng (580–643) and others, completed in 631. The essential passages dealing with principles of good government from sixty-seven classics, histories, and other sources were extracted and arranged by classifications. According to Morohashi et al. (1981–82, vol. 3, 264c) the work was lost in China around the beginning of the Sung dynasty (960–1127), but survived in Japan and was later reintroduced to China.

With Princess Hua-yang he could at least place some small measure of hope in the vows they had exchanged to meet again, and in the crystal jewel she had given him as a symbol of those vows. Even so, he had spent endless nights in despondent brooding. Now with this lady he had not the slightest keepsake to console him in his longing, and, as each new day of fruitless longing was added to the last, he scarcely felt he could still be among the living.

"Why must I be torn apart like this?" he cried out. "Why does not the smoke from the fire of my longing blow in a single direction?"[136] He was filled with shame at his own weakness of heart. The frequency with which his daily duties brought him before the empress dowager now seemed capable only of exacerbating his grief.

A new month came, and now the red plum blossoms in the palace garden were in full bloom, their fragrance carried everywhere on the evening breeze. The other courtiers had taken their leave, but Ujitada remained on, gazing out at the changing sky, which as it changed reminded him more and more of the night when he had been so taken by the moon.

41. Towaba ya na   "Where is the straight path
    Sore ka to niou   To one once seen as in a dream
    Ume ga ka ni   And then never again?
    Futatabi mienu   Oh, that I could ask this scent of plum,
    Yume no tadaji o   Which so reminds me of her."[137]

The choking tears came again; if anyone had been there to see Ujitada brushing away his tears, and if he had known the true origin of those tears, he would no doubt have felt the deepest pity for him.

136. *Senzaishū* 731, Tadamori:

    Hitokata ni   In a single direction
    Nabiku moshio no   Blows the smoke from the salt kilns;
    Keburi kana   Oh, if only I could believe
    Tsurenaki hito no   The same were true of the feelings
    Kakaramashikaba   Of the coldhearted one I love.

    The phrasing of the present line suggests that Teika may have been thinking of Tadamori's poem, but the allusion is to a much older tradition, going back to a poem found in the fourth book of love poems in *Kokinshū*, in which the direction of the smoke from salt-kiln fires is invoked as a metaphor for one's (or the beloved's) sentiments of love. *Kokinshū* 708, Anonymous:

    Suma no ura no   The smoke
    Shio yaku keburi   Rising from the salt kilns
    Kaze o itami   On the Bay of Suma,
    Omowanu kata ni   Is blown by a sudden wind
    Tanabikinikeri   In an unexpected direction.

137. The last line of the Japanese ("the path so straight in dreams") echoes the second line of poem 33, recalling the similar way Ujitada felt after his final meeting with Princess Hua-yang at the Pavilion of the Five Phoenixes.

Since the emperor had retired, Ujitada left the palace as the early rising moon came into the sky. He continued to stay in the apartments provided him by the court, so he did not have far to go. He had lost all interest in his studies as day after day went by offering no relief from his sorrow, and tonight, too, he removed his formal court cloak and cap and retired directly to bed. Lying awake, he gazed sadly at the moon.

42. Itsu to naku   "Ever and again
    Tsuki koso mono wa   The radiant moon in the sky above
    Kanashikere   Brings such wistful sorrow;
    Haru to aki to no   Its especial glow in spring and autumn,
    Aranu hikari ni   Brings the greatest sadness of all."

By the time the moon sank beyond the mountain rim, the whole world seemed to have gone quietly to bed. Then suddenly Ujitada heard someone drawing his door shut. He turned to look, but recognized the unmistakable perfume that filled the room even before he could see who it was. His heart leaped.

Now that he once again held the lady in his arms, gone were the frustrations of a flower so heartlessly beyond reach.[138] She was completely without reserve and so irresistibly charming that Ujitada was more helpless than ever to awaken from his dreampath of love. What could it have been in his former lives that condemned him to experience such an uncontrollable passion? he wondered. Over and over he reproached her for allowing not so much as a whisper on the wind to reveal where she lived, but her only response was to go on weeping pitifully.

"Surely you can at least tell me if there is someone else whose feelings you must consider, or whose displeasure you fear," he pressed.

She gave no sign of having any such concern.

"Then are you the spirit of the clouds of Mount Wu, or a goddess from the river Hsiang come to bewitch me?" he asked.[139]

Still she would not speak.

Cocks crowed and she quickly began making ready to leave, but when Ujitada said he would not let her go she did not seem unwilling to stay.

He appealed with a poem:

43. Omou ni mo   "No thoughts can contain,
    Iu ni mo amaru   No words express, the way I feel
    Yume no uchi o   In this wondrous dream;

---

138. A possible allusion, though no specific source has been identified.

139. Mount Wu is a mountain in the east of Szechwan; the Hsiang flows through the eastern part of the province of Hunan. As Ujitada's words show, both places are associated with supernatural legends. The story associated with Mount Wu is told in the prose preface to "Kao-t'ang fu," by Sung Yü (third century B.C.E.), which is quoted at some length in chapter two, pp. 42–43.

The goddesses of the river Hsiang were the two former queens of the legendary Emperor Shun, Ngo-huang and Nü-ying, who threw themselves into the river when they heard of his death and thenceforth were worshipped as divine spirits.

Samete wakarenu   If only there were a night so long
Nagaki yo mo ga na   We would never need wake to part."[140]

The lady at long last broke her silence, though in a barely audible murmur
under her breath.

44. Furisutsuru   "For him who goes away,
     Hito ni wa yasuki It may be an easy parting—
     Wakareji o   But the forsaken one
     Hitori ya samenu   Is doomed to remain forever trapped
     Yume ni madowan   In a dream of endless anguish."[141]

So piteously affecting was the sight of the lady's distress, even Ujitada's all-possessive longing to return home now yielded to the grief of the immediate parting. At this moment there seemed nothing capable of rousing him from the stupor of his passion.

He knew it would be scandalous to be discovered thus by others, but even greater was his fear that this mysterious lady might disappear like a mayfly at dusk. He held her tightly in his arms, determined to keep her with him even into the full light of day. For her part, she seemed in no great hurry to depart, and continued to lie pliantly in his embrace.

Then she was gone, vanished without a trace, before Ujitada could realize what was happening. He was stunned. Could she have hidden herself in a magical cape?[142] he wondered, and groped frantically at the space beside him,

---

140. *Sagoromo monogatari*, book 4, Prince Sagoromo (Mitani and Sekine 1965, 430):

Nanakuruma   No thoughts can contain,
Tsumu tomo tsukiji No words can express, how wildly grow
Omou ni mo   The grasses of my love;
Iu ni mo amaru   Still more would there be left to load
Wa ga koigusa wa   After seven wagons had been loaded full.

This poem alludes in turn to *Man'yōshū* 694, in which the poet speaks of grasses of love sufficient to load seven wagons.

141. The lady refers to Ujitada's plans to return to Japan, implicitly accusing him of being all too willing to forgo further meetings.

142. The idea of a *kakuremino*, a cloak or cape that makes one invisible, appears to have developed in Japan sometime around the turn of the eleventh century. Such a cape is mentioned in both *Makura no sōshi* ("The Pillow Book," ca. 1001) and *Shūishū* (ca. 1006), and these references may already have been alluding to events in a tale, now lost, called *Kakuremino no monogatari*. *Sagoromo monogatari* in several places mentions a man who must be the protagonist of this tale, and *Fūyōshū* (1271) contains eleven poems selected from the tale; these two documents are the principal sources of information used by scholars seeking to determine the nature of the tale. The cape quite clearly allowed the protagonist to do things not normally possible. The protagonist apparently did not have the greatest of success in his relations with women, but there is no evidence to suggest that he used his cape to force his attentions upon unwilling women. Rather, he appears to have been something of a champion of good over evil: in one instance he spoke as the voice of the Buddha to prevent a priest's straying from his vows; in another he spoke as the goddess of Ise to rescue a former vestal virgin from violation by an unwanted suitor. It is not possible to determine whether any use of the cape in the tale parallels the use Ujitada thinks the mysterious lady has made of such a magical cape in the present scene. Matsuo 1963, 1–19; Ogi 1973, 317–19.

but to no avail. She was gone, more elusive than a dream, leaving Ujitada in utter darkness as to which direction he might turn his tenderest longings.

Nothing remained but her singlet, scented with the indescribably marvelous perfume that had permeated the room from the moment she entered. No patterned robes of any sort had been worn in the palace since the late emperor's death, but this was a most attractive *zōgan* gossamer.[143] The lady had left no promise of another meeting. If this proved to be their last, was this singlet to be his only memento of her? The thought threatened to send forth a fresh flood of inconsolable tears.

With this new shock added to his already overburdened heart, Ujitada felt quite unwell, and would have preferred to remain in his apartments today. Unfortunately, however, the emperor had emerged from his chambers early, and the great commotion that accompanied the gathering of the courtiers at the palace was such that Ujitada could scarcely pretend not to have noticed. He forced himself to go, in the end, and tried to make the best of things by seating himself at some distance from the throne where he might remain relatively inconspicuous. Inwardly his heart remained in utter turmoil over the events of the night, but, lest his feelings show and someone guess that he suffered from the sickness of love, he made every effort to present a normal, composed appearance.

The emperor spoke to him in his customary, casual manner, dispensing with formalities.

"When the spring has passed, you will leave us, and the days remaining to be counted before your departure have dwindled far more rapidly than I could wish," he said. "Even when a person knows just how long a separation will last, to be parted from one he has grown fond of leaves him longing anxiously for the day of reunion. But for us, this parting may mean we will never meet again. It saddens me beyond words."

He brushed away tears. He had matured most remarkably in the time Ujitada had known him, presenting now so fine a figure of grace and majesty that Ujitada felt honored beyond his powers of gratitude to receive such kind words from him.

143. *Zōgan*, a gauzelike fabric of the finest quality, which, when made into robes, was generally decorated with a small design or picture painted with a paste made of gold or silver dust, or embroidered with gold or silver thread. As the context implies, it is not the sort of robe normally worn during a period of mourning.

There is an echo here of the story of Utsusemi ("the lady of the locust shell") in chapters 2 and 3 of *Genji monogatari*, though the situation is somewhat different in that Utsusemi escapes and makes herself altogether inaccessible, while here the mysterious lady comes to visit Ujitada of her own accord. In both cases the singlet is a keepsake, but here it also acts as a kind of bridge between reality and dream, or between the real and the unreal: on the one hand the singlet is concrete proof for Ujitada that the meeting actually took place, but on the other, the circumstances under which he acquired it—from a lady who first came from nowhere and then vanished in his very arms—are such as to make him wonder if even what he thinks is waking and real is in fact a dream.

What nature of curse from a previous existence could have brought him such a bitter fate? Ujitada wondered. What was it that made him so desperate to return home when he was blessed with such benevolent favor here? As if his poor heart did not already have enough cause for distress, these new inner doubts were added to its many burdens.

"If Your Majesty will but grant your gracious leave to this humble servant from beyond the sea, I would make my journey across the waves a full circuit, so that I might serve you again. How could I ever forget the benevolent favor you have shown me?"

Across the room, a flicker of a smile crossed the empress dowager's lips.

"You so long to go home," she said, "that you would hurry off over treacherous mountains and across the wide sea, even when you could choose instead to stay here and spend your days and months without the least fear for your safety. If anyone truly believed you would decide to make the journey again, to return to this court, he would be very foolish indeed."

Ujitada was struck again by the uncanny resemblance between Her Majesty and the mysterious lady, and found himself wondering if there was perhaps someone among her close relatives who bore a sufficient likeness to her that one could be mistaken for the other. He knew this could not be, however: Her Majesty was the daughter of a former general, Teng Wu-chi. She had been chosen to serve at court in her thirteenth year, and, because of her peerless beauty, had advanced rapidly in rank until named empress when she was but seventeen. She was an only daughter, with no sisters either elder or younger. Her father had died an untimely death, and her sole surviving relative was her brother, Teng Li-ch'eng, general of the Imperial Guard.

As brother of the empress dowager, Teng Li-ch'eng would normally have entertained considerable expectations for prestige and influence at court once the rebellion had been quelled and peace restored. But Her Majesty had purposely avoided according him any special favors over other servants of the court, declaring that rule by the relatives of an empress could lead to little good for the state.[144] The men she chose as her advisors, she chose for their wisdom and

144. Abundant examples from Chinese history bear out the truth of the empress dowager's declaration: When Empress Lü became the de facto ruler of China upon the death of Emperor Kao-tsu of the Former Han, she ruled through members of her own family and came close to bringing the Former Han dynasty to an end almost as soon as it was established (see translation n. 108, above). At different times during the Latter Han dynasty (25–220 C.E.), members of the Tou and Liang families gained great power through the influence of empresses that came from among their kin, and caused difficulties for the imperial family. During the T'ang dynasty (618–907) there was the Empress Wu, who succeeded her husband most ably but was condemned by Chinese historians as a usurper because, after initially adhering to the form of ruling in place of the youthful male successors (683–90), she took the title of "emperor" for herself (r. 690–705) and went so far as to change the dynastic name (see Reischauer and Fairbank 1958, 157). Also, although the temporal setting of the tale would technically exclude it as an example the empress dowager could know, a power struggle between the brother and the adopted son of Yang Kuei-fei, the favorite consort of Emperor Hsüan-tsung (r. 712–56), led the adopted son, An Lu-shan, to launch just such a revolt as is mounted by the King of Yen and Yü-wen Hui of this tale (see translation n. 95, above).

virtue; they were without exception men who had the good of the nation at heart, and they worked together to spread peace and order to the farthest corners of the land. In addition, the empress dowager herself provided an example for the entire court by applying herself tirelessly to the needs of the people, vigilantly guarding the peace, and never losing herself in the pride of power. To witness such virtue and gaze upon her person as flawlessly beautiful as a polished jewel made one wish truly to know the nature of the bounty she had brought from a previous life to make it all possible. Indeed, it seemed quite impossible that there could ever have been another like her at any time in the past.

"It is truly deplorable," she said one day, "that throughout the history of our land, for a woman to take it upon herself to conduct the affairs of state has been to lead the nation into turmoil. Although rulers may be blind to their own failures regardless of their sex, how much more likely it is that a humble woman such as myself will unwittingly err in her attempts to conduct affairs of state that are beyond her full understanding. If those who have grievances are too reticent to come forward and speak directly to me of my mistakes, but instead complain of my actions in private, it can be of no benefit either to myself or to the nation. My subjects must come forward and criticize my errors without fear, as in the reigns of old."

She ordered that grievance boards be erected in public places so that those with complaints could submit them.[145] Since there had been no cause for discontent in the time she had governed, however, no one offered any criticism no matter how long she waited. She wept in shame.

"Even the sage emperors of old received the remonstrances of their subjects by erecting grievance boards. Yet, when I, a woman both humble and ignorant, wish to follow in their path, my subjects doubt my intentions and fear that they will be punished for speaking out. No one will tell me of my errors. It is clear that my failings are too great for my subjects to have any faith in my word. Can there be any greater shame?" she lamented.

At long last one of the courtiers came forth with a petition: "In the short time since Your Majesty first undertook to rule this land, you have not only rescued us from a precipitous national calamity and restored peace, you have comforted and strengthened the people with your many benevolent decrees. Not in the least measure has your conduct of government differed from the sage rule of Yao and Shun. There is one matter, however, that is without precedent in this country: the case of the dragon general, a youth of but few years come to us from among our foreign subjects. The youth's rapid ascent to high rank is itself unprecedented. But this is not all: no such man bestowed with rank at this court has ever been known to return to his homeland, yet it is said that the dragon general is even now counting the days until he will cast off the moorings of his ship. In your many actions as our sovereign, the only instance in which

---

145. Such boards were said to have been erected upon bridges during the reign of the legendary sage emperor, Shun. The other sage emperor, Yao, was said to have established "remonstrance drums."

you have not followed the example of the past is in your treatment of this man. I humbly submit that Your Majesty must abandon any reservations you may have owing to his race or his youthful years, and reward him fully for his unparalleled service to this court. Then, surely, he will be persuaded to put aside his plans for returning to his homeland, and he will remain in the service of His Majesty our emperor for many long years. If you continue to treat him as now, it will stand as a blemish upon your enlightened rule."

"Your concern is indeed well taken," the empress dowager said after reading the petition. "Under a cloud of ill fortune, a ruler as wise as Yao and Shun was suddenly taken from our midst, and our entire land was plunged into a war as cruel as those of the Ch'in and Han.[146] Throughout the twenty-two districts north of the Yellow River, not a single man loyal to the throne could be found to fight against the outlaws, and the advance of the rebel horde on the capital was swifter than the flowing of water. We were forced to flee the ninefold security of this palace to seek refuge beyond the perilous footbridges of the Chien-ko Path. Alas!—the rebel army threatened to overtake us before we could reach our sanctuary, and there was nothing for us to do but turn and face their arrows in the open field. Even at such a pass, of all our loyal servants in the hundred offices and six armies, not one man stepped forward to offer a plan or to lead us into the desperate battle. By the strength of the dragon general alone were we able to prevent the King of Yen from establishing his rule; by his strength alone have we returned to worship at our ancestral altars.

"History has shown that in extraordinary times men will accomplish extraordinary feats. Such feats must not go unrewarded, and so I granted the young man court rank. In truth, he is worthy of a domain of ten thousand houses, and a purse of a thousand pieces of gold. What I have given him falls short of a tenth part of what he is due. Yet he has refused to accept any further rewards.

"That this man should leave us to return to his homeland is no more my wish than yours. But he is not an ordinary man; he is a man who lives under the special protection of divine spirits. To stand in the way of such a man's deepest desire would be to forget the burden of our great debt to him. Though I have agonized at length over what might be done, I have been unable to think of any acceptable means of preventing his departure. Discuss this matter again among yourselves and advise me what to do."

There were among the courtiers a few men who secretly would have preferred to see Ujitada dead. They remembered, however, that twenty ordinary men could hardly have hoped to overpower Yü-wen Hui, yet Ujitada had single-handedly cut down not only the fearsome general himself but his eight stalwarts as well; at his hand seventy ferocious barbarians had been reduced to dust and ashes.[147] It was quite obvious that no ordinary weapon would bring him down,

146. The wars through which these dynasties were established.
147. In spite of the empress dowager's open references to the divine assistance she knows Ujitada to have received, we are clearly meant to understand that the others remain in the dark about the true circumstances of Ujitada's feats of heroism. See p. 112.

and, since nothing at all escaped his notice, he would be sure to discover the plot were anyone to attempt to poison him. Knowing this, everyone continued to affect the greatest of deference toward Ujitada both publicly and privately, and as the months went by no one really hoped any longer to see any harm inflicted upon him.

Now, too, it became quite clear that there was nothing more the empress dowager could do with regard to Ujitada, and no further criticisms were leveled against her rule. The more elderly and experienced among the courtiers still felt it a great shame for their country that nothing could be done, but they knew as well as any that this one man and no other had been their salvation from certain death. Nothing could have been farther from their minds than to show disrespect or speak ill of him in any way.

Ujitada for his part was profoundly sensible of all that the other courtiers were thinking, but could find in his heart no more inclination than before to consider a change of plan in accordance with their wishes. Instead he passed the days and months losing himself more than ever on his mountain path of love.[148]

Although many of the courtiers had been critical of Ujitada's intention of returning to Japan, even those who had spoken most harshly of the plans were now quite happy to see them progress. It would in fact be a considerable relief to have Ujitada depart, for once he was an ocean away, they would no longer have to be reminded day in and day out of his peerless accomplishments or their own shortcomings.

When he finally learned that a date had been set and his ship would sail before the end of the summer, Ujitada ought to have been overjoyed, and more anxious than ever to embark. Instead, the unforgettable image of the mysterious lady who had appeared so dimly and fleetingly before him, and the desolating fear that he might never see her again, pushed all else from his mind. What could the bond have been that fated their time together to be so brief? Was he destined to row out to sea still feeling as though rudely awakened from an unfinished dream? A new wave of grief came over him and he collapsed in a flood of tears—tears now tinged with red. The sleeves of his night clothes still held the scent of the lady's perfume, but even in this he found no comfort for it

---

148. *Hamamatsu Chūnagon monogatari*, chapter one (Matsuo 1964, 182; translated in Rohlich 1983, 77):

Arakarishi	I was drenched by many rough waves
Ōku no nami ni	On the voyage here,
Sobochi kite	Only to now find myself lost
Koi no yamaji ni	On the mountain path of love.
Mayou koro kana	

This is the first allusion to *Hamamatsu Chūnagon monogatari* in the course of Ujitada's meetings with the mysterious lady. The reader familiar with *Hamamatsu Chūnagon monogatari* may have already noted some resemblances between Chūnagon's encounter with a mysterious lady in that tale (see translation n. 65, above) and Ujitada's affair with the mysterious lady in *Matsura no miya monogatari*. The parallels become even clearer when the identity of the mysterious lady is revealed at the end of the tale.

pained him the more that he "knew not which way to place his pillow." How had he slept that night when the lady came to him as if in a dream?[149]

45. Madoromazu   "Since that dream
    Nenu yo ni yume no   On a night that brought no sleep,
    Mieshi yori   Nor even dozing,
    Itodo omoi no   The burning passion in my heart
    Samuru hi zo naki   Has not cooled for a single day."[150]

After a day of unceasing rain, the night sky had turned much darker than usual. With no means to console his grief, Ujitada left the shutters open and gazed sadly out into the blackness. Suddenly the air filled with that unmistakable perfume, and his heart leaped with excitement. He could tell she had entered at the back of the room. Almost delirious with joy, he hastened to close the shutters.

46. Ukite miru   "If you truly longed
    Yume no tadaji no   To walk again the path of the dream
    Shinobareba   That so stirred your heart,
    Nagaki wakare o   Not likely would you be so anxious
    Isogazaramashi   For the parting that must be our last."

In spite of the resentfulness of her tone, the lady's infinite beauty could do nothing but make Ujitada's heart grow fonder with each meeting, and how much greater then was the anguish of knowing that this love could be theirs for no more than a few passing moments. There was between them tonight not the least reserve as they spread their robes one on the other and lay down together; it seemed scarcely possible that their meetings had been so few. The depth of their mutual passion showed itself in the burning glow of their faces.

Ujitada showered the lady with reproaches for behaving as elusively as clouds or mist and leaving him so helplessly uncertain of the ground on which he stood. The lady for her part lamented how rapidly Ujitada's date of departure approached. They had grown more familiar with each new meeting, and when

149. *Kokinshū* 516, Anonymous:

    Yoi yoi ni   Night after night
    Makura sadamen   I know not even which way
    Kata mo nashi   To place my pillow;
    Ika ni neshi yo ka   How did I sleep on that night
    Yume ni mieken   When my love came to me in dream?

    There was apparently a belief that the direction of one's pillow could affect one's dreams.
150. The spelling *omohi* for *omoi* creates a double meaning through the conventional pun on *hi* (fire). *Samuru* in the last line means both "to cool," in association with the image of fire or burning passion, and "to wake," from a slumber or dream. Thus, the last two lines might also read, "Not for a single day have I awakened/ From the torments left me by that dream." Earlier, Ujitada wished for a dream from which he need never awaken (poem 43), but that was when he was with the lady. Now he laments that he can never wake from the "dream" that is the source of such torment precisely because it was not really a dream at all.

they were together like this Ujitada quite nearly forgot that the lady remained a mysterious stranger to him.

47. Te ni toreba   "You are in my arms;
    Ayanaku kage zo   Yet why is it my eyes can but see
    Magaikeru   The image of another—
    Ama tsu sora naru   One no more within my reach
    Tsuki no katsura ni   Than the laurel on the moon?[151]

"What could it have been in another life that leads me now to such an unspeakable confusion?" He burst into tears again.

She replied:

48. Kusa no hara   "A drop of dew
    Kage sadamaranu   Resting upon the grass of the moor
    Tsuyu no mi o   But for a fleeting moment—
    Tsuki no katsura ni   How could anyone ever mistake me
    Ikaga magaen   For the laurel on the moon?

"It is not because I wish to keep distance between us that I have been reticent to tell you where I live. I merely fear you will find it a most unpleasant and disagreeable place. And, in any case, now that things have come to this, I must insist that you 'say no to those who ask if you have seen me.'[152] I think it not too great a favor to ask of one who intends to abandon me."

151. *Man'yōshū* 632, Prince Yuhara (translated in Nihon Gakujutsu Shinkōkai 1969, 86):

    Me ni wa mite   What can I do with you—
    Te ni wa torarenu   You who so resemble
    Tsuki no uchi no   The laurel in the moon
    Katsura no gotoki   That I see with my eyes
    Imo o ika ni sen   But cannot touch with my hands?

   The *katsura* is more properly the redbud, or "Judas tree." Chinese legend held that a katsura tree some five hundred *jō* in height (one *jō* was approximately three meters, or ten feet) grew on the moon.

152. *Kokinshū* 811, Anonymous (translated in Seidensticker 1976, 43):

    Sore o dani   As one small mark of your love, if such there be,
    Omou koto tote   Say no to those who ask if you have seen me.
    Wa ga yado o
    Miki to na ii so
    Hito no kikaku ni

   Or somewhat more literally: This one thing,/ If you would show me your love,/ You must promise:/ Tell no one you have seen my house,/ Lest everyone learn of our love.

   The poem appears also in *Yamato monogatari*, episode 26 (Takahashi 1972, 287), where it is said to have been composed by Princess Katsura following a clandestine meeting with "a man she should not have seen."

   The phrasing of the present passage makes it quite clear that the allusion comes by way of *Genji monogatari*, where *Kokinshū* 811 is alluded to in chapter 2 ("Hahakigi," see Abe et al.

It was for her a speech of remarkable length, and her voice carried not the least hint of insincerity. A new surge of passion convulsed Ujitada's heart.

"Spring nights are short and the cock's crow is not far off," he said. "And still I have no means of knowing whether I hear it crow truly or in dream. How am I ever to be released from the anguish of such helpless uncertainty?" He reproached her again and again for her stubborn concealment of her secret.

She responded with another verse:

49. Ada ni tatsu   "If we are parted
    Ashita no kumo no   Like a bank of morning clouds
    Naka taeba   Suddenly breaking up,
    Izure no yama o   To which mountain will you look
    Sore to dani min   As the place where I dwell?[153]

"The truth is that I have no place to go. But you, it would appear, are under a bond from a former life that drives you anxiously back to your homeland: I suppose I should not let myself hope for even a pretense of undying love from you.

50. Tazunete mo   "Where I live
    Towaba ikuka no   You must not seek, must not inquire,
    Tsukihi to ka   Lest everyone learn
    Mayou yumeji o   How many days and months I have been
    Hito ni shiraren   Lost on the dreampath of love.

"Neither bonds from former lives, nor rebirth in future lives can ensure that we will ever meet again. I fear this very meeting is destined to be our last." She was in tears.

Ujitada was overcome with the profoundest of pity, but knew there was nothing he could do to ease her distress.

51. Kabakari mo   "This dream of love—
    Yonayona miyuru   Could it recur night after night
    Yume naraba   Even so much as this,
    Wakare no michi o   Who would then be so anxious
    Tare ka isogan   To take the path of parting?

1970–76, vol. 1, 178), and the rendering of the poem given by Seidensticker serves excellently in the present context. In the *Genji monogatari* passage, as in this passage, the allusion is shortly followed by the crowing of cocks and a complaint (from Prince Genji) about their fearsome clamor.

    The allusion in *Genji monogatari* appears during the liaison between Genji and Utsusemi, the wife of the governor of Iyo. Thus, in both *Yamato monogatari* and *Genji monogatari* there are overtones of forbidden love—something that goes beyond the secretiveness that would be quite natural in any affair—in the plea for secrecy. (Another association with Utsusemi has been noted in translation n. 143, above.)

153. The first two lines (lines two and three of the translation) evoke the imagery of the preface to "Kao-t'ang fu" (see chapter two, pp. 42–43), where the Lady of the Morning Cloud is described as going through many sudden transformations.

"If you persist in telling me no more about where you live than where the clouds go, what inducement do I have to remain in this country?" he asked resentfully.

"You would wait for neither the autumn of the seasons nor of our love to depart. This is all the more reason 'a homeless fisherman's daughter' must not speak her name,"[154] the lady said, unyielding as ever.

Her stubbornness vexed him to no end, and yet he was incapable of thinking of her with anything but warmth and tenderness. They clung to each other as dawn neared, grieving together that the time had come when "lovers must retrieve their separate robes."[155]

---

154. *Arika sadamenu ama no nanori mo mashite.* . . . If a single specific allusion was intended, none has been identified. However, the line unquestionably alludes to the broader tradition of ladies who hid their identities by saying they were fishermen's daughters.

    For example, the present utterance distinctly echoes a conversation in chapter 4 ("Yūgao") of *Genji monogatari* in which Prince Genji presses "the lady of the evening faces" to identify herself (Abe et al. 1970–76, vol. 1, 236; translated in Seidensticker 1976, 70):

> "I hid my name from you because I thought it altogether too unkind of you to be keeping your name from me. Do please tell me now [*ima dani nanori shitamae*]. This silence makes me feel that something awful might be coming."
> "Call me the fisherman's daughter [*Ama no ko nareba, tote* . . .]." Still hiding her name, she was like a little child.

    The lady's reply to Genji is in turn an allusion to a well-known anonymous poem (*Wakan rōeishū* 722; *Shinkokinshū* 1701):

Shiranami no	I spend my days
Yosuru nagisa ni	On sandy beaches where white waves
Yo o sugusu	Rush to shore—
Ama no ko nareba	I am but a fisherman's daughter
Yado mo sadamezu	Without even a place to call home.

    A poem by Sei Shōnagon is also part of the tradition. It seems possible that the second line of the version found in *Goshūishū* may have influenced Teika's choice of words in the present passage. *Goshūishū* 1156:

Kazuki suru	The fisherman's daughter,
Ama no arika o	As she dove deep beneath the waves,
Soko nari to	Gave you a special glance;
Yume iu na to ya	Did you not see she was asking you
Me o kuwaseken	To tell no one where she stays?

    (In *Makura no sōshi*, the second line reads *Ama no sumika o*.)

155. *Kokinshū* 637, Anonymous:

Shinonome no	The light of dawn
Hogara hogara to	Softly, softly brightens the fringe
Akeyukeba	Of the eastern sky,
Ono ga kinuginu	And lovers, sadly, from their common bed
Naru zo kanashiki	Must retrieve their separate robes.

"Well, then, 'even so much as this,'[156] again tonight," the lady promised.

It was but slight comfort for Ujitada. When the lady drew the door closed behind her, he quietly slid it open again a crack. Nothing—not even a wisp of cloud drifting off into the empty sky—remained where she had been the briefest instant before.[157] Only the scent of her perfume lingered behind, now a cruel reminder of one who was gone, rather than a longed-for sign of one who had come. As one meeting had followed on another, Ujitada had quite lost the power to free himself of this infatuation, and yet the manner in which the lady departed left him with scant assurance that it was anything but a fantastic dream. Indeed, he was tormented increasingly by the fear that the mysterious lady was a manifestation of some demonic spirit.

156. The lady quotes a phrase from Ujitada's last poem (poem 51).
157. Thus, she is even more elusive than the lady in "Kao-t'ang fu," who was always present in the clouds over Mount Wu.

Book Three

The lady came and went as though she were the spirit of the clouds at dawn and the rain at dusk,[158] and she shrank from the faintest glow of light, whether of the moon in the deep of night or the torches before the dawn. She had done nothing to dispel the dreamlike uncertainty of events, however true, that take place amidst darkness,[159] and Ujitada's longing was magnified the more by the disquieting doubts that continued to weigh upon his mind. Night after night, he had met her in his dreams,[160] it was true, and in this he found a glimmer of hope; but neither could he forget that she had left him without a word on which he might rest such hope.[161] Even could he somehow confirm that he was the victim of some demonic trick, how much better that would be, he thought, than this wretched uncertainty.

The meetings as futile as the existence of a mayfly had now broken off,[162] and Ujitada spent his days brooding ever more mournfully over his endless

158. Another allusion to "Kao-t'ang fu."

159. *Kokinshū* 647, Anonymous:

Ubatama no	The true events
Yami no utsutsu wa	Of a meeting amidst the darkness
Sadaka naru	Of a jet-black night
Yume ni ikura mo	Offered but little more comfort
Masarazarikeri	Than a vision in a lucid dream.

160. *Gosenshū* 767, Anonymous:

Omoine no	Thinking of her,
Yonayona yume ni	I fall asleep, night after night,
Au koto o	To meet her in my dreams;
Tada katatoki no	Oh, that in waking I could meet her so,
Utsutsu to mo ga na	If only for a single moment.

161. *Kin'yōshū* 448, Mototoshi's Daughter:

Tanome oku	Without a word
Koto no ha dani mo	On which I might rest my hope,
Naki mono o	How will I endure?—
Nani ni kakareru	My life is even less certain
Tsuyu no inochi zo	Than the time of the dew upon the leaves.

162. *Shinkokinshū* 1195, Anonymous:

Yūgure ni	Like the fragile mayfly,
Inochi kaketaru	I lived this day but for the evening,
Kagerō no	Hoping you would come;
Ari ya arazu ya	But it seems my waiting was as futile
Tou mo hakanashi	As asking, "Does the mayfly live or die?"

troubles. Having to go on mixing with the world had become a severe trial to him, for inwardly his feelings were in as wild a tangle as the leaves of the *shinobu* plant.[163] But since this confusion was a private matter of the heart, he did his best to keep it to himself and to conduct himself with composure at all times.

To proceed with his plans for departure would be to relinquish all hope of another meeting in this world, Ujitada knew, and so no longer did he wish, as he had before, to rush homeward at the earliest opportunity. He had in fact become quite reluctant to leave, and it was with a measure of cheer that he greeted the official postponement of his ship's departure: reports of continuing stormy weather along the coast indicated that it would be unsafe to attempt an ocean crossing any time soon; the ship would not sail until autumn.

Although the postponement could to some extent relieve the sense of urgency, however, Ujitada remained as deprived of means to communicate with the lady as he had ever been. He spent his days as before, gazing out at the gloomy sky, lost in melancholy brooding.

At court, the scent of the empress dowager's incomparable perfume reached Ujitada on even the slightest movement of air, regardless of how far away he seated himself. Inevitably it reminded him of the other lady's perfume, which it seemed so to resemble, and on a number of occasions he quite nearly forgot himself and said something to her about the likeness. Tears overflowed his eyes when he thought of the unforgivable offense he had been about to commit. She was the unreachable laurel on the moon, a shining jewel on which not even the tiniest speck of dust might lodge.[164] It was not for Ujitada to presume upon the sentiments of such an exalted lady.

It must have been an extraordinary spirit indeed, he thought, that could appear before him in such a close likeness. He did not generally give much credibility to stories about supernatural spirits appearing in human form, but perhaps this was just such a case, in which even the seeming likeness of the perfume was an illusion deliberately created to confuse him. Though no one could have guessed it, such thoughts remained constantly on his mind.

163. The *shinobu* plant created a tangled pattern when used to dye fabrics, and was therefore frequently cited as a metaphor for disorder—especially the disorder of feelings of love, because *shinobu* also means "to yearn."

164. A reference to the laurel on the moon appeared in poem 47.

The second half of the sentence would seem to take its phrasing from *Eiga monogatari*, "Tama no utena," the Katano Nun (translated in McCullough and McCullough 1980, 566):

Kumori naku	Not a speck of dust
Migakeru tama no	Might lodge
Utena ni wa	On the mansion of jade
Chiri mo igataki	Where every blur
Mono ni zarikeru	Has been polished away.

Tama no utena ("jeweled dais" or "jeweled mansion") is a metaphor for magnificent structures, such as the imperial palace. In the context of *Eiga monogatari* it refers to the Amitābha Hall.

On the fifteenth of the Fourth Month, as the courtiers were departing for their various destinations after a busy morning in attendance upon the emperor and his mother, His Majesty approached Ujitada.

"I know that you cannot stay with us forever," he said, "but it is a special joy to me that your departure has been delayed. My wish has come true, at least for the moment. If only it could last!"

Ujitada wanted to tell the emperor that he was too much honored by His Majesty's frequent attentions to his plans. He wanted to explain that even his inordinate desire to return home—which for so long had cast a dark shadow over his heart—had recently given way to such regrets over cutting short his service to the Chinese court that he could hardly bear to see the days go by. But he had scarcely begun to speak before he became too choked with tears to go on.

Watching from across the room, the empress dowager was overcome with pity for Ujitada. In a voice no one could have heard, she murmured a verse to herself:

52. Akikaze no   "When autumn winds come
    Mi ni shimu koro o   To chill not only the body
    Kagiri nite   But the heart as well,
    Mata aumajiki   Then will be the final parting:
    Yo no wakare kana   We will never meet again."[165]

She barely breathed the words.

Watching her at this moment, Ujitada marveled again at the resemblance between her and the other lady. How was it possible that they could be so alike? It seemed preposterous to think that some supernatural spirit had assumed the empress dowager's features down to the tiniest detail, yet it was too great an insult to Her Majesty even to contemplate that they might be the same person. Having no other means to soothe his painful bewilderment, he silently composed a poem:

53. Yuku fune no   "My departing ship
    Ato naki kata no   Will leave no trace of where it sails;
    Aki no kaze   When I am gone
    Wakarete hatenu   May the autumn wind remember the way
    Michishirube seyo   And forever be my guide to you."

The moon climbed higher, casting its brilliant light everywhere. "Just so . . . on Mikasa Hill,"[166] Ujitada murmured, brushing away tears as he gazed on and on at the moon.

The empress dowager could not bear to see Ujitada in such a state of distraction; her heart went out to him, with pity now quite beyond the bounds of the ordinary. So, too, the emperor, who graciously went on speaking with

165. There is a pun on *aki*, "autumn" and "to grow tired of" someone or something.
166. An allusion to Abe no Nakamaro's poem given in translation n. 45, above.

Ujitada "into the deep of night."[167] He ranged over many topics, even to weighty and intricate matters of scholarship, but returned again and again to his disappointment over Ujitada's unbending determination to leave China.

So moving were His Majesty's laments that Ujitada began to feel his resolve weakening. Which was truly his greater desire, he wondered: to return home, or to remain on the path of love? Was he perhaps making a terrible mistake? Had the lady made any promises, he might have found in them now the additional inducement he needed finally to make up his mind to stay. But she had not, and Ujitada's thoughts continued to be drawn first one way and then the other by his helpless dilemma.

Morning was not far off when Ujitada left the palace. As had become his custom of late, he left the shutters open and lay gazing out at the nighttime sky. His waiting was in vain, however. Soon the cocks began to clamor and the moon disappeared behind a cloud.

54. Tori no ne no   "The cock's crow
  Matsu yo munashiki Announces the end of another night
  Soragoto ni   Waited all in vain;
  Ware nomi akenu The gate of my heart, alone, remains unopened,
  Mune no seki kana And my bursting feelings locked within."[168]

A gentle rain began to fall in the morning, adding to the dampness of Ujitada's sleeves, already wet with tears. Feeling unwell, he asked his attendants to make excuses for him and did not leave his bed. When word of his

167. *Fukeyuku made ni*. Hagitani notes that the particle *ni* is unnecessary for the prose syntax, and on this basis claims an allusion to *Senzaishū* 991, Kiyosuke:

  Ima yori wa   From now on,
  Fukeyuku made ni I will not gaze upon the moon
  Tsuki wa miji   Into the deep of night,
  Sono koto to naku For every time I raise my eyes
  Namida ochikeri I weep without knowing why.

 The poem would have been relatively recent at the time the tale was written, and it is difficult to know how familiar it was to readers of the tale, or how effective an allusion to it might have been. Some modern readers may find the claim of an allusion dubious, especially since the line in question is not particularly distinctive. Kiyosuke's poem *is* the only instance listed in *Shinpen kokka taikan* of the phrase *fukeyuku made* (into the deep of night) followed by the particle *ni*, however, and since the line appears in a scene where Ujitada is gazing tearfully at the moon and thinking of another famous lunar poem, with its overtones of sadness and longing for home, the larger context can be seen as helping to establish an allusion. If the allusion is accepted, Kiyosuke's poem brings to the present scene a heightened sense of the emperor's solicitous concern for Ujitada: he does not go on speaking with Ujitada merely to pass the time, but expressly to draw his attention away from the moon that is the source of such great sadness to him—just as it was a source of sadness for the speaker of Kiyosuke's poem.
168. The third line carries a double meaning: *soragoto*, "false illusion" or "deception," and *sora goto ni*, "with each [new dawning of the] sky." The line also is important in establishing an allusion to a famous poem by Sei Shōnagon, and through it to the Chinese story of how Prince

illness reached the palace, His Majesty sent a messenger to inquire what could be the matter.

"It is nothing so serious as to arouse concern," Ujitada asked the messenger to tell the emperor. "I am sure it is only a mild cold. But I thought caution the best policy, and so have stayed away from the palace for this one day."

As he lay lost in his heavyhearted brooding, a second messenger arrived, bringing from the empress dowager many words of concern and comfort along with medicines for Ujitada to take. The man she had chosen for this mission was her nephew, Teng Ying-ch'eng, and Ujitada rose from his bed so that he could thank him properly. The youthful Teng thought Ujitada struck an even finer figure out of court dress than in, and found him so naturally warm and approachable that he could scarcely believe such perfection had been born into this world. The elegance and beauty of his every feature were exactly as one would wish to find them in a woman, he exclaimed to himself,[169] and yet this very man had on the battlefield stained his sword like no other and won fame as a warrior without peer. He was indeed a rare figure of a man.

Teng, like the emperor, had been guided in his studies by the wise teachings of the empress dowager, and he was universally regarded as a man with a great gift for learning. Indeed, he acquitted himself most admirably in an exchange of Chinese poems with Ujitada before taking his leave to return to the palace.

Meng-ch'ang escaped capture when one of his men imitated a cock's crow and caused the gatekeeper to open the gate of the frontier barrier before dawn. Sei Shōnagon's poem comes in the course of an exchange with Fujiwara Yukinari, in which the latter falsely pretends he has spent the night with her. *Makura no sōshi*, section 139, "Tōben no, shiki ni mairitamaite. . . ." (Matsuo and Nagai 1974, 274; the section number varies from text to text):

Yo o komete	Try though you may
Tori no sorane wa	With all your heart to imitate
Hakaru to mo	The cock's morning crow,
Yo ni ōsaka no	The barrier gate on your path of love
Seki wa yurusaji	Will never open in the deep of night.

This allusion could not have been made until after the turn of the eleventh century, long after the tale is set and long after the date given in the colophon of the tale.

To return to poem 54: in association with the sky image, *akenu* (not open) also means "to dawn" (in the positive form, since the negative *nu* applies only to the speaker's heart). In the translation, "dawn" has been collapsed into "end of night," but whatever it is called, the time when night gives way to day is when the futility of one's waiting is finally known. Thus: "The barrier gate opened for Prince Meng-ch'ang, the gate on the path of love opened for me (unlike for Yukinari), and the sky continues to dawn ('open') each morning; the only thing that does not open is the gate of my heart, bursting with the pent-up torments of night after night waited in vain—the painful truth of which futility is impressed upon me afresh with each new dawn."

169. *Onna nite mimahoshū.* The phrase by itself may mean either that the speaker wishes the other were a woman, or that the speaker wishes he were himself a woman and looking upon the other as a woman would look upon the ideal man (see, for example, Abe et al. 1970–76, vol. 1, 390, n. 10). In the present passage, the way in which the sentence continues calls for the former meaning.

Ujitada watched the moon, one night past full, rise above the mountain rim. Tonight would no doubt be the same, he thought disconsolately: he would gaze in solitary reverie at the moon until it disappeared beyond the opposite mountain rim. But suddenly the air filled with that unmistakable perfume, and a frenzy of excitement gripped his heart. He hurried to close the shutters.

With the lady beside him again, gone in an instant were all the resentments that had piled up in night after night of wretched longing, and Ujitada had not the heart to cast the least shred of reproach upon her. When the palace bell sounded the approach of dawn, he could hardly believe that more than a few moments had passed, and he felt quite as though the bell were announcing his own impending demise. No more on this morning than on any other could he bear to think of being separated from the lady again, and it was clear that she felt the same. But, as always, the growing light of the dawn drove her away as if fleeing from mortal danger. There was nothing Ujitada could do.

55.	Kumo no iru	"Even could I learn
	Yama mo izure to	To which peak the cloud goes to rest,
	Shirarete mo	Still would I grieve—
	Mine ni wakaren	When from the mountaintop it flees
	Koto zo kanashiki	Into the morning sky."

The verse formed in his mind, but he could not bring himself to utter it aloud.

56.	Tachinaruru	"On which peak
	Yama wa soko to mo	The white cloud is wont to rise
	Shirakumo no	I do not know;
	Taete tsurenaki	Yet it heartlessly breaks away,
	Ato no kanashisa	Leaving me stricken with grief."[170]

He felt as though once again his torments had been multiplied. There seemed nothing he could do to relieve his aching heart.

Still too distraught to rise the next morning, he made excuses again that he did not feel well. Word spread quickly, and brought a stream of alarmed visitors to Ujitada's bedside—people he had grown familiar with in his daily attendance at court. Those who came, however, were unable to obtain any explanation for the "soundless waterfall" they encountered,[171] and went away feeling no more reassured than before about Ujitada's condition.

---

170. There is a pun on *shirakumo* (white cloud) and *shirazu* (not know). The allusions to "Kao-t'ang fu" continue in both of these poems.

171. I.e., they found Ujitada in tears for no apparent reason at all. There were several actual waterfalls known by the name "Otonashi no taki" (literally, "waterfall of no sound") in Japan, the most famous of which was in Ōhara, to the northeast of the Heian capital (modern Kyoto).

Ujitada passed the time gazing languidly out at the sky, which, in spite of its emptiness, remained as before his best hope for relief of his longing. It was not likely, however, that she would come again so soon.

He would have preferred to continue to stay at home, but he knew he could not keep his absence from becoming known, and then there would be more visitors to receive, with all manner of questions to answer. It would be much less trouble to pretend he had recovered, he decided, and so from the next day he resumed his daily attendance at the palace. His nights, however, were still spent waiting in vain. The severity of his affliction increased with each disappointing night, and he seemed gradually to lose all power of reason. The studies for which he had come to China had now fallen into complete neglect.

Toward the end of the month, the peonies in the palace garden reached the height of their bloom, and as one might well have expected in this country, exclamations over their beauty fell from every lip.[172] Indeed they seemed veritably to shine out in their color, and Ujitada, too, was at once captivated by their loveliness. He plucked one to take with him when he withdrew for the day.

He spent the evening as he had spent every other evening of late, gazing off at the changing colors of the sky and hoping against all hope that the lady would come to him once again. Tonight the sky seemed more than usual to match his feelings, as the gathering clouds let loose a sudden shower in the deepening dusk. Then came the call of a cuckoo, the first of the season. Its power to move the human heart was no different here than in Japan.

57. Hototogisu   "O cuckoo,
    Nare o zo tanomu   You are my only comfort
    Murasame no   On this rainy night;
    Furusatobito wa   When the person of the village
    Toi mo konu yo ni   Neither comes nor sends word."[173]

The shower passed quickly, and stars appeared in the sky as the clouds moved away. Ujitada sensed a change in the air and hurried to close the shutters. He could not see her yet, but as always the smell of her perfume alone was sufficient to send a tremor of happiness through his heart. Then she spoke.

58. Shinobaruru   "No word comes
    Furusatobito wa   From the person of your village, of whom
    Toi mo kode   You so long to hear;

172. The Chinese were known to especially favor the peony, as the Japanese favored the cherry blossom.
173. *Furu*, in addition to being the first part of *furusatobito* (person of the village), completes the phrasing of the third line with its meaning of "falling (rain)."

| Itou kumoi no | Instead you are startled by the unwanted call |
| Tori zo ayashiki | Of the bird from above the clouds.[174] |

"This dreampath we walk—it would be most disagreeable if anyone were to discover it, and each time I come to you I feel that I am increasing the burden of sin for which I will someday be held to account. But when I count the few days remaining before your departure I am so overcome with sorrow that I cannot bear to stay away. I shudder to think how I will feel about all of this when it becomes no more than a memory."

She was apparently as conscious as Ujitada that reason and prudence dictated the utmost of restraint, and yet her repeated visits testified that in the battle between prudence and passion the latter had been continually the victor. Perhaps even supernatural spirits were susceptible to the weaknesses of the human heart when they adopted human form. Still, Ujitada could not forgive the lady for her inflexible refusal to reveal where she lived—where she vanished when she left him, like a mayfly eluding his grasp[175]—and now he entreated her once again, invoking every persuasion at his command, to put an end to her perverse silence.

"Tonight I have opened my heart to you in all its weakness," the lady said, "and I would no more continue to conceal my name than did the lady of the morning clouds.[176] But if you were to learn the full extent of our bond from former lives, I would have no words to explain how I could have allowed myself to become so entangled in a worldly attachment. It is from shame that I hesitate even now to reveal who I am. Yet almost equal to that shame is the pain of continuing to keep such a secret from you, for, if I am to blame for preventing

---

174. The mysterious lady identifies herself with the cuckoo (*hototogisu*). Although the first call of the cuckoo was awaited with great anticipation each year at the beginning of summer, she suggests that Ujitada finds her call startling rather than pleasing because he actually has someone else on his mind—someone from his home in Japan. *Furusato* is most commonly used to signify one's own native place, but it can also signify any place that one has frequented in the past. Ujitada, in his poem, uses it in the latter sense to refer to the small mountain village where he first met the mysterious lady, but the lady chooses to interpret it instead as a reference to his home. In essence, she is repeating her complaint that Ujitada's feelings for her are not deep enough for him to change his mind about leaving China.

The description of the bird as "from above the clouds" recalls the frequent references to the lady's behavior as resembling that of the cloud-spirit in "Kao-t'ang fu"; it also hints that the lady is the empress dowager, since imperial palaces and personages are frequently referred to metaphorically as "above the clouds."

175. *Genji monogatari*, chapter 52 ("Kagerō"), Kaoru (Abe et al. 1970–76, vol. 6, 264):

Ari to mite	The elusive mayfly—
Te ni wa torarezu	Though I see it, and reach for it,
Mireba mata	It escapes my grasp;
Yukue mo shirazu	When I look again, it is gone,
Kieshi kagerō	Vanished I know not where.

176. The lady in "Kao-t'ang fu" revealed her identity to the king without the slightest reserve. See chapter two, p. 43.

the release of your torments, then I would be guilty of leading a fellow being into greater suffering. Before long, I hope, you will be able to understand."

She still would not tell him her name.

In the darkness her fingers touched the peony Ujitada had brought that day from the palace. She picked it up and turned it in her hand.

"Perhaps this flower can tell you where I live," she said with a playful laugh. "When you find it, you will know who I am. But I know you will despise me."

Even the charm of her gentle laugh seemed only to press home all the more painfully the feeling of helplessness that had been Ujitada's from the beginning of this love.

The echo of the bell that announced the dawn lingered not even so long as the cock's crow, and the short summer night seemed to have passed in a briefer span than either. The lady went away as before, taking the flower with her, and from that moment a new quest was added to all the other concerns already weighing upon Ujitada's mind. He would have liked nothing better than to set out immediately, to wander over the hills and moors in search of his beloved.

This morning of all mornings, however, the imperial audience commenced even earlier than usual. Summoned several times, he hurried to the palace and attended to the day's proceedings. Afterward the emperor detained Ujitada and spoke to him in the casual manner he had been wont to adopt of late. Among other matters, His Majesty was particularly concerned to indicate the texts he wished to have discussed the following day. One subject led to another and soon it had grown dark.

The day had thus been filled with public concerns, and left no time for Ujitada to apply himself to the search for the flower—the search in which he had no clue but the clouds. With so many others nearby, it had been out of the question that he should approach the empress dowager. And to make matters worse, she had remained all day behind her curtains of state, far away from where Ujitada sat. It made him feel quite forlorn that today not so much as a whiff of the marvelous perfume that had always reminded him of the mysterious lady carried to him across the room.

The Fifth Month came. Preparations for the autumn sailing began in earnest now, and the men with whom Ujitada had been associated in his offices at the Chinese court came one after another to call upon him. The feelings of his heart were forced to yield to duty as he passed the days receiving such visitors. Indeed, there seemed to be no end to the matters requiring his attention and preventing him from going in search of the lady. If only he could get away, he might happen upon something that would lead him to the flower, but this was difficult. Finally he hit upon the pretext of touring, before his departure, those places he had not yet had a chance to visit. He traveled in various directions, but found no trace of the peony blossom he sought.

He returned once again to the village of the plum blossoms where he had first come upon the lady. The summer grasses growing thickly in the grounds showed no sign of human passage, but neither did the buildings look as though they had been completely abandoned. The rooms appeared to have been carefully swept and cleaned, for there was not a speck of dust anywhere to be seen. On the floor near the back wall, however, lay a single petal of a peony blossom. The time for these flowers had long since passed, yet this petal remained as fresh and unfaded as if it had just been plucked. Could he be dreaming? He looked everywhere for someone to ask about who might have come there—who might have left behind such a token—but could find no one. Tears streamed down his face as he departed for the city, heartbroken.

It was mystifying in the extreme that a single flower petal could have remained unwithered and unfaded. He sank again into his desolate brooding, paying attention to little more than the dawn and the dusk as the passing days carried him closer and closer to the time when he would have to leave the Chinese capital behind. Night after night he lay awake with his shutters open, but always in vain. By the time the Fifth Month came to an end, Ujitada felt that his soul had quite left his body and had taken with it all his capacity for regret.

Since the port from which his ship would sail was itself a distant journey from the capital over land, it was decided that Ujitada and his party should start out around the twentieth of the Sixth Month.

The lady's behavior, so like the elusive mayfly, continued to disturb Ujitada, and he began even to contemplate a change of plans—to stay through the autumn. But then he would think of his mother, waiting so anxiously for his return. And he would think of the other, no doubt waiting just as anxiously—Princess Hua-yang, who had given him the precious jewel that he kept always with him. With every such reminder that his affections had not taken a single direction, his sorrow increased, and he passed the days knowing no relief from his inconsolable anguish.

59.	Shirazarishi	"When the embassy boat
	Morokoshibune no	Reached calm harbor in unfamiliar China
	Minato yori	Little did I guess
	Ukitaru koi ni	I would soon find myself broken apart
	Mi o kudakitsutsu	On the shoals of uncertain love."[177]

The tenth of the month came and went, and the summer heat reached its peak. When the day's business of state was over, the emperor and his mother retired to rest in an open gallery overlooking the garden lake. An occasional cool breeze came in from over the water. They had with them only a few close attendants, but after a short while they summoned Ujitada. He came and seated himself on a stone bench in the shade of the deep eaves.

177. *Shirazarishi* carries the meaning of "unfamiliar (China)" as well as "to not know (or guess)." *Morokoshibune* (embassy boat), *minato* ("port" or "harbor"), and *ukitaru* (<*uku*, "to float") are associated words; as a modifier for "love," *ukitaru* means both "uncertain," and "intemperate" or "indiscreet."

"We have long known you would leave us," the emperor said, "but with the remaining days now so few, our sorrow is deepened and our regrets multiplied." There were tears in his eyes.

Ujitada, too, was near tears, feeling most undeserving of the emperor's gracious sentiments.

The empress dowager was close by. With the middle of the Sixth Month approaching, the heat of the sun was almost too great to bear, even when dressed in the lightest of clothes; there was no one who did not suffer. Yet, at such a time as this, when the glare of the summer sky was all but blinding, the empress dowager seemed to be improved in her dazzling beauty—if such can be said of that which was already beyond the power of words to describe; she seemed veritably to glow with a light of her own. Ujitada felt as though his eyes had only now been opened. Unaffected by the sweltering heat, she was like a cool, clear moon risen in a deep blue sky.[178] Ujitada gazed in awe at her shining figure, quite speechless with wonder. Could such a lady really be of this world? The gentle breeze brought to him the scent of that special perfume, no mere aloe or sandalwood, which seemed in every way identical to the perfume of the mysterious lady of his dreams. Was he imagining things? Or had he indeed been transported to the land of paradise? He gazed on and on at Her Majesty, quite without regard for rudeness, thinking that the sutras spoke of worshipping the Buddha just so.[179] He feared he was being irreverent, but could not help himself. Tears streamed down his cheeks.

The emperor and empress dowager, for their part, found no words adequate to express their sadness over Ujitada's impending departure, or the depth of their gratitude for the unforgettable, devoted service he had rendered the court. They, too, could but give themselves over to weeping.

"Though I am not one for the lewd songs of Cheng and Wei,"[180] the emperor said, "I am also aware that our traditional rituals and music must not be abandoned, and I would so have liked to entertain you with concerts while you were here. Unfortunately, we have been in mourning during most of your stay, and our strings and pipes and bells and stones have had to be kept silent. It will remain as a lasting regret for me. I do not know if I will be able to forgive you for rushing away so impatiently, without waiting until the full cycle of days and months has passed,[181] even though it would have passed in next to no time at all. I fear it may be enough to make me forget how deeply devoted you have otherwise been to us."

Still, since he had vowed not to betray Ujitada's deepest wish, even such reproaches were of no use in the end.

---

178. *Midori no sora*, said of a clear daytime or evening sky.
179. The *Lotus Sutra* frequently describes the Buddha's disciples as gazing up into his face with folded palms, in reverent worship or troubled appeal. See, for example, Hurvitz 1976, 157, 168, 202–3, and passim.
180. Two kingdoms of the Spring and Autumn period (722–481 B.C.E.). Various sources describe the music of these kingdoms as lewd and immoral, with a disruptive effect on public morals. See Hagitani 1970, 287–88, n. 282.
181. That is, until the year of mourning was over. Ujitada's total period of stay in China has extended beyond a full year.

"Knowing there are many who anxiously await your return, I cannot bring myself to stand in the way of your most ardent desire. Life holds constant uncertainties for us all, but if we, if both of us, should happen to have been allotted a lengthy span of years, you must promise that you will someday visit this court again. Only then will I be able to contain my regret and permit you to go; only then will I know the true depth of your devotion to this court."

Ujitada's assent was lost in a flood of tears.

60. Kagiri aran   "Though nothing can change
    Inochi o sara ni   The allotted span of my life,
    Oshimite mo   Yet will I hold it dear;
    Kimi no mikoto o   How could I ever fail to heed
    Ikaga wasuren   My Lord's gracious command?"[182]

The emperor replied:

61. Kore yue zo   "For such words
    Ware mo inochi no   I, too, shall hold my life dear—
    Oshimaren   Though they may be
    Tada naozari ni   But empty answer to fill the moment,
    Tanomeoku to mo   And I a fool to believe them.

"I can but hope that we will both be long in this world." He was a beautiful child, and his manner was of one far beyond his years.

Darkness descended slowly upon them, and the empress dowager, who had had little to say, now withdrew to her apartments. A short while later the emperor also retired. Just as he did so, one of the empress dowager's ladies-in-waiting appeared with a message for Ujitada.

"I do not wish to startle you, but will you be angry with me for treasuring so long this flower out of season?" The lady held out a single peony, as fresh and beautiful as if it had just that moment been plucked. Its color had not faded the slightest shade. Ujitada then realized that the lady-in-waiting was none other than the lady he had seen standing by the gate on that spring night. He was struck completely dumb.

"Her Majesty asks that you stay a while longer," the lady said. "There are some things she wishes to tell you in person."

Ujitada bowed his assent and waited as he was. He discovered a verse attached to the flower:[183]

62. Mata wa yo ni   "In all the world
    Iro mo nioi mo   No other flower could be alike
    Naki mono o   In scent or in color—
    Nani no kigusa no   With what blossom of tree or grass
    Hana ka magawan   Could you have confused this peony?"[184]

---

182. In *Hamamatsu Chūnagon monogatari*, Chūnagon makes a similar promise to come back to China to see the Hoyang Consort. Matsuo 1964, 210; Rohlich 1983, 98.
183. Hagitani (1970, 106, n. 5) suggests also the possibility that the poem was written upon the petals of the flower itself.
184. Implicitly identifying herself with the peony, the empress dowager asks, "How could you ever have been in doubt about my identity?"

The flower, however, seemed to have lost its natural scent, and was infused instead with the marvelous fragrance of the empress dowager's perfume.

The moon came into the sky. Through her lady-in-waiting, the empress dowager bade Ujitada come to her apartments. He seated himself on the veranda, separated from Her Majesty by a blind.

The empress dowager now told Ujitada all she knew, all the things that had so profoundly affected her feelings for Ujitada. He could find no words to reply. He turned his face away to hide the tears that streamed from his eyes, hoping the glistening on his cheeks would be taken merely as the brilliant light of the moon.

"If I failed to tell you the truth about how we 'drifted . . . onto the path so straight in dreams,'[185] it would but further multiply my sins. The one called Yü-wen Hui was in fact an incarnation of an evil asura.[186] Seeing that Yü-wen was about to bring the nation to ruin, the late Emperor Wen[187] asked the Reverend Hsüan-tsang[188] to relay urgent appeals for help to Śakra.[189] Śakra took pity on Emperor Wen and determined to help him. I was in service in the Second Heaven then, and, although I had given no cause to be sent back to a lower world, Śakra relieved me of my duties and arranged for me to be reborn in this country—to quell the insurrection and ensure the legitimate continuation of Emperor Wen's line.

185. See the poem by Toshiyuki cited in translation n. 86, above. Although the translation can only reproduce the effect partially, the phrasing used here takes not only line four of Toshiyuki's poem, but line two as well, and thus establishes the allusion more clearly than anywhere else in the tale.

186. Asuras are devils of an especially belligerent character, at odds constantly with Śakra, in Buddhism (see n. 189, below), or Indra, in Hinduism.

187. The former emperor is here given a name for the first time. He was most likely named after the second T'ang emperor, of the same name, whose reign (626–49) was so successful that the era name—Chen-kuan in Chinese, Jōgan or Teikan in Japanese—thereafter became a synonym for good government. The name of Wen is clearly intended to underscore earlier descriptions of the late emperor as a sage ruler. Use of *Jōgan no chi* (*chi*= "government") as a superlative for good government gained double force in Japan owing to the flourishing of the court (or, more particularly, of Fujiwara fortunes) under the leadership of Chancellor Fujiwara Yoshifusa during the reign of Emperor Seiwa, 858–76, which was also known by the era name of Jōgan. Also see following note.

188. Hsüan-tsang (600 or 602–64) traveled to India between 629 (or 627) and 645 and brought back several hundred Sanskrit texts, as well as the teachings that became the doctrine of the Fa-hsiang (Japanese, Hossō) sect in China. After his return, he translated a great many Buddhist texts into Chinese, beginning a new tradition of translations distinct from older translations. He also wrote a detailed account of his journey that later became a source for Ming dynasty author Wu Ch'eng-en (ca. 1505–80) when he wrote *Hsi-yu chi* ("Journey to the West," ca. 1570), a considerably more fantastic tale of a monk's pilgrimage to India. The aptness of his selection by the fictional Emperor Wen for this heavenly mission to Śakra becomes clear when we consider that he was sent on the mission to India by none other than the historical Emperor Wen. See previous note.

189. The god Śakra, lord of the Trāyastrimsa Heaven (the second lowest of the six heavens in the World of Desire—hence the "Second Heaven," below), together with the god Sikhin, lord of the Mahābrahman Heaven (the highest of three levels in the first heaven in the World of Form), is a guardian of the Buddhist Law. In Buddhist mythology he leads the heavenly legions in the battle against the asuras, and, from his palace on the summit of Mount Sumeru (Japanese, Shumisen), keeps a tutelary watch on inhabitants of the world below heaven, taking pleasure in acts of virtue and chastising evil.

"I was chosen because I already had certain ties to this country. But as a woman I did not have the strength to achieve my purpose all alone; I needed someone to assist me. From among his many pages, Śakra chose you. 'Here is my bow,' he said. 'Take it. Go and destroy this incarnation of an asura.' You were without connections in this country, and, furthermore, if you were born here, there would be no place to hide the bow until it was needed. For this reason, Śakra arranged for you to be born in Japan, and he charged the god of Sumiyoshi with your keeping.

"I knew all this when I was born into this world; I thus had no cause for genuine fear or despair. But having entered the flesh of a human being, I strayed onto an evil path. My heart's true vision clouded over, and I became trapped in the darkness of this diabolical world. When the national crisis came, I could not help myself—I fled desperately, in fear and grief.

"Then you came forward, true to the bonds you brought with you from the other world. I cannot tell you what a relief it was to see you—to see your determination and faithfulness. I lamented then as now that I could not tell you of my joy even in the vaguest way. Though I had been born into this world, I had thought of the inhabitants of this world as unclean, and had always kept my distance from them. But you were one I had known from the Second Heaven, and I was instantly filled with feelings of warmth and tenderness toward you. Perhaps I was wrong to try to keep you from suspecting how I felt, or perhaps I failed to understand the extent to which I was susceptible to the desires of the flesh: I became lost in an indiscreet love, a futile dream from which I could not wake. I was behaving quite irresponsibly, I knew, and I could think only of the chastisement I would receive from Śakra—of the great shame I would feel when I faced him again. This, too, was a heavy burden on my thoughts, added to the burden of the secret I had so long kept from you, and in the end it was a greater burden than I could bear: I determined to reveal everything. But I fear that this, too, may be a simpleminded mistake, and I find myself wondering if I will ever be able to redeem myself from my many sins."[190]

The empress dowager's words had awakened in Ujitada long forgotten memories of life in another world, and, perhaps because of this, one sad thought after another passed through his mind. With the empress dowager so close by, Ujitada was quite on the verge of losing all reason and yielding to

---

190. Or possibly read in place of the last two sentences, "I find myself wondering if it will be held against me as an error of simplemindedness that I was unable to detain you in China, and I worry that I will never be able to redeem myself from my many sins." Hagitani 1970, 109, n. 8. While this alternate reading may place less strain on the language of the original, however, it makes little sense in the context either of what has actually taken place or of the explanation the empress dowager has given.

In light of the empress dowager's revelation that she has come from the celestial world, the story of Ch'ao Hsü in "T'ung-yu chi," included in *T'ai-p'ing kuang-chi* ("Extensive Gleanings of the Reign of Great Tranquility," 978), is of interest for its resemblance to the meetings between Ujitada and the mysterious lady: Ch'ao Hsü first dreams of a fairy, then actually has her come to him for a night of love. She identifies herself as being from the celestial world. Her arrival is preceded by the blowing of a wind, which brings a wonderful fragrance to the room. Toward morning, a waiting woman appears to warn her of the imminent cock's crow.

impulse—such was his yearning for just one more journey down their dream-path of love.

In revealing the true circumstances of their love, however, the empress dowager had released herself from the tremendous burden she had been carrying in her secret, and she was already drawing back from the murky and impure affairs of this transient world. She could think only with profound sadness of the unbreakable bonds that determine the course of every life and soul.

"The time I was given to be away from the Second Heaven is brief. I will not continue to govern this country for long—surely not beyond my fortieth year. I know I will return to the place from which I came, and so I need have no regrets upon leaving this world. Yet, having been born of a mother and father into this ephemeral life, whenever I think of it coming to an end I am as loath as any to leave it behind. It pains me especially that there will be no one close by who can truly understand my feelings. So at my hour of death, at least, I beg you, however difficult it may be for you to get away from your duties at home, please find a way to come back to this country and be at my side.

63. Yuku kata mo   "In the clear sky
    Kumoranu tsuki no   Not a cloud blocks the path
    Kage naredo   Of the brilliant moon;
    Iru yama made wa   Promise me you will be there to attend
    Tazunete mo miyo   When it sinks beyond the mountain rim."[191]

Knowing, as she did, what the future would hold, there really was no cause for her to be so heartstricken over her parting with Ujitada, yet she had grown accustomed to the ways of the human world and was quite as susceptible to feelings of grief as any other mortal.

"It will not be possible for you to return immediately to the Second Heaven," the empress dowager resumed. "You have longstanding ties with the palace of the immortals on Mount P'eng-lai,[192] as well as other bonds from former existences that destine you to live long in this lower world, and one of my ladies tells me that your connections with the music of the zither also require you to remain here for some time. But this was all ordained by an

191. The poem repeats metaphorically the sentiments the empress dowager has expressed above: she can take some comfort in knowing exactly where she will be going when she leaves this life, but the time of departure will be as difficult for her as for any ordinary mortal.

192. Japanese, Hōrai. A mythical mountain, or island, said to be located in the eastern sea, by which was meant, originally, the Gulf of Po Hai, and later, the vicinity of Japan. Japanese references also place it in the east, which is to say, to the east of Japan. In *Taketori monogatari*, for example, Kaguyahime charges one of her suitors with the task of fetching a jeweled branch from a tree on P'eng-lai, "in the eastern sea" (Katagiri 1972, 57). On the island were said to be gold and silver palaces, whose inhabitants knew neither aging nor death. From a distance the island would appear like a cloud, from nearer it seemed to be under the sea, but it was not possible for ordinary humans to actually reach the island.

In Po Chü-i's "Song of Unending Sorrow," which tells of Emperor Hsüan-tsung's boundless love for Yang Kuei-fei both before and after she was killed by men of his own army during the An Lu-shan rebellion (see translation nn. 95 and 96, above), a Taoist sage commanded to search for Yang Kuei-fei after her death finally finds her living on P'eng-lai.

irresistible fate; you need not fear that it was caused by any shameful failing of your own heart.

"I have spoken to you in this way in order that you might know the nature of your past. As for those meetings in which you would not forgive me for vanishing like the morning clouds, even though we are both still of this world, still the same man and woman, now that I have revealed to you our true nature, it would not be proper for us to continue such dreamlike wanderings."

She spoke firmly, with a tone of finality, and yet she wept as though nothing could have pained her more. No one who saw her thus, brushing away tear after tear, could, even in jest, have thought that such beauty belonged naturally to this world. With the blind partly raised, the light of the moon illumined her face in a marvelous glow no words could describe.

It was the custom of the country to speak forthrightly, and perhaps it was because of this that she boldly recited,

64. Minarete wa	"If we remained together,
Koizu mo araji	Not for long would you be able
Omokage no	To restrain your love,
Wasurarenubeki	For I am not the kind of person
Wa ga mi naraneba	Whose face can be easily forgotten.[193]

"You can remember me with this." She pushed under the blind a small box containing a mirror.[194]

65. Onozukara	"In this mirror
Sugata bakari wa	Perhaps, at least, an image of me
Utsurinan	Can appear before you—
Koto no ha made wa	Even if the words that I speak
Kayoikozu tomo	Cannot ever reach your ears.

"I would be most embarrassed if this box were discovered by a certain person who could recognize it as mine.[195] Still, she would not likely be able to guess its true significance. 'Say no to those who ask if you have seen me.'"[196] She pressed her sleeve to her face and slipped away into her private rooms.

Ujitada was beside himself with grief. He would have raised his voice in a wailing cry, but he could not, for now that Her Majesty had withdrawn there were others nearby. He forced himself to remain silent. Let me die now, just as I am, he thought. How much easier that would be than to go on living and suffering like this. In the end, he somehow found the strength to keep his

---

193. I.e., "It is therefore best that we part." Now that Ujitada knows who she is, if they remained together, he would wish more than ever to be with her and show his love for her. But it would be no more acceptable for them to love openly now than it was before; they must remain strangers. Since Ujitada is not likely to be able to become indifferent toward her beauty, it is best that they part.

Hagitani (1970, 111 and 217) reads *Koi su mo araji* in the second line, which makes the first two lines an expression of the idea that those who are always together do not fall (or stay or grow) in love. This does not seem to fit as well with the rest of the poem, however.

194. In folk belief, a mirror was believed to embody the soul of the one reflected in it.

195. That is, Princess Hua-yang.

196. See translation n. 152, above.

composure, and to refrain from making a spectacle of himself in the presence of others. But nothing could compare to the desolation he felt as he got up and made his way home from the palace.

Back in his own apartments, a crowd of young courtiers had ordered up a banquet with all manner of delicacies and wines, and their servants were waiting nearby with special farewell gifts that each had prepared for Ujitada. He longed to cry aloud, but even here he was forced to hold his grief in check.

He spent the night with his well-wishers, joining as best he could in the entertainments, but his heart was elsewhere. Was it all to come to an end just like that? he wondered, and he could think of nothing else. Gone was the anguish of believing his beloved must be a spirit of the clouds and rain. But it came to him now that, had he ever known who the lady really was, not for a moment would he have allowed himself to contemplate exchanging vows of love with her. It was frightening to think of what he had done—even now, after it had become an affair of the past. He became more and more choked with emotion as he recalled everything that had taken place.

The next morning he no longer wished to rush off into the countryside as he had on recent mornings. Instead he was anxious to get to the palace, where he could at least look upon the empress dowager from afar and imagine he was meeting her in private. He arrived much earlier than usual, and passed the time of the day's proceedings gazing at the faint outline of the empress dowager's figure visible through her curtains of state, pondering over and over the fate that had brought him such uncommon sorrow. Afterwards, Her Majesty withdrew to her apartments, and Ujitada was deeply disappointed when she did not appear for the usual private lectures held for the emperor.

Both publicly and privately, elaborate preparations were in progress for Ujitada's impending departure. Even those who were not directly involved were caught up in the flurry of activity. Ujitada, however, remained preoccupied with other concerns. "As if you were you and I were I," he sighed.[197] Hoping

197. *Ware wa ware*, an allusion to the second poem in the following exchange found in *Izumi Shikibu nikki* ("The Diary of Izumi Shikibu," ca. 1008; Fujioka Tadaharu 1971, 138–39):

Ware hitori	How useless it is
Omou omoi wa	For me, all alone, to be thinking
Kai mo nashi	These thoughts of love;
Onaji kokoro ni	If only I knew that you and I
Kimi mo aranan	Were of the selfsame mind.

The reply:

Kimi wa kimi	To set us apart,
Ware wa ware to mo	As if you were you and I were I,
Hedateneba	I would not think—
Kokorogokoro ni	How is it possible that you and I
Aran mono ka wa	Could be of different minds?

Hagitani (1970, 112, n. 7) appears to see Ujitada's sigh merely as an expression of his having his own concerns, distinct from the preparations for departure, which are commanding everyone else's attention; he notes that this is an unusual usage of the phrase *ware wa ware*. Ujitada does of course have his own concerns; however, the nature of the exchange in *Izumi Shikibu nikki* would suggest his sigh is one of lamenting the apparent ease with which the empress dowager has been able to set the two of them apart—to put an end to her visits.

beyond hope, he spent endless hours gazing longingly up at the sky, but in vain. The nearly full moon gave the courtiers an additional excuse to gather at his apartments night after night, toasting him with unwanted wine, and so he was deprived even of the chance to lose himself in a genuine dream.

From the empress dowager were delivered mountains of official gifts as well as assorted medicines for Ujitada to take back with him to Japan. There seemed nothing she did not think of, and she spared no effort or kind word to ease the pain of departure for him. Messengers went back and forth between them constantly.

The visitor Ujitada truly wished to see, however, was the elusive mayfly of all those meetings amidst the darkness.[198]

The day before Ujitada was to depart, a magnificent ceremony was held in the main hall of the palace. The emperor appeared in his most formal and majestic robes. Ujitada was reminded of the one no longer of this world, who had received the embassy party in this hall only the year before.

The ceremony had been planned with a maximum of pomp and solemnity but, perhaps for this very reason, failed to be truly extraordinary in any way. The sun was still high in the sky when those who had attended the ceremony began dispersing in their several directions. As before, however, the empress dowager detained Ujitada and had him shown to the open gallery that led to the fishing pavilion on the lake. Several of her ladies were in attendance. Having dressed for the ceremony in their finest robes, they were at their loveliest, every one of them, and yet next to the empress dowager they seemed to be quite without advantage. As on the last occasion when Ujitada had been summoned to this gallery, even beneath the brilliant sun clouded not by the slightest wisp of a shadow, the empress dowager seemed to shine out with a light of her own. Ujitada thought again that such pure and resplendent beauty, together with the quiet charm that made her seem not the least bit distant, could scarcely have been the features of an ordinary mortal.

"Our days have passed in listlessness beneath the merciless heat of the sun, and now the time has come for us to make our final farewells. There are so many things I want to say—I really do not know where to begin. Tomorrow I'll no doubt think of all the things I neglected to say and wonder how I could have forgotten."

In spite of herself, tears welled in her eyes. Ujitada had been struggling not to lose his composure in front of so many others, but when he saw the empress dowager's eyes fill, his own quickly overflowed. Bowing his head, he wept without restraint.

Her Majesty's ladies had many of them been with the imperial palanquin when it fled to the western mountains. They had not forgotten those events. They, too, dampened their sleeves as they remembered all that Ujitada had done.

198. "Meetings amidst the darkness" echoes the allusion noted in translation n. 159; "the elusive mayfly" continues the imagery drawn from the poems cited in translation nn. 162 and 175.

"I forget that my allotted span in this fleeting world is short, and imagine the day when we can still meet again in this life," the empress dowager said. "Or I find myself wishing you had no parents awaiting you, so that you might decide even now to remain in China. I just can't help myself." Over and over she wiped tears from her eyes.

Ujitada felt honored beyond his due to know that he was the object of such strong sentiments from the empress dowager. It was a demonstration of favor such as none could have taken lightly.

The manuscript states: "The binding is damaged and some pages are missing."

Many of the younger courtiers had decided to see Ujitada to his port of embarkation, and, in consequence, the journey to the sea became a rather noisy affair, offering no time for quietly gazing up at the sky or for thinking of love and the sadness of parting. Ujitada's companions plied him constantly with wine, and there was nothing for him to do but join them in composing poems and extolling the scenery of the mountains and lakes that they passed. Inwardly, however, he longed to turn back, though eightfold clouds might stand in the way.[199] Time and again his eyes were drawn in the direction of the capital, now left so far behind.

The ship set sail on the fifteenth day of the Seventh Month. Those who had come to see him off continued to the end to pour out their regret over his departure, no doubt just as anyone would expect.

As the oarsmen rowed the ship out onto the vastness of the sea, where the waves rise up to meet the clouds, all Ujitada could think of was the matchless countenance of the empress dowager. Her image remained constantly before his eyes. She was indeed a lady he would never forget, he thought, with greater conviction than he had ever felt before.

Guided by a strong protector, Ujitada's ship made the crossing without incident. The reader may imagine the joy with which Ujitada's mother welcomed him home in Matsura.

Oh yes, I neglected to mention: before Ujitada left the Chinese capital, the empress dowager had quietly arranged that a zither and some other personal effects Princess Hua-yang had left behind would be included among the things Ujitada would take home with him. No one else was aware of it because she made the arrangements herself.

Fearing that even now it might be too great a shock for his mother if she were to hear of the stormy rebellion they had been through in China, Ujitada extracted vows of silence from all those who had been with him.

The Japanese emperor was beside himself with joy at Ujitada's safe return. Since Ujitada had been given such high rank even in the great land of China,

---

199. *Yae no shirakumo.* The phrase is used as a pillow word for *tachikaeru* (to return), and does not appear to be an allusion.

the emperor declared that he should join the ranks of the senior nobles at home as well. He was appointed to hold concurrently the offices of imperial advisor, controller of the right, and middle captain of the Imperial Bodyguards.

Anxious to be reunited with Princess Hua-yang, Ujitada followed her instructions and went to the temple at Hatsuse to conduct the twenty-one-day services. Everything took place exactly as she had said: on a moonlit night, the sound of a zither descended upon the temple from high up on the mountainside, where great zelkova trees towered overhead. Ujitada hurried to the spot.

The princess greeted him with a poem:

66. Hatsuse no ya   "On this Hatsuse peak,
    Yutsuki ga shita ni   Beneath the tall zelkova tree,
    Teru tsuki no   I waited for you—
    Hikari o sode ni   For this day when I would see you again
    Machiukete miru   Close as the moonlight upon my sleeve."[200]

    Ujitada replied:

67. Omoiiru   "Drawn by a tender vow
    Chigiri shi hikeba   Held deep and true within my heart,
    Hatsuse naru   And by your wondrous play,
    Yutsuki ga shita ni   I have found you on this Hatsuse peak
    Kage wa miekeri   Beneath a great zelkova tree."[201]

They returned together to the temple, and from there to Ujitada's home in the capital. His mother could scarcely contain her delight to see them.

The zither that Princess Hua-yang had sent off beyond the clouds had flown here to Japan, and so she had been able to keep it with her while she waited for Ujitada's return. Ujitada had recognized the sound instantly as the sound of the zither he sought. Now that he had found the Princess again, his love and affection for her returned in even greater measure than before, and he was certain she could have no equal in beauty. He seemed to have utterly forgotten the one who had spoken to him of his ties with the palace of P'eng-lai.

200. Implicit in the moonlight upon her sleeve are tears of longing, for it is only upon a wet sleeve that moonlight can be caught and reflected.

   Both this poem and Ujitada's reply are based on *Man'yōshū* 2353, a *sedōka*, or "head-repeated poem," by Hitomaro:

   Hatsuse no ya   My secret lover,
   Yutsuki ga shita ni   Hidden in a village at the foot
   Wa ga kakuseru tsuma   Of the Peak of Zelkovas, in Hatsuse—
   Akane sashi   I wonder,
   Tereru tsukuyo ni   Might someone perhaps have seen her,
   Hito miten ka mo   In the bright light of the moon.

   For Hitomaro's poem, there is some question as to whether *yutsuki* is intended as another name for *tsuki no ki* (zelkova tree) or as the name of a mountain in Hatsuse. The separate mention of zelkova trees high on the mountainside in the line preceding poem 66 indicates that Teika intended the meaning of "beneath the tree(s)" rather than "at the foot of the mountain." Also see appendix B, pp. 187–88.

201. *Hiku* (*hikeba*) means both "to draw" and "to play (an instrument)."

They could now play their zithers together without the slightest need for secrecy. As Ujitada's mother listened, her heart warmed with ever deeper feelings of love for them both.

Ujitada had steeled his heart, thrown off his all-consuming attachment to the empress dowager, and determined to return home, but now that he gazed once again upon the trees and grasses of the countryside, and listened to the calls of the birds, he found everything about his country and its ways to be embarrassingly inferior to what he had seen and heard in China. Indeed, was there anything that might have induced Princess Hua-yang to come to this strange land save her ties to the Chinese zither and her own steadfast faithfulness to a vow she had made? It touched him to the quick to realize that there was not.

With Princess Hua-yang so completely occupying his affections, Ujitada had also quite forgotten about Princess Kannabi. He had not sent her so much as a simple greeting since returning to Japan.

"How he has changed!" she exclaimed in annoyance, and sent the following poem.

68. Morokoshi ya	"Far Cathay—
Wasuregusa ouru	Is it perhaps a land where grow wild
Kuni naran	The grasses of forgetfulness?
Hito no kokoro no	So far now from your mind am I,
Sore ka to mo naki	You think not even to ask of me."[202]

The poem awakened many old memories for Ujitada. His reply:

69. Morokoshi no	"Rising and falling
Chie no namima ni	Upon the thousand waves that lead
Ukishizumi	To far Cathay,
Mi sae kawareru	The trials of my journey have changed me
Kokochi koso sure	Both in body and in soul.[203]

202. *Wasuregusa* (the grasses of forgetfulness), because of their name, were conventionally spoken of—and planted, or picked and worn within the sash of one's underrobe—as having the power to relieve the torments of love by allowing one to forget one's longing or grief. For example, *Tosa nikki* ("The Tosa Diary," 935), Second Month, Fifth Day (Matsumura Seiichi 1973, 59; translated in Miner 1969, 83):

Suminoe ni	O take our ship
Fune sashiyoseyo	To rest upon the beach of Sumiyoshi!
Wasuregusa	For I would like to pick
Shirushi ari ya to	The grasses of forgetfulness to see
Tsumite yukubeku	If they can prove the promise of their name.

Conversely, as in poem 68, they could be referred to when reproaching another for neglect and loss of interest in a relationship.

203. *Ukishizumi* refers both to the rising and falling of the waves and to the trials Ujitada went though in China. *Mi sae* carries the two senses of "even in body (as in soul)" and "even I (as you)." By quoting the first two lines of the poem Princess Kannabi sent him when he was about to depart for China (poem 13), Ujitada reminds her of the sentiments she expressed then, implicitly contrasting them with the sentiments of her poem now and suggesting that she has changed as much as he.

"I did not write for fear that I might cause offense to your new rank."
Princess Kannabi felt quite defeated when she read the note.

The love between Ujitada and Princess Hua-yang continued to grow and it
was not long before the princess began to experience the unmistakable signs of
approaching motherhood. At such a joyous time, Ujitada could hardly have been
expected to turn any part of his boundless love for the princess to others. In his
delight over the princess's pregnancy, he allowed many days to pass without
once thinking of the empress dowager or the solemn promise he had made
regarding her final days in this world. How sad it was!

The mirror given him by Her Majesty had been sealed tightly in its case,
and an attached note instructed him to open it only in a place of stillness and
purity. Saying that he wished to arrange prayers and services for a safe delivery,
Ujitada managed finally to get away to a temple, and there he broke the seal of
the case. In the mirror was reflected, with vivid clarity, the world he had left
behind in China.

It was now early in the Eleventh Month. The evening sky was filled with
heavy clouds, swirling before gusting winds and threatening at any moment to
burst forth in shower. Her Majesty was seated in the open gallery overlooking
the lake in the palace garden. The waters of the lake below, though not visible,
would be turbulent with choppy waves.

The period of mourning for the late emperor had come to an end, and Her
Majesty had changed to robes of colorful, figured silk—though it seemed she
was not one for making an ostentatious display of the brightest of colors. Lost in
melancholy, she plucked absently at a *shō* zither.[204] Could any words do justice
to such beauty? Ujitada wondered. How could he so easily have forgotten the
agony it had been to leave her? Saddened by his own faithlessness, he wept in
great sobs. How vexing it was that she could not see him as he saw her.

The light of day began to fade, but still he gazed into the mirror and still he
wept his fruitless tears. Even after the room had fallen into complete darkness
he could not bring himself to put the mirror away. Was it from the memory of all
those meetings, now so vividly with him again, or did it come from her image in
the mirror?—he thought he could smell the fragrance that had always announced her arrival, the perfume with which none other could compare. It
seemed to wipe from his mind all thoughts of Princess Hua-yang, whose side he
had been loath to leave even for a moment.

He called for a light and looked into the mirror again, but the flame of the
lamp was reflected in the mirror and he could not see as well as before. Holding
the mirror within the folds of his robe, he lay down for a short time. His heart
seemed ready to burst. He knew, however, that his grief would not be easily
consoled, and he must not neglect the one who was near at hand. It would be
too cruel to Princess Hua-yang if he were to stay away the entire night. When it
had grown quite late, he carefully returned the mirror to its box for safekeeping,
and set out for home.

204. The thirteen-stringed Chinese koto. Not to be confused with the *shō* pipes (flageolet) of
Ujitada's first mysterious meeting with the empress dowager.

Princess Hua-yang was not feeling well, and had been waiting anxiously for Ujitada to return. She greeted him cheerfully, glad to have him beside her again, but then saw that he was quite downcast and had been weeping. Had something happened? she wondered. This was most unusual.

He came to her and spoke of one thing and another. But what was this extraordinary scent his robes gave off? A wondrous perfume—so like one she had known in her former existence. The empress herself had been quite certain none other could compare, but was there someone in this land who used a perfume equally exquisite?

It was a severe shock—something she had never expected. Suddenly she was embarrassed at the innocent joy with which she had welcomed Ujitada home, and she turned her face away as tears of bitterness began to fall from her eyes. When had she learned the ways of jealousy? she wondered miserably.

70.	Mi o kaete	"In my new life
	Shiranu ukiyo ni	Reduced to wretched wandering
	Sasuraete	In an unknown land—
	Nami kosu sode no	Am I fated to see my sleeves soaked
	Nururu o ya min	By waves that break over mountains?"[205]

How quick she was! Was she, too, a lady of unclouded perceptions?[206] It was a daunting thought, but Ujitada managed to reply without losing his composure.

71.	Shiranu yo mo	"Even in an alien land,
	Kimi ni madoishi	Willingly, for you, did I wander astray
	Michi nareba	Onto a path of passion—
	Izure no ura no	From which bay could waves now arise
	Nami ka koyubeki	To break over the summit of our love?

"Am I hearing things? I seem to have been accused of something I would not dream of doing. Why am I suddenly the object of such mystifying reproaches?"

He drew her to him, but she continued to weep and would not easily yield to his embrace. As he tried to calm the princess's tears, Ujitada thought again of the empress dowager. He had learned from her that he was not the same as other men. Yet even though he had met her and exchanged vows with her under circumstances scarcely of this world, it seemed he had been born quite like any other man in the degree of suffering and torment his love brought him. Would the princess sooner or later guess the full truth? he wondered. The anticipation brought him a twinge of bewildered embarrassment.

205. An allusion to *Kokinshū* 1093, Anonymous:

	Kimi o okite	If I ever,
	Adashigokoro o	With fickle heart, turned away
	Wa ga motaba	From you to another—
	Sué no matsuyama	It would be when the waves of the sea rose up
	Nami mo koenan	To break over the pine mountains of Sué.

206. Like the empress dowager.

The manuscript states: "Here, too, the binding is damaged and the remaining pages have been lost."

This tale is about events that took place long ago, and, indeed, both the poetry and the language are pleasantly old-fashioned. Beginning with the flight to Mount Shu, however, the text appears to have been revised by some clever fellow of our own age and contains many unsightly passages. I wonder what the truth of the matter is. And when the grand lady of China speaks of drifting onto the path of dreams[207]—what a charming tale within a tale it is![208]

Jōgan 3, Fourth Month, Eighteenth day.
Finished writing in the western wing of the Somedono Palace.[209]

She seems a flower, but is not; she seems a mist, but is not.
In the deep of night, she comes; as the heavens dawn, she departs.
She comes like a spring night's dream, for but a fleeting moment;
She departs like a morning cloud, leaving no trace to follow.[210]

How true it is! But I am mystified why one so sober of heart—one who preferred not to meet beauty that can topple cities[211]—would have left such a poem behind him. Or is it that in China a mist like this really does exist?

207. The empress dowager began her account of the ties she and Ujitada had to the Second Heaven by saying she felt she must tell him "the truth about how we 'drifted . . . onto the path so straight in dreams'" (p. 151).
208. Or, "her telling of the story behind the story is such a delight!" *Soragoto no naka no soragoto okashū. Soragoto* literally means "lie," "deception," or "falsehood," but was often used in reference to fictional stories, as here.
209. Jōgan 3 corresponds to the year 861 on the Western calendar. The Somedono Palace was the residence of Fujiwara Yoshifusa (804–72), who was serving as chancellor at the time, and the western wing would likely have been occupied by his daughter, Meishi (829–900), empress of Emperor Montoku (827–58; r. 850–58) and mother of Emperor Seiwa (850–80; r. 858–76). Teika apparently wished to give the impression that the manuscript was written under her auspices. The choice of date may also have been intended to recall the Jōgan period as an era of good government. See translation n. 187 and chapter one, pp. 24–25.
210. A poem by Po Chü-i (*Haku Raku-ten shishū*, book 2, 248). The entire poem is quoted, though a character is missing in the third line. Since all manuscripts of the tale are missing the same character, it is quite possibly an inadvertent error by Teika himself. In alluding to "Kao-t'ang fu", "she" is the spirit of Mount Wu; in reprising Ujitada's marvelous, mysterious affair, "she" is the empress dowager; in encompassing both, and much more, "she" is love.
211. An allusion to the last lines of "Lady Li," by Po Chü-i (*Haku Raku-ten shishū*, book 4, 354). The poem describes Han dynasty emperor Wu's great grief at the loss of his favorite consort, Lady Li. First he commands a portrait of the lost lady, but the portrait neither speaks nor smiles, and so merely increases Emperor Wu's anguish. Next he asks a magician to summon her soul back to this world, but the image that appears lasts so fleetingly that he cannot be certain it was indeed she, and he is still unable to speak with her. The emperor would have grieved had her soul not returned, but he grieves equally for her having returned. King Mu of Chou and Emperor Hsüan-tsung of the T'ang, the poet notes, each suffered the same painful grief upon losing his beloved; the hold love has upon the human heart remains the same whether one's beloved is living or dead. The poem concludes:

Men are not like trees or rocks; all are moved by passions.
How much better, then, never to meet beauty that can topple cities.

The "one so sober of heart" is therefore Po Chü-i.

Appendix A: Evidence on Dating
Matsura no Miya Monogatari

All evidence regarding when *Matsura no miya monogatari* was written clearly discredits the date given in the colophon (861), whether that date is assigned to the extant version of the tale or to a different, earlier version; the evidence is also wholly consistent with ascription of the tale to Teika. The three charts presented here collate a wide variety of evidence put forth without reference to the tale's authorship; the discussion in section 4 briefly outlines the still-inconclusive efforts of scholars who, at least tentatively accepting Teika's authorship, have attempted to determine a more precise date for the tale by looking to Teika's biography and oeuvre.

1. Chart I: External Evidence

As this chart shows, no reference to *Matsura no miya monogatari* occurs in any secondary source before *Mumyōzōshi*, with the possible exception of *Waka iroha* ("Essentials of Poetry") just three years earlier. Subsequently, however, the tale appears three more times during the thirteenth century, in the letters of Cloistered Prince Sonsei, in the miscellany *Chiribukuro* ("Bag of Dust"), and in the poetic anthology *Fūyōshū* ("Leaves in the Wind"); further, the two best manuscripts extant today are believed to date from the fourteenth century. The pattern of no mention before *Mumyōzōshi* and what may be termed regular, though not frequent, mention thereafter makes it far more likely that the tale was written relatively close to the time when its title first appears in a secondary source, ca. 1201, than that it was composed some three to four centuries earlier as the colophon claims.

Underscoring this view is the prominent play *Matsura no miya monogatari* receives in *Fūyōshū*, a collection of poems selected from some two hundred tales of the Heian and Kamakura periods, including those tales that have come down to us as the major works of Heian fiction: *Utsuho monogatari, Genji monogatari, Sagoromo monogatari, Hamamatsu Chūnagon monogatari,* and *Yoru no nezame.* Even in the company of these much longer tales, the nineteen poems from *Matsura no miya monogatari* represent the twelfth largest number selected from any single tale (Ogi 1973, 10–11). When considered in proportion to the total number of poems in the tale (71) and the size of the tale as a whole, the significance of the figure grows still greater, for not even the major tales of the Heian period are represented by so large a percentage. The comparable figures for the major Heian tales are: for *Utsuho monogatari,* 110 of 1004 (Maeda

Chart I. External Evidence for Dating

TEXT	DATE	COMMENT
Sanbō ekotoba Kanjo ōjō gi Makura no sōshi Genji monogatari Rokujō Sai-in mono- gatari utaawase Sagoromo monogatari Genji ippon kyō	984 late 10th– early 11th C ca. 1001 ca. 1010 1055 ca. 1070s ca. 1166	No mention of Matsura in any of these standard Heian-period sources scholars look to for information on tales of the period. (See Ogi 1973, 23–63 for brief but useful commentary on the information found in each of these works.) The absence of mention does not in itself prove the tale did not yet exist, but stands in sharp contrast to the record of Mumyōzōshi and after.

Waka iroha
  (poetic treatise by
  the priest Jōkaku)
	1198	Matsura not included in list of fourteen tales: not yet written? But list is far from exhaustive and other major titles are also missing (see Jōkaku 1956, 114–15).
		
		"Katsura no miya," found in one variant, may be copyist's error for Matsura, since one of hentaigana for ma is easily mistaken for ka (Nakano 1971a, 259). Would push terminus ad quem three years earlier; no help for terminus a quo.

Shūi hyakuban
  utaawase (poetry
  contest on paper
  compiled by
  Teika)
	1195 or 1206	Poems from Matsura not included: not yet written? But poems come from only ten tales besides Genji; nothing requires inclusion of Matsura.

Mumyōzōshi	ca. 1201	Matsura called "recent."

Letters of Cloistered
  Prince Sonsei
  (d.1239)
	1233.v & vi	Remark upon matters connected with the preparation of a picture scroll of a tale referred to as "Matsura (or Matsuura) monogatari," a common variant title for the tale; the tale in question is said to have battle scenes.

Chiribukuro (a miscellany)	ca. 1260–90	Contains reference to Matsura (Tesaki 1940, 44).

Fūyōshū (or Fūyō
  wakashū, an
  anthology of
  poems from
  monogatari)
	1271	Contains 19 of the 71 poems in Matsura; no other tale is represented by so high a proportion of its poems.

(continued)

Chart 1. Continued

TEXT	DATE	COMMENT
Fushimi manuscript Go-Kōgon manuscript	before 1317 before 1374	Extant manuscripts said to have been copied by their namesake emperors. Positive identification of copyists not possible.
Shōtetsu monogatari (commentary on poetry)	ca. 1448	Cites two poems based on *Matsura* as if they were written in 1193 (Hisamatsu and Nishio 1961, 211–12); poems were actually written in 1207 and 1216.

manuscript, Utsuho Monogatari Kenkyūkai 1973–75); for *Genji monogatari*, 180 of 795; for *Sagoromo monogatari*, 56 of 216 (Naikaku Bunko manuscript, Mitani and Sekine 1965); for *Hamamatsu Chūnagon monogatari*, 29 of at least 134 (as figured by Suzuki 1965, 174–80); for *Yoru no nezame*, 25 of at least 113 (as figured by Suzuki 1965, 167–73).

While it is difficult to know what the compilers' intentions might have been in selecting so many poems—was it an expression of esteem for the tale itself, or for the quality of the poetry; or was it perhaps a gesture of veneration for Teika the man and all his many achievements?—the magnitude of attention given the tale confirms in no uncertain terms the expectation that *some* earlier source would have mentioned *Matsura no miya monogatari* if the tale had been circulating since the ninth century or before. It is virtually inconceivable that a tale treated so prominently in *Fūyōshū*, and mentioned three other times in secondary writings from the thirteenth century, could have circulated three to four centuries previously, as the colophon would have us believe, without ever receiving a single secondary mention.

Waka iroha, *Shūi hyakuban utaawase* ("Poetry Contest in One Hundred More Rounds"), and *Shōtetsu monogatari* ("Conversations with Shōtetsu") have been cited principally in efforts to pinpoint the date of composition within a narrower time span, but are in fact of little use—as the comments on the chart suggest. While it is possible to argue persuasively that *Matsura no miya monogatari* should have received *some* secondary mention in the course of several centuries, the absence of its name in a particular text cannot prove that it did not exist at the time that text appeared—unless it can first be established that the text attempted, and successfully achieved, an exhaustive list of tales then extant. Neither the list in *Waka iroha* nor the selection of tales included in *Shūi hyakuban utaawase* can be considered exhaustive in any sense. As for *Shōtetsu monogatari*, the correct dates for the poems cited make them useless in determining when the tale was written.

Of some slight assistance may be the title *Katsura no miya*, found in a variant manuscript of *Waka iroha*: the title may well be a copyist's error for

Chart II. Internal Evidence for Dating

	ITEM	DATE
LINGUISTIC ITEMS— SPECIFIC	*keimei-su* (<*keiei-su*) and *motamaeru* (<*mochitamaeru*).	Linguistic forms that developed much later than Jōgan era (Fujioka Sakutarō 1915, 211).
	nōshi refers to cloak only, rather than full suit.	Usage from after mid-Heian (Sakurai 1933, 80).
LINGUISTIC ITEMS— GENERAL	"Style and language suggest that it was written around the beginning of Kamakura."	End of 12th C (Kurokawa, n.d.).
	Sinified vocabulary.	Second half of 12th C or Kamakura period (Kaneko 1934, 41).
TEXTUAL PRECEDENTS	Opening section modeled closely on *Utsuho* (tr. n. 4).	Ca. 983 (Nakano 1981, 405–9).
	Kakuremino no monogatari, a tale now lost, believed to be source for reference to magical cape of invisibility (p. 127 & tr. n. 142).	End of 10th C or later (Oyamada 1829, 101).
	Some of China events modeled closely on *Hamamatsu* (tr. notes passim).	Late 11th C (Hagitani 1970, passim).
	Numerous poetic allusions.	Range from *Man'yōshū* (ca. 759) through most of 12th C; none clearly identified from 13th C (Ishida 1940; Mizuno 1940; and Hagitani 1970, passim).
	Chinese names, places, events can be traced to sources as late as *Hsin T'ang-shu* (1060).	Late 11th C (Hagitani 1970, 261, nn. 129, 134).
	Poem 11, line 2 follows reading of *Man'yōshū* 2530 that was standard before Sengaku's edition.	Sengaku's *Man'yōshū* appeared in 1246 (Mizuno 1940, 56).

(continued)

Chart II. Continued

	ITEM	DATE
HISTORICAL FEATURES	Apparent observance of *nochi no meigetsu* (p. 83 & tr. n. 64).	Observance began in 919 (Fujioka Sakutarō 1915, 211).
	Armed rebellion as subject of courtly tale.	Difficult to imagine before mid-12th C (Kaneko 1934, 41; Sakurai 1933, 83).
	Japan described as *tsuwamono no kuni,* "land of warriors" (p. 103).	Suggests mid-12th C or later; some say suggests period after Minamoto triumph in 1185 (Sakurai 1933, 83).
	Flight of imperial train from Chinese capital quite possibly modeled on flight of Heike with Emperor Antoku and his mother from Heian capital during Genpei Wars (p. 98 and tr. n. 95).	After 1183.
	Linking of Buddhist and Shinto deities (Śakra and Sumiyoshi).	Earlier references to such links are found, but full theoretical formulation and their claiming of a distinct place in Japanese religious consciousness belongs to 11th–12th C (Kitagawa 1966, 68).
	The numerous allusions to *Man'yōshū.* Setting of tale in China.	2nd half of 12th C, which saw a strong revival of interest in *Man'yōshū* and in things Chinese (Sakurai 1933, 81–86).

Matsura no miya, since one of the *hentaigana* characters for *ma* is easily mistaken for a *ka.* If this view is accepted, the terminus ad quem for the tale can be moved to 1198, but no ground has been gained toward determining a more precise terminus a quo.

2. Chart II: Internal Evidence

This chart separates into several categories evidence deriving from the content of the tale itself, and notes for each item either the particular date of that item, which serves as evidence in establishing a terminus a quo, or a more general date that the item indicates as the most likely time of composition. All items listed discredit the date given in the colophon; most indicate a date toward the end of the eleventh century or later; and a few point to a late twelfth-century date in at least a general way. The identification of allusions to poems composed through most of the twelfth century provides strong concrete evidence of a date near 1200. Strict constructionists may quibble that some of the allusions are not legitimate because the foundation poems are too recent, but indications that *some kind* of influence flowed from foundation poem to tale poem are too clear and numerous to be dismissed. No further evidence emerges to alter the terminus ad quem provided by *Mumyōzōshi*.

The most specific help in setting a terminus a quo comes from the observation that the child emperor's flight from the Chinese capital was most probably modeled on the flight of Emperor Antoku from the Heian capital in 1183. Coincidental resemblance remains a possibility, of course, as it does with any identification of fictional event or personage with historical, but the parallels are sufficiently striking to make it seem highly unlikely. (And it may be noted parenthetically that, once Teika's authorship is accepted, other evidence pointing to a somewhat later date—see below—strongly encourages affirmation of the suggested link between historical event and fictional analog.)

For details on many of the textual precedents, see the notes to the translation. It bears noting here that *Matsura no miya monogatari* could not have been the model for *Utsuho monogatari* and *Hamamatsu Chūnagon monogatari*. Even if there were no other indications that *Matsura no miya monogatari* is the later tale, it would be all the more incredible that *Matsura no miya monogatari* was twice imitated and yet not once mentioned in a secondary source during the tenth and eleventh centuries.

With regard to the second and third items under "Historical Features," it may be noted that the *monogatari* genre was from its inception a thoroughly peaceful form of fiction concerned with the elegancies and vicissitudes of courtly life and love. Depictions of warriors in action or armies on the march, or even individual displays of physical prowess on the part of civilians, do not appear in the fiction that members of the Heian court produced. As briefly mentioned in the introduction (pp. 16–17), the only exceptions are found in the final section of *Taketori monogatari* and in the first chapter of *Utsuho monogatari*. Thus, the depiction of an armed rebellion as part of a work that otherwise falls fully within the courtly love-tale tradition is most credibly explained as a reflection of the massive military upheavals that shook Japan in the latter half of the twelfth century.

3. Chart III: The Possible Existence of Different Versions

This chart summarizes the observations that have been, or could be, construed to show that the tale must have circulated in more than one version, along with rebuttals to each. As already shown by the evidence presented in charts I and II, the suggestion that an early version existed around (or even

Chart III. The Possible Existence of Different Versions

ARGUMENT	REBUTTAL
Textual inconsistencies in extant tale (e.g., the ambassador is left behind in China) suggest it must be incomplete.	Similar minor inconsistencies appear in all Heian fiction.
Entry A of colophon says text must have been revised or extended (*tsukuri-kaetaru*); with entry B, this suggests an original writing followed by revisions before 861, or an original writing in 861 followed by revisions at later date.	9th C or earlier date impossible for any version of tale: debt to *Utsuho* and *Hamamatsu* too great (see chart II)—especially in book 1, which would have to have been the main body of any earlier version.
Reasons to conclude two hands involved in creating extant tale: General style: shift at end of book 1 reaffirmed by almost all students of tale. Man'yō language prominent in book 1, none in book 2, little in book 3; Chinese compounds in books 2 & 3 but not book 1. Poetic style: systematic study shows allusions to *Man'yōshū* numerous in book 1, none in book 2, few in book 3 (Hagitani 1969). Usage of humble verbs *kikoyu* and *mōsu*: *kikoyu* far outnumbers *mōsu* in book 1; *mōsu* far outnumbers *kikoyu* in book 2; almost even balance in book 3 (Ōtsuki 1967). Appears to reflect historical shift in usage by which *kikoyu* increasingly gave way to *mōsu* in course of Heian period (Akita 1962, 1964, and 1965).	Single author may have abandoned effort at archaism after book 1 because too difficult to sustain (e.g., Fujioka 1915, 211), or because already planned fictitious colophon to create spurious textual history for the tale. Tales written in 13th C "in the manner of tales of old" (*giko-monogatari*) retain earlier usage (Akita 1965, 45). Usage of *mōsu* abounds in prose containing numerous Chinese expressions regardless of period; usage shift in *Matsura* matches increase in Chinese expressions (Ōtsuki 1967, 24–25). Author may have intended Japan scenes to be in archaic, Man'yō style, and China scenes to be in contemporary idiom, which, appropriately enough, made greater use of Chinese vocabulary.

(*continued*)

considerably before) 861 is clearly impossible. Otherwise, the brief rebuttals given in the chart are in some cases as speculative as the arguments, but they are in every case wholly plausible, showing that none of the evidence advanced requires the conclusion that there have been two different versions of the tale.

The strongest evidence against all two-version theories can be found not in any of the rebuttals on the chart but in the simplicity of the manuscript tradition (see chapter three). Given the absence of any significant variant lines, the natural assumption would be that the tale has circulated in only a single version,

Chart III. Continued

ARGUMENT	REBUTTAL
Mumyōzōshi fails to mention colophon, style shift, or even the extraordinary military section; description of tale by reference to *Man'yōshū* and *Utsuho* seems to apply only to book 1. *Mumyōzōshi* author must have seen only book 1, or a shorter version without succession struggle and empress dowager episodes.	Cannot expect full description in two or three lines; description does fit overall frame of tale—i.e., the ending as well as the beginning.

Fūyōshū and Shōtetsu also saw book 1 as having greatest literary interest (Kikuchi 1981, 21–22).

Military section may have seemed too aberrant or nonliterary to be worthy of comment.

Ch. 1 and overall frame of *Utsuho* are informed by fantastic and supernatural elements; *Utsuho* remark may refer to these qualities throughout *Matsura*.

The shorter form imagined would leave nothing but elements borrowed from *Utsuho* and *Hamamatsu*, and surely would not have elicited *Mumyōzōshi's* final exclamation. |
| *Mumyōzōshi* criticizes *Hamamatsu* for being unrealistic; should have done same for extant version of *Matsura;* different version must have existed (Ogi 1961, 245–46). | *Matsura* never raises expectations of realistic tale, unlike *Hamamatsu* (see Rohlich 1983, 20ff., for analysis of what *Mumyōzōshi* author found "unrealistic"); criteria of judgment would have been different; cannot assume *Mumyōzōshi* author likes only realism. |
| Shōtetsu's description of *Matsura* differs from extant tale on several counts; suggests Shōtetsu read longer version. | Poetic references in same passage show Shōtetsu is speaking from memory, and memory is unreliable; probably is mixing up *Matsura* and *Hamamatsu* in his mind, an easy confusion owing to resemblances.

The two earliest surviving manuscripts, from which all other manuscripts emanate, date to 14th C, long before Shōtetsu's time; both have lacunae already in place. |

and it will take arguments more substantial than those noted on the chart to overturn that natural assumption.

4. Seeking a More Precise Date

The majority of scholars who have looked into Teika's other work and diary for clues to when the tale might have been written appear to favor a date within a year or two of 1190.

Imai (1954, 20) cites an unidentified source as suggesting a date shortly before Teika turned thirty (1191 by traditional Japanese count, or 1192 by Western). He presumably concurs.

Ishida (1957, 205) suggests a date shortly after 1191, apparently on the basis of the increasingly romantic qualities of Teika's poetry, which he sees as reaching something of a climax around the time of *Roppyakuban utaawase* (1193).

Yoshida (1959, 34–35) suggests 1189 as the most likely year, and cites a specific poem in which Teika speaks of *fude no susabi* (playful scribblings) as the grounds for his claim, along with several more general qualities of Teika's poetry of the period. He also asserts that the tale must have been written after 1186, when Teika became a household officer of the Kujō house and began to deepen his Chinese learning through his contacts there.

Hagitani (1969, 2) appears to concur with Yoshida while expressing reservations regarding certain parts of his argument.

Ishikawa (1958, 328, n. 1) suggests a date near the time of *Ninnaji no miya gojusshu* (1198—though Ishikawa is under the impression that the sequence was written in 1194), in which are found two poems with close affinities to the tale. Assuming Ishikawa is correct to link Teika's poems and the tale, it is not necessary to conclude as he does that the poems and the tale date from around the same time. Other scholars have pointed out that poems from 1187 and 1190 can be considered essentially similar to those Ishikawa cites (Higuchi 1980, 26; Kikuchi 1981, 25).

Kusano 1979 draws attention to a passage in Teika's diary dated 1199.ix.12, in which Teika recounts a story told him by his sister about a person who saw six identical figures sitting in a row at the carriage stand of a certain princess's residence. Claiming that this story must have provided the inspiration for the miraculous appearance of the eight identical warriors when Ujitada is about to be cut down by Yü-wen Hui, Kusano argues for a date of composition between 1199 and 1201 (the date of *Mumyōzōshi*). The imaginative leap from six static figures in an otherwise ordinary setting to eight warriors saving the day in battle is a considerable one, however, and no link need be assumed. Further, Nishiki (1988, 136) observes that a legend illustrated in *Suwasha engi ekotoba* ("Legends of Suwa Shrine"), a picture scroll that draws on material from the Nara period text *Sumiyoshi taisha jindaiki* ("The Sumiyoshi Shrine Record of the Age of the Gods"), has the god of Sumiyoshi appearing out of the sky as two warriors to assist Empress Jingū's ships in their third century campaign to the Korean peninsula, and he concludes that such acts were probably part of accepted lore about the god of Sumiyoshi in the twelfth century.

In an article responding to Kusano's argument, Higuchi (1980, 28) points to the early 1190s as the most likely time of composition for *Matsura no miya monogatari*, on grounds that the manner in which the tale draws upon *Man'yōshū* differs from the manner of Teika's later poetry of around 1200.

In short, all efforts to pinpoint the date of the tale on the basis of Teika's poetry or diary remain quite speculative in nature. At most it may be said that the best guesses currently available place the tale's composition within a year or two of 1190.

While my own study did not take me into Teika's biography and work deeply enough to allow me to offer a full and rigorous argument, based on observations made in the course of the study that is outlined in appendix B, section 5, I am inclined to look for a date before 1193. The two poems by Teika composed in 1193 and 1194, which bear extensive resemblances to poems in the tale, could indeed have preceded the tale (see appendix B, p. 187), but the opposite seems more likely. Even in an age when the male members of the court were beginning to show a more open and avid interest in fiction, fiction writing by men would have been regarded as "playful scribbling" (see remarks on Yoshida 1959, above), and as a context for composing poetry it would have been considered essentially "off the record." On the one hand I would imagine that poets in their moments of "playful scribbling," whether the scribbling includes fiction or only poetry, were far more likely to try out new lines and phrases than simply repeat ones already published; on the other, I cannot doubt that it was a matter of course for poets in formal and public settings to use (i.e., "publish") lines, and entire poems, they had already tried out in private, or among a few close associates but "off the record." (As a postscript I might note that in Lammers 1987, appendix A, 416–19, I develop an admittedly speculative—but I believe plausible—view in which Teika's 1194 poem is a kind of private allusion to the tale.)

Appendix B: The Authorship of *Matsura no Miya Monogatari*

Presented in this appendix is an outline of the essential evidence supporting Fujiwara Teika's authorship of *Matsura no miya monogatari*. A more complete discussion and compilation of data may be found in Lammers 1987, chapters 4 through 6 and appendixes.

1. External evidence: *Mumyōzōshi*

As noted in the introduction, the passage in *Mumyōzōshi* where *Matsura no miya monogatari* is mentioned contains an ambiguity that has allowed some scholars to deny that any ascription to Teika was intended. Tesaki 1940 resolves this ambiguity by examining the entire *Mumyōzōshi* and discovering two consistent characteristics of how the author carries forth her discussion.

The first is the author's frequent use of the conjunction *mata* ("now" or "again") to signal a shift in topic or subtopic. Tesaki observes that the sentence in which *Matsura no miya monogatari* is mentioned does not begin with this conjunction, while all three of the preceding sentences do (for reasons of English flow, the conjunctions have been omitted from the translation given in the introduction). The three conjunctions quite appropriately signal shifts in topic, first to a group of recent tales, then to a tale by Takanobu, and then to several works by Teika. Since no shift in topic is signaled between the reference to Teika's several works and the remarks on *Matsura no miya monogatari*, the author does indeed seem to be treating the tale as one of Teika's works rather than as a work by yet another, unnamed author.

The second characteristic Tesaki notes is that the author of *Mumyōzōshi* never mentions an author by name without also making some comment on one or more of his works (*sakka nomi o ronjite sono sakuhin ni genkyūshinai to iu koto wa hoka ni mitomerarenai*). Implicit here is that the broad, unspecified reference to "several works" by Teika is not a substantial enough "comment" to compare with other examples: i.e., if the present case is not to break a rule that is otherwise consistent throughout the rest of *Mumyōzōshi*, the reference to *Matsura no miya monogatari* must be read as the author's comment, following her usual pattern, upon a particular work by the author she has just mentioned, Teika.

A review of *Mumyōzōshi* shows that both of Tesaki's points are well taken. A slight qualification is perhaps necessary with regard to the second point: most of the nearly thirty *monogatari* mentioned in *Mumyōzōshi* are discussed without reference to their authors; the pattern *is* consistent where authors are mentioned, however, whether for works of fiction or other genres, and when all genres are considered together the total number of examples is sufficient to make the observation a meaningful one (Lammers 1987, 95–97).

In the face of these observations, to insist that we cannot assume any integral link between the two key sentences, and therefore to deny that *Mumyōzōshi* provides positive external evidence of Teika's authorship of the tale ultimately raises more questions than it answers or turns away. Of course, to establish that *Mumyōzōshi* is indeed speaking of the tale as belonging to Teika's hand does not immediately guarantee that it is correct and reliable in doing so, but it means that any denial of Teika's authorship must be accompanied by a plausible explanation of why someone known to be close to Teika would have made a false statement of this kind regarding his fiction writing, whether erroneously or deliberately.

2. Internal Evidence: Some General Observations

A broad survey of the tale suggests three qualities the author of the tale must have had: (1) Though not a specialist, he must have been quite well versed in Chinese studies and sources—well versed enough to rule out not only a female author (compared with *Matsura no miya monogatari*, the treatment of China in *Hamamatsu Chūnagon monogatari* is extremely vague and superficial) but also a male author whose knowledge of China was merely average. (2) He must have been quite familiar with *Man'yōshū*. (3) He must have been someone who, aesthetically speaking, showed an inclination toward the ethereal and the romantic.

Teika fulfills these conditions so well that we can be quite certain he would ultimately have been considered a potential author for the tale even had it not been suggested by *Mumyōzōshi*. In particular, notwithstanding objections that the tale is unworthy of Teika, the prominence in the tale of qualities associated with the poetic ideal of *yōen* ("ethereal charm," discussed in chapter two) would have made it impossible to ignore him as a potential candidate for long once serious consideration of the authorship question had begun, for this ideal is more closely identified with Teika than with any other poet. (For a more complete development of how Teika fulfills the conditions especially well, see Lammers 1987, 104–15.)

Once Teika has come under consideration, his suitability as author can be noted in more specific terms as well. He had a particular fondness for the image of the full moon, an important image in the tale (Hagitani 1970, 32, n. 5 and 254, n. 98; Ishida 1979, 50, 60). The Kujō house, for which he served as a household official and on whose patronage he relied, was a house of considerable Chinese learning (Ishida 1957, 298–99). We know from Teika's diary that he took pleasure in reading the Chinese histories and classics (Ishida 1940, 81–82), and he is also one of very few *waka* poets whose name appears in records of Chinese poetry gatherings as well as *waka* gatherings (Ishida 1957, 299). Teika frequently alluded to poems from *Man'yōshū* in his own compositions, in contrast to both his father Shunzei and members of the rival Rokujō house of poetry, who studied *Man'yōshū* extensively but held that its archaic language should be used in only very unusual circumstances in actual composition (Brower and Miner 1961, 245–46). Against the background of a centuries-old disdain for fiction among male aristocrats, Teika not only embraced but extended the progressive attitude toward fiction his father had shown, both in his avid reading and copying of *monogatari*, and in his use of *monogatari* as the basis for allusion in poetic composition (Konishi 1976, 188; Misumi 1979, 282, with reference to Teramoto 1970, 44–58 and Hagitani 1960; Ishikawa 1958, 280).

3. Internal Evidence: Ishida Yoshisada's Study of Poetic Style

Ishida 1940 focuses his attention upon poetic style, searching the indexes of *Kokka taikan* (Matsushita and Watanabe 1903, hereafter *KT*) and *Zoku kokka taikan* (Matsushita 1925–26, hereafter *ZKT*), for lines of poetry identical, or nearly so, to lines found in the tale. His premise: since poetic style is by nature highly idiosyncratic and peculiar to its author, comparing the poetry in the tale with the poetry in Teika's private collections may well provide a set of matching "fingerprints" to positively identify Teika as the author.

Ishida's findings are impressive. He manages in the space of a few pages to document a remarkable array of resemblances between Teika's poetry and the poetry in the tale—resemblances that are closer or more extensive or more numerous than he finds for any other poet, or that he cannot find at all for other poets. While Ishida's assertions of significance are not uniformly strong, a few of the examples are so striking as to seem capable by themselves of concluding the argument.

Unfortunately, a careful examination of his evidence reveals a number of potentially damaging irregularities: inconsistent means of gathering data, unequal handling of primary data and control data, questionable assumptions, summary disposal of certain crucial questions, impressionism, and the appearance of circularity. Though none of these irregularities necessarily commands immediate, outright rejection of Ishida's argument—the flaws may be in the presentation of evidence, and not in its substance—taken together they are sufficient reason for careful scholars to reserve judgment, and to speak of Teika only as the *possible* or *probable* author of the tale. Some scholars have continued to find reasons to question the ascription outright (Nakano 1971a; Ōtsuki 1967).

4. Internal Evidence: Hagitani Boku's Study of the Chinese Sources

Hagitani 1941 carefully examines the nature of the knowledge of China—correct and erroneous, well-known and obscure—displayed in the tale, and, by documenting in detail the most likely sources of that knowledge, corroborates in concrete and specific terms the more impressionistic assertion made by earlier scholars that the author must have been above average, but not a true specialist, in his Chinese learning. The particularity of the information given in the tale—names and descriptions of places, persons, official titles, buildings, document titles; references to historical precedents and principles of government; obvious modeling of characters on historical figures—attests to the author's familiarity with a wide variety of dynastic histories, Confucian classics, literary anthologies, and scholarly compilations, even when the information proves to be inaccurate in one way or another. By contrast, Rohlich 1983 documents how little concrete knowledge of China and Chinese sources the author of *Hamamatsu Chūnagon monogatari* must have had (see his chapter 1, nn. 5, 9, 10, 31, 35, 36), and shows that the knowledge needed to write the tale came primarily from literary sources and did not require familiarity with the histories or classics (see his chapter 1, nn. 10, 18, 21, 23, 27–29, 37, 42, 48, and chapter 3, nn. 26–28).

In the second part of his argument, Hagitani examines Teika's own writings, and discovers explicit references to all of the important sources reflected in *Matsura no miya monogatari*, thus establishing a close correlation between things Chinese reflected in the tale—some items being far from household words among members of the Japanese court—and things Chinese that had caught Teika's interest.

Hagitani establishes beyond any doubt that Teika *could have* composed the tale—that his knowledge of Chinese history, politics, customs, geography, and so forth, was both adequate and appropriate in nature for him to do so. Further, the specificity of the correlation he discovers between Teika's interests and the Chinese features of the tale suggests quite strongly that Teika *must have* written the tale, for even if there were a dozen others who fit the more general stipulation that the author be well versed in Chinese studies, it is difficult to imagine such a close and specific correlation being duplicated by another man.

The evidence is admittedly circumstantial, but when combined with the testimony of *Mumyōzōshi*, certainly comes very near to closing the case.

5. Internal Evidence: Ishida's Study Revisited

My claim, in the introduction to this volume, that Teika's authorship of *Matsura no miya monogatari* should now be considered confirmed beyond any doubt is based not only on a review of all previous authorship studies, but on my own extensive reevaluation, update, and expansion of the study Ishida Yoshisada conducted in 1940, as detailed in Lammers 1987. The data compiled there is too voluminous to repeat in its entirety here, and so a generalized description and summary must suffice, at least for immediate reference, as evidence that my claim is well founded. I must emphasize, however, that neither the procedures followed nor the data compiled in this study lend themselves to abstracting, for both were highly case-specific at every stage of data gathering and analysis. The reader who remains unpersuaded by the summary, or who otherwise wishes to evaluate the procedures, data, and analysis in full, is asked to seek out the complete treatment given in Lammers 1987—particularly the three appendixes.

The principal reference tool for my analysis was *Shinpen kokka taikan* (Henshū Iinkai 1983–87, hereafter *SKT*, with volume numbers indicated in

Roman numerals). Although this massive line-index of classical court poetry continues to grow—ten volumes are now projected; only five had been announced at the time of my study—with the advancement of publication through *SKT* III, which contains the full *Rokkashū* (see below), I judged that the study could go forward without awaiting the appearance of further volumes because:

(a) the first three volumes of *SKT* already provided a reference tool far superior to what had been available to Ishida, containing as they did a much larger body of poetry than *KT* and *ZKT*, and permitting full, five-line access to the whole;

(b) volume III included the complete *Rokkashū*, the most crucial set of private collections for the control portion of the study;

(c) use of *Monogatari waka sōran* ("Comprehensive Index to *Monogatari* Poems"), together with the sections covering diaries (*nikki*) and histories (*rekishi*) in the older *KT*, would compensate for large parts of the missing *SKT* V, which was scheduled to include poems from these various prose texts;

(d) although a few private collections potentially of interest were still missing (scheduled for inclusion in *SKT* IV and V), whether and to what degree they might alter the figures compiled from *SKT* I–III could at least be estimated by using the more limited index (first and fourth lines only) in *ZKT*; and

(e) since the "completeness" of even a full *SKT* would be essentially illusory, creating merely an impression of completeness where no such thing is actually possible, more important than the inclusion of all five volumes then projected would be the use of uniform and consistent means for gathering data from the three volumes available.

In the discussion that follows, references to "poem 1," "poem 35," etc., always signify poems from the tale as they are numbered in the translation. In references to "line 1.5," "line 19.2" (or simply "35.1"), etc., the poem number precedes the period and the line number follows. Poems not from the tale are referred to by their *SKT* numbers, in the form, "<volume number>.<collection number>.<poem number>": e.g., *SKT* III.133.2050.

When *SKT* IV and V became available after completion of my original study, I conducted a few recounts, selecting lines and phrases that showed particularly striking usage patterns in the counts based on *SKT* I–III (lines 19.1–5, 24.4, 29.4, 31.1, 33.2, 40.1–3, 66.1). No significant surprises emerged from the recounts, and I am satisfied that a comprehensive rehearsal of the study would alter only the numbers and not the substance of my earlier conclusions: further checking might still cause an individual line or two to be thrown out as evidence, but it could not overturn the broader pattern of stylistic affinities observed between Teika and the tale. Since a full recount is thus unwarranted, and since any effort to incorporate the partial figures would mean mixing incompatible data, I have chosen in my discussion here to adhere to the evidence presented in Lammers 1987 (with one parenthetical exception). I should note, too, however, that the analysis presented here *does* supersede Lammers 1987. It includes a number of changes, ranging from minor corrections to more substantial adjustments, based on further reviews of the data drawn from *SKT* I–III—including new observations as well as the discarding of one to which I previously attributed considerable significance.

The Divisions of the Study

The study was divided into three parts. The first two parts corresponded to Ishida's separate discussions focusing on (1) *kotoba* (diction) and (2) *sugata* (style or cadence), respectively, and in them I reexamined the data for every line and phrase of poetry Ishida presented as evidence of affinity between Teika and the tale.

In the third part of my study, as an independent check on Ishida's selective approach, I examined all lines from the first twenty-five poems in the tale. The potential circularity suggested by Ishida's statement that he had eliminated lines of the sort anyone might have used, and focused only on lines with a "Teika-like fragrance," raised concerns that he might have overlooked stylistic resemblances between the poems in the tale and the work of other poets.

The second and third parts of the study may be dispensed with quickly, prior to discussing part one.

Since none of the indexes available provide access to the broad patterns of syntax and rhythm on which Ishida based his claims of affinities of *sugata* between Teika's poetry and the poetry in the tale, part two of my study could not be as systematic as the others, but it took only a very limited survey of several poetic sequences by Teika and by Fujiwara Ietaka (1158–1237) to reveal that the criteria for claiming affinity would have to receive much more precise definition than Ishida gave them before any meaningful conclusions could be drawn. The evidence *does* seem to show, in its nebulous and impressionistic way, that Teika's poetic style is consistent with the style of the poetry in the tale, and that therefore Teika could have been the author, but since it seems to do much the same for Ietaka's poetic style, it can hardly be claimed to provide a positive link between Teika and the tale.

Part three involved the systematic compilation and analysis of usage tallies in a manner essentially similar to the procedure described below for part one; because the number of lines being examined was over three times as many as in part one, however, the scope of the search was limited to *SKT* III. Teika emerges at the top of the figures at each level of analysis, and there are a few individual cases where Teika's pattern of usage seems quite remarkable by comparison to others. The differences observed between Teika and the others are not as great here as in the findings of part one outlined below, and it is difficult to know just how much statistical significance they carry, but at least marginally they serve to reconfirm the findings of part one. With regard to the question of circularity, certainly none of the evidence from part three suggests

Ishida's method of selecting lines for consideration caused him to overlook evidence of striking affinities between other poets and the tale that are on the same order of consistency and magnitude as those he found for Teika.

Procedures for Part One

The principal procedure for part one of my study involved searching the indexes of *SKT* I–III (supplemented by *KT*, *ZKT*, and *Monogatari waka sōran* as noted above) for individual lines and for a number of longer phrases identical with or similar to those found in the poetry in the tale. The number of times Teika matched a line or phrase from the tale, either exactly or closely, was then compared with the total number of matches on record, as well as with the number of matches by other individual poets. In order to eliminate duplicates, since many poems appear in more than one of the sources included in *SKT*, the full text of each poem listed was examined before being counted—except in cases where it was immediately obvious that there would be no point in establishing a precise count.

In analyzing and discussing the data, I established the practice of characterizing lines as rare (4 instances or less on record), relatively rare (5 to 10 instances on record); intermediate (11 to 30 instances on record), and common (more than 30 instances on record). The ranges chosen for each of these designations were not set beforehand, arbitrarily, but rather reflect what was actually observed in the course of the study; the figures for each would need to be somewhat larger in evaluating counts based on more volumes of *SKT*.

The nature of the resemblances and affinities counted varied from one example to the next. In each case, the starting point was a line or phrase from a poem in the tale, and the initial search was for an identical line—an *exact match*. Next, whether an exact match was found or not, the neighboring listings in the indexes were examined, to see how the line being searched related to similar lines—*near matches*. In some cases, as a means of gaining further perspective, auxiliary searches were conducted for *near matches of the near matches*, though usage information thus gained was always kept separate from the main usage tallies.

The scope of what actually counted as a "match" in each case depended entirely on what was discovered in the indexes. Where the unit of significance (i.e., the part of the line that had to match *exactly* for the line as a whole to be considered a near match) was not immediately apparent, several different units were considered—the full line (a–b–c–d–e–f–g), part of a line (a–b–c–d–x–x–x), the full line with variation allowed somewhere other than at the end (a–b–c–x–e–f–g; a–b–c–d–x–x–g), all of one line and part of another (a–b–c–d–e/f–g–h–x–x–x–x), etc. Five- and seven-syllable lines were counted in separate tallies, so they could be considered both together and apart. Each case was evaluated individually as to the significance of any variations. For example, if counting near matches increases Teika's use of a line while the overall occurrence of the line remains rare, it increases the impression of an affinity between him and the tale. On the other hand, if including near matches allows other poets to join Teika as users of the still-rare line, it reduces that impression—though the degree will depend to some extent upon other factors, such as the dates of the other poets (see following items). Yet again, if including the near matches turns a rare line into a common one, then the significance of any use of the line drops sharply—unless, of course, Teika's use of the line dramatically outdistances all others. The need for this kind of flexible approach in counting and evaluating matches should be obvious: no two lines or phrases examined hold precisely the same place in the context either of the Japanese language or of court-poetry conventions and prior expressions; each is unique as to the number of times it occurs in an identical or similar form, and as to its relationship to other similar lines and phrases.

Control

In order to gain perspective on the relative significance of the figures from one case to the next, the figures for Teika were compared with figures for other individual poets throughout. By keeping watch on comparative figures for other individual poets, attention could also be given to shifts in usage over time. This contrasts with Ishida, who mainly compared the figures for Teika with those for all other uses combined, without regard to when those uses occurred in history, and who gave other individual poets (in fact, only the *Rokkashū* poets) no more than a cursory glance at the end of his discussion, in a manner that left many open questions.

To my knowledge, no student of the tale has ever suggested any specific candidate besides Teika as author of the tale, on any grounds. Nevertheless, as part of my attention to historical usage, I considered whether the dates of all poets whose names appeared in the usage tallies made them potential candidates for authorship of the tale. Broadly speaking, any male aristocrat who was born ca. 1180 or who lived until at least a few years after 1180 could be considered such a candidate. This date allows for the possibility that someone in his upper teens composed the tale just before 1201 (the date of *Mumyōzōshi*), or that an elderly man composed it just before his death, shortly after the flight of the Heike from the capital in 1183 (the probable model for a similar flight in the tale—see translation, p. 98). It also allows for composition any time in the second half of the twelfth century, which encompasses the likely farthest limit of what the *Mumyōzōshi* author meant by "recent years," and which is the period to which all of the less specific evidence on date points.

Most of those who were designated potential candidates under this broad definition failed to show any resemblances of usage with the tale, and at an advanced stage of analysis it became both possible and useful to eliminate them from the discussion and speak of only the "serious" candidates. "Serious" in this case does not mean that they were in genuine contention for consideration as author, but simply that they had in some instance(s) shown resemblances of usage similar to those observed for Teika, and therefore had not been eliminated as potential candidates. If any such candidate had shown a repeated pattern of close stylistic resemblances to the poetry in the tale, it would have signaled the need to reassess the entire premise of Ishida's style study.

The most suitable poets for comparison with Teika are the five poets whose private poetry collections are frequently grouped together with Teika's and called *Rokkashū* (literally, "The Six Private Collections"): Teika's father, Fujiwara Shunzei (1114–1204; 652 poems); the priest Saigyō (1118–90; 2634 poems); Fujiwara Yoshitsune (1169–1206; 1611 poems) and the abbot Jien (1155–1225; 5803 poems), both of the Kujō house on whose patronage Teika depended in his youth; and Fujiwara Ietaka (1158–1237; 3201 poems), foster son of Shunzei and Teika's closest poetic associate. They are particularly suitable as a control group because (a) they are contemporaries of Teika, and hence potential candidates all; (b) their close association with Teika makes them the most likely ones to show stylistic affinities to Teika, and, by extension, the most likely to show a similar degree of affinity to the tale; and (c) four of them have private collections whose sizes are on the same order of magnitude as Teika's (3755 poems), enabling more meaningful comparisons based on *frequency* than are possible with poets whose collections are smaller by factors of ten and more.

Classification of Data

Finally, whereas Ishida relied on the simple, cumulative effect of data— one striking usage tally for Teika followed by another, and then another—to carry his argument, my study categorized the data in terms of several statements that can be made comparing Teika's usage to (a) all other poets on record, (b) all other poets of his time, (c) all potential candidates, and (d) all "serious" candidates.

The Quantitative Findings

In tallies of the number of times Teika and other poets used lines identical (or nearly so) to forty of the individual lines of poetry in the tale, and to a handful of two- to three-line phrases, the figures for Teika show a striking contrast to all other poets. The contrast is summarized in the following statements; in reading them, it is important to remember that they refer to Teika's, and other poets', use of lines found in the poetry in the tale, not their use of just any line.

(1) For eleven individual lines, Teika's usage may be declared unique: (a) among all poets on record (none), (b) among all poets in his time (5 cases: 40.2, 45.3, 49.5, 60.2, 66.1), (c) among potential candidates (3 cases: 19.1, 24.4, 38.4), and (d) among "serious" candidates (3 cases: 40.4, 46.4, 54.2). All but two of the lines in question are of rare to relatively rare occurrence, which increases the significance of Teika's use. (It is important to note, too, that in several of these cases, Teika uses the line more than once—see statement 3, below.)

   In only one case can any statement of unique usage be made for another poet, and it can be made only within the least significant category of comparison: Yoshitsune is the only poet among "serious" candidates to use line 5.4, a line that is otherwise of intermediate occurrence.

When compared to this single case for all other poets, the eleven cases observed for Teika alone represent a truly extraordinary figure.

Examples: 66.1 is discussed at length below. 60.2 has only two matches, one by Teika and one by Fujiwara Motosuke (908–90). 24.4 occurs only four times, twice in poems by Teika, and once each in poems by the priest Gyōson (1055–1135) and Fujiwara Shigeie (1128–80).

(2) For eight individual lines, Teika was one of only two poets to use an identical or similar line: (a) ever (2 cases: 40.2, 60.2—both are counted in statement 1b, above); (b) in his time (2 cases: 31.1, 33.2 [41.5 and 46.2 are the same line as 33.2]); (c) among potential candidates (3 cases: 39.2, 39.5, 69.4); (d) among serious candidates (1 case: 55.4). Since two of the eight were already listed under statement 1, we have six new lines, two of which are relatively rare, two of intermediate occurrence, and two quite common but unused or rare in Teika's time.

In all six cases where the other poet belonged to Teika's time (i.e., all but the two cases in statement 2a), the other poet is Ietaka, which is to say, the same statements can be made for him as for Teika.

For all other poets combined, this statement can be made in only a single case: line 52.4 was used by both Saigyō and Shunzei in Teika's time; it occurs only three times overall.

Once again, the number of cases noted for Teika (and Ietaka) is quite remarkable when compared to the single case for all other poets.

Example: Line 31.1, *Tama kiwaru*, is quite common, with 41 uses recorded overall, but more than half belong to the Man'yō period. Of the eighteen uses from later periods, Teika is responsible for five and Ietaka for four; no other poet from Teika's time used the line. Teika is the only poet ever to use *Tama kiwaru* at the beginning of a seven-syllable line, and he uses it three times, further underscoring his favor for this expression. (The discovery in *SKT* V of one other use from Teika's time would move this example to statement 4 below, but with virtually no change in the significance it carries. At the same time, confirmation from *SKT* IV and V that the line was never used by Minamoto Sanetomo, the poet of Teika's day most known for composing in the Man'yō style, would seem to bolster further the significance of Teika's frequent use of this line.)

(3) For seven individual lines, Teika was the only poet to use an identical or similar line more than once: (a) ever (6 cases: 24.4, 39.5, 40.2, 49.4, 49.5, 56.4); (b) in his time (none); (c) among

potential candidates (1 case: 19.1); (d) among serious candidates (none). Of the seven lines noted, five have already been listed under statements 1 and 2; three of the seven are of rare occurrence, two are relatively rare, and two are intermediate.

In no case is any other poet the only one who used a line identical with or similar to a line from the tale more than once. The closest statements possible are that Ietaka and Teika were together the only poets (a) ever (33.2 [41.5 and 46.2 are the same line as 33.2]), or (b) in their time (39.2, 66.2, 69.4), to use a given line more than once. Three of these lines are of intermediate occurrence, and the fourth is quite common.

Example: Line 39.5 occurs seventeen times, three of them from Teika's hand. The line first appears in *Genji monogatari*, and Teika was the next to use it; among Teika's contemporaries, Ietaka and Emperor Juntoku (1197–1242) also used the line once each, but all other uses are from later periods and never more than once by a single author.

(4) For three individual lines (18.1, 29.4, 40.3), Teika's usage of identical or similar lines is dramatically higher than any other poet.

This is not true in a single instance for any other poet.

Example: Reducing a complex count to rough figures, Teika alone accounts for nearly one third of all instances of line 40.3, a construction that was rare until Teika's time but became very common thereafter. Two close associates, Ietaka and Yoshitsune, are the only others to use the line more than twice, and even their usage is only about one third of Teika's.

(5) For ten individual lines, Teika's usage of identical or similar lines is higher than all other poets (5 cases: 19.4, 31.1, 33.2, 39.1, 69.4), or all candidates (5 cases: 15.4 [16.2 and 17.4 may be considered the same line], 19.1, 19.2, 45.1, 66.3)—though not as dramatically higher as in Statement 4.

A similar statement can be made of Ietaka for two lines (48.1, 66.2) and of Yoshitsune for one (45.2). Thus, *only three cases appear among all other poets, against ten cases for Teika alone.*

Example: Line 33.2 is matched twenty-one times, three by Teika and two by Ietaka. No other poet used the line more than once, and none other used it at all in Teika's time.

In addition, the following observations can be made regarding phrases spanning more than a single line. Although the individual lines making up these longer phrases have already been included under statements 1 through 5 where appropriate, their significance multiplies when they are seen to form longer expressions that were duplicated or approximated by Teika or other poets.

(6) For eight phrases spanning two or three lines, Teika was the only poet to use an identical or similar phrase: (a) ever (6 cases: 19.1–3, 40.2–3, 45.1–3, 49.4–5, 60.1–2, 66.1–3); (b) in his time (none); (c) among potential candidates (one case: 19.1–2, a smaller part of the phrase cited under statement 6a); (d) among serious candidates (one case: 19.4–5).

   No similar statement can be made for any other poet. Several of these cases are discussed below.

(7) For three phrases spanning two or three lines, Teika was one of only two poets to use an identical or similar phrase: (a) ever (none); (b) in his time (one case: 19.1–2, already cited under statement 6c because the other poet is not a serious candidate); (c) among potential candidates (two cases: 39.1–2, 66.1–2); (d) among serious candidates (none).

   Kujō Ieyoshi (1192–1264) is the other poet for the poem cited under statement 7b, and Ietaka is the other poet for the poems cited under statement 7c, which is to say, the same statements are possible for them as for Teika.

   Ietaka and Yoshitsune are the only two poets of their time to match 56.3–4. In this particular case, however, the two-line match is no more significant than matching 56.4 alone, for which Teika's showing is stronger: of only four additional matches for 56.4, two belong to Teika, and one is the poem being alluded to by all of the others.

   No other statements of this kind can be made of any other poet.

(8) For two phrases spanning two or three lines (49.4–5, already cited in statement 6a; 66.1–2, already cited in statement 7c), Teika was the only poet ever to use an identical or similar phrase more than once.

   No similar statement can be made for any other poet.

Finally, observations of a slightly different kind emerge from the tracking of historical usage—though these are on more precarious ground because in any given case a single new listing in *SKT* IV or V could, depending on its date, remove that case from inclusion here.

(9) In nine cases, Teika was the first poet to use an identical or similar line (a) ever (2 cases: 19.2, 54.2), or (b) after centuries of disuse (7 cases: 19.1, 33.2, 39.5, 40.2, 56.4, 60.2, 66.1). For the latter group, the earlier occurrences range from the Man'yō period (1 case), to the Kokin period (4 cases), to shortly after 1000 (2 cases). In five of the seven cases the line occurs only once before Teika; in the others, two and five times. The number of later occurrences for both groups range from zero to eighteen. In five of the cases Teika uses the line two or three times, but in only one case has any other potential candidate used the line more than once.

In just three cases, another potential candidate (for purposes of the present argument, it would be meaningless to make these statements of anyone who is not a candidate) was the first to use a line (c) ever (1 case: Saigyō, 52.4), or (d) after centuries of disuse (2 cases: Shun'e, 49.5; Ietaka, 55.4). For the cases cited in (d), earlier uses were once and twice, respectively, and occurred in the early to mid-tenth century. The number of subsequent uses for both (c) and (d) range from two to twelve. In all three cases, the "first user" uses the line only once, as did all but one of the subsequent users. The single exception among the subsequent users is Teika, who used line 49.5 four times.

In addition, there is one case that may belong in Teika's group (b) but has been left out because the span for its possible date remains too broad (38.4), and there are four cases where inability to date poems precisely prevents final determination of whether Teika or someone else was the first to use the line (e) ever (1 case: Teika or the priest Gyōnen, 46.4—a variant reading in *KT* would move this to statement 9f), or (f) after centuries of disuse (3 cases: Teika, Ietaka, or Ietaka's Daughter, 39.1–2; Teika, Saigyō, Sadanaka, or Jōzeimon'in Hyōe, 60.1; Teika or Ietaka, 66.2). Ietaka's Daughter and Jōzeimon'in Hyōe, as women, are not potential candidates even though they belong to Teika's age.

Thus, among other individual poets, Ietaka could be the "first user" in three cases at most, Saigyō in two, and no one else more than one. By contrast, Teika has already been confirmed as "first user" in nine cases, surpassing the highest total possible, based on *SKT* I–III, for all other potential candidates *combined*, and his total could swell to as many as fourteen.

Needless to say, when other factors are considered, credit for first use is not equally significant for every line. For example, for line 49.5, Shun'e was the first in over two centuries to use the line, but Teika is responsible for four out of eight subsequent uses (and out of ten uses total). What is important in the present analysis, however, is the overall picture that emerges when distinguishing cases strictly on the basis of first use, matching—from a different perspective—the patterns that emerged from the statements based on total number of uses, above.

The pattern is clear and undeniable: Teika's poems show numerous resemblances to the poems in the tale—in quantities that stand out as truly extraordinary when compared to other poets. The only other poet to show any sign of recurrent resemblances that might be considered sufficient to speak of a "pattern" is Fujiwara Ietaka, and even for him, the pattern observed is barely a shadow compared to that observed for Teika. Other poets show random resemblances, but in no case do they even begin to show a recurrent pattern that could support claims of overall stylistic affinities with the poetry in the tale. Since the usage patterns of the *Rokkashū* poets and other potential candidates were monitored throughout, for every line and phrase examined by Ishida and on exactly the same terms as for Teika, the failure to find, for these other poets, patterns of resemblance similar to Teika's cannot be attributed to unequal treatment.

The Qualitative Findings

The close inspection of the poetic usage that yielded the data for the essentially quantitative analysis outlined above also facilitated, in fact required, a simultaneous qualitative examination—an examination of the particular nature of resemblances found for Teika as opposed to others. Although Ishida gives little attention to qualitative questions in his article, in the final analysis it is when qualitative observations are added to the numerical tallies that the evidence speaks most persuasively in favor of accepting Teika as author of the tale. They are capable of silencing any lingering doubts that the evidence summarized above may not be statistically significant, or objections that literary matters of this nature simply do not lend themselves to quantitative study at all.

Four of the resemblances of phrase noted under statement 6—lines 1–3 of poem 19 and *SKT* III.133.865; lines 1–3 of poem 45 and *SKT* III.134.535; lines 4–5 of poem 49 and *SKT* III.133.1740, and lines 1–2 of poem 60 and *SKT* III.133.2656—are of particular importance, each being unique to Teika, and each being of a nature and magnitude that cannot be explained as accidental. If any of these four phrases had precedents in earlier poetry, as several other phrases noted under statements 6 and 7 do, then the resemblances could be attributed to the precedents held in common rather than to any direct link between Teika's poems and the poems in the tale. In the absence of such precedents, however, some conscious relationship must be assumed between Teika's poems and the poems in the tale: whichever poems came first, their language has been intentionally appropriated for the poems composed later.

Citing Teika's proscription against composing allusive variations (*honkadori* —"taking a foundation poem") upon "poems written just yesterday or today," which is found in his *Kindai shūka* (see chapter one, p. 15), Ishida dismisses out of hand the possibility that Teika would have drawn on poems from a tale written in his own age. Since by definition any allusive variation, regardless of authorship, must contain language identical (or nearly so) with the poem it takes as a foundation, Ishida wishes to rule out the possibility that Teika's poetry resembles poetry in the tale merely because he chose to use the tale as a source of foundation poems for his own compositions, rather than because of affinities of style that can support an argument for common authorship.

Given the extensive appropriation of language involved in these four phrases, however, Ishida cannot achieve his aim merely by dismissing resemblances due to allusive variation. Any direct appropriation of language has the same effect no matter the purpose to which it is put: i.e., the later poem resembles the earlier poem whether the two are of common authorship or not. It is, therefore, entirely immaterial whether a particular appropriation was intended as a bona fide allusive variation or was merely a borrowing of previously used language that happened to be suitable for expressing a new, wholly independent conception. The important point is that in all the searches conducted for this study, no one but Teika shows resemblances of two- and three-line phrases that cannot be dismissed as accidental, and Teika shows not just one but four such cases. Thus, if we assume that the poems in the tale came first, as is most likely, Teika is the only poet known to have alluded to *Matsura no miya monogatari*, or he is the only poet known to have borrowed quite freely from the poetry in the tale. The most—and, I submit, only—plausible explanation for this circumstance is that Teika was indeed the author of the tale. He alone could allude to, or borrow from, the tale in this way because he himself had written it.

Two of Teika's four poems, composed in 1193 (*SKT* III.133.865, resembling poem 19) and 1194 (*SKT* III.133.1740, resembling poem 49), could have preceded the tale, though the possibility seems quite remote. This would not alter the conclusion that the resemblances between them and the poems in the tale owe to common authorship, however. It is most unlikely that any second party would have duplicated language immediately recognizable as belonging originally to Teika—even in the context of a literary endeavor, such as the writing of fiction, that would not have been considered serious.

In another of the cases included under statement 6, a poem from the tale (poem 66) and two poems by Teika (*SKT* III.133.1125 and *SKT* III.133.2263) draw upon the phrasing of a *sedōka* by Hitomaro (*SKT* II.1.2357) in almost identical ways. In most such instances, we must assume that the resemblances of phrase come from the shared precedent, and this prevents us from arguing credibly that the resemblances owe to common authorship. What makes this case different is the exact duplication of Hitomaro's first line, "Hatsuse no ya," in *Matsura no miya monogatari* and in the first of Teika's poems, but nowhere else in any poetic collection or work of literature listed in the indexes consulted.

Modern scholarship appears to prefer a reading of "Hatsuse no" for Hitomaro's first line, as indicated by the *hiragana* gloss provided for the poem in *SKT* II, but this in no way affects the present argument. What matters here is Teika's actual reading, not Hitomaro's intended one. Even so, it is worth noting that the indexes yield no matches at all for "Hatsuse no" (not surprising for an irregular line), which leaves Teika the only poet ever to have quoted Hitomaro's first line in either reading. If we accept the modern view, technically speaking Teika is the only poet on record ever to use the line "Hatsuse no ya." This would move the line from statement 1b to 1a in the quantitative analysis above. I have counted it under 1b, however, because it is virtually certain that Teika was directly quoting the reading of Hitomaro's line current in his day, rather than inventing a new variation upon it. "Hatsuse no ya" is the gloss given for Hitomaro's *sedōka* in the Nishi-Honganji manuscript of *Man'yōshū* (the *katakana* gloss in *SKT* II), which derives from Sengaku's (or Senkaku, b. 1203) third and final edition of the anthology completed in 1266, as well as the reading given in both *Fubokushō* (ca. 1310) and *Shokusenzaishū* (1318–20).

The absence of any further duplications of "Hatsuse no ya" dramatically contradicts expectations, not only because Hatsuse is a popular *utamakura* (place name of frequent poetic reference) that occurs at the beginning of some two hundred similar lines of poetry, but also because a number of other poets, including Ietaka (*SKT* III.132.2498), take Hitomaro's *sedōka* as a foundation poem in their own compositions. If the line in question were one that anyone might have matched casually, quite by accident, then several of the other poets responsible for the two hundred odd lines beginning with "Hatsuse" ought to have matched it. On the other hand, any poet who set about composing an allusive variation upon Hitomaro's *sedōka* could have quite deliberately duplicated his first line, thereby inadvertently matching the line in *Matsura no miya monogatari* as well. But none did. These circumstances make Teika's unique match all the more remarkable, and in fact speak much more strongly for affirming a direct link between Teika and the tale than a line for which he has a half-dozen or more matches, or a line for which he produced two or three matches out of only three or four in existence. Only Teika and the author of *Matsura no miya monogatari* quoted Hitomaro's line exactly, and the most plausible explanation is that Teika and the author were one and the same person.

The Question of Teika's Allusions to Other Tales

Teika alluded in his poetry to tales other than *Matsura no miya monogatari*, and, if it could be shown that the appropriation of language involved in such allusions is essentially similar to that found for *Matsura no miya monogatari*, it might call into question my conclusion that Teika could draw on *Matsura no miya monogatari* in such a way only because he was its author: perhaps the patterns noted here merely represent Teika's technique of allusion to any tale rather than a signature telling us he was the author of this one. To dismiss this possibility with complete certainty would require a monumental study examining several other tales along the same lines as I have done for *Matsura no miya monogatari*. There are several good reasons for not allowing this issue to detain us, however:

First, we know that Teika was not the only author to allude to other tales, which is to say, no matter how extensive his record of allusions to other tales may be, the question of why no one else alluded to *Matsura no miya monogatari* would lead us back to the conclusion already drawn. In this connection it is well to remember the prominent treatment *Matsura no miya monogatari* received in *Fūyōshū* (see appendix A, pp. 163–65), which raises the expectation that Teika would not have been the only one to allude to it unless there were special circumstances.

Second, the quantitative analysis based on individual lines (i.e., not on two- to three-line phrases) made this a study not only of conscious allusion and borrowing, but of style, which is to say, a study that could—and quite clearly did—reveal unconscious stylistic habits and inclinations held in common by

Teika and the author of *Matsura no miya monogatari* but by no one else. Once again, no matter how abundant Teika's record of allusions to other tales may be, the likelihood that extensive affinities of style (completely unrelated to deliberate borrowing or allusion) would also exist between Teika and *several* tales by *several different* authors must be virtually nonexistent—especially in light of how few affinities between different poets surfaced in the present study.

Third, from a logical perspective it would be circular to claim here that the quantitative findings can erase our uncertainties about the qualitative findings, after claiming earlier that the qualitative findings can silence lingering doubts about the quantitative findings (p. 186). But when one considers it as a question of odds, circularity is no longer an issue: the likelihood that such striking quantitative findings could coexist with such striking qualitative findings *without* being significant in any way must be, as above, virtually nonexistent.

In short, the chances that the conclusion drawn—i.e., that Teika could allude to and borrow from the tale only because he was indeed its author—would be negated are so negligible that it may be accepted with all necessary confidence without any further studies. In fact, unless some compelling new reason for questioning the conclusion should arise, the circumstances simply do not warrant the immense amount of time and effort that would be required for an expansive examination of Teika's (and others') poetic styles and allusive techniques as they relate to several more tales.

6. Possible Objections

Most objections to accepting Teika as author of the tale are based on false premises, assuming, for example, that Teika would have had something to say about the work in his diary if it were his own creation, or that a well-educated man, especially the heir to a poetic house of such stature, would never have dabbled in fiction writing.

The error of the first assumption is easily demonstrated: Teika certainly *might* have mentioned the tale in his diary, but then again he might just as likely have chosen not to mention it, as he chose not to write anything about *Monogatari nihyakuban utaawase*, a mock poetry contest he compiled pitting poems from various Heian period tales against one another. The purpose of a diary of this kind was primarily to preserve a record of one's activities as an official of the court, for the future reference of oneself and one's descendants. Thus, while the diary naturally would include references to such literary matters as were connected with formal poetic events at court, there would be no reason to record a strictly private literary activity such as the writing of a fictional tale. Even Murasaki Shikibu, who, one would presume, had less reason to be reticent about her involvement with fiction writing, mentions *Genji monogatari* in her diary only incidentally, in the context of reporting other occurrences in her life at court (Nakano 1971b, 201–2, 243–45, 249–50; Bowring 1982, 91, 137–38, 143–44); while one of these references does clearly link her to the writing of the tale, it remains the case that she never saw fit to discuss her writing directly and overtly—not even a cryptic, "Finished another chapter today." In spite of being a very personal record in many ways, her diary, like Teika's, is fundamentally a record of her public activities—the events she participated in at court, her contacts with the leading men of the court, her relationships with and observations of other ladies at court, and so on—and it is easy to imagine that she thought of her fiction writing as belonging to an entirely different sphere.

The second assumption is even more quickly dismissed: Hagitani has shown beyond any doubt that *some* well-educated man obviously *did* dabble in fiction; why could it not be the heir to a poetic house, especially one who is known to have taken a great interest in fiction?

The appearance of Ishida's and Hagitani's articles in 1940 and 1941 put an end to most objections of this kind. As already noted, however, some scholars remained wary of accepting these studies as definitive proof. Two relatively late objections may be rebutted as easily as the above:

Ōtsuki (1967, 26) questions the ascription on grounds that a man as well educated as Teika would not have made the mistake of using official Japanese bureaucratic titles inconsistent with the period in which the tale is set. Ōtsuki's error is twofold. First, no matter how well educated Teika was, we cannot assume that his knowledge of the Japanese histories, or his library holdings, were so specialized as to allow him to avoid the kind of minor historical contradictions, vaguenesses, and inaccuracies that have been pointed out by modern scholars with the aid of extensive reference works (see Hagitani 1970, passim—especially supplementary notes 2–5 and 12–15—for brief discussions of some of the historical inaccuracies). Second, as a literary man rather than a historian, Teika may well have been striving only for a general effect of historical authenticity, and been quite unconcerned about precise historicity. The specificity of the time setting given in the tale's opening line should not be taken as an indication that he was striving for precision and accuracy in all historical references (see translation, n. 1).

Nakano (1971a, 260–61), noting that *waka* and *renga* poet Shōtetsu (1381–1459) speaks of two Teika poems based on *Matsura no miya monogatari* as representative of the way Teika took fictional stories as foundations for allusive variations (see Hisamatsu and Nishio 1961, 211–12), asserts that Teika would not have used *Matsura no miya monogatari* as a foundation unless it had been written by someone else in an earlier age. This view, like Ishida's perfunctory pronouncement that resemblances of phrase between Teika and the tale could not owe to allusive variation, derives from an overly rigid and one-dimensional view of Teika's rules for allusive variations. It fails to recognize the variety of forms allusion and appropriation of language can take, not all of which would fall under Teika's proscription, and it admits no flexibility in applying Teika's proscription to the particular situation or occasion (Is the foundation a poem or a story? Is the new poem intended to be formal and public, or informal and private?). It also allows no variance between a rule Teika set down for a young and still inexperienced pupil of poetry, and Teika's own poetic practice in his middle age—in spite of the fact that precisely such a variance can be observed between Teika's preaching (Fujihira 1975b, 513–14; Brower 1985, 410) and practice (see pp. 174–75, section 2, above) as pertains to the use of Man'yō diction. In the end, Teika's apparent allusions to *Matsura no miya monogatari* suggest the need for reevaluating some of the standard assumptions about techniques of allusion, rather than a need to set aside the entire body of evidence confirming the tale's late twelfth-century date and its authorship by Teika. As argued in section 5, above, there is no reason to assume that Teika would not have composed poems based on his own tale; in fact, such compositions provide a strong link between Teika and the tale.

In sum, none of the objections that have been raised offer a serious challenge to the evidence amassed in support of the ascription.

7. Conclusion

The circumstantial nature of Hagitani's study, and the lapses in rigor of Ishida's, had left sufficient lingering uncertainties to allow those who felt the tale unworthy of Teika to go on resisting the ascription, if only by always retaining a conjectural or interrogative locution when referring to it: "Fujiwara Teika saku *ka*" ("By Fujiwara Teika?"—emphasis mine). That Higuchi Yoshimaro and Misumi Yōichi, both of whom have written articles in which they appear fully to accept Teika's authorship (Higuchi 1980; Misumi 1974, 1975, 1979), nevertheless use this conjectural locution in their brief textual remarks on *Matsura no miya monogatari* for the fifth volume of *SKT*, published in 1987, testifies to the caution scholars still feel compelled to exercise in addressing this issue.

As the present survey of the principal evidence has shown, however, support for the ascription made in *Mumyōzōshi* ranges from the broad and general (what is suggested about the author's knowledge and temperament by some of the obvious features of the tale) to the deep, or very particular (what is revealed about the author's knowledge of China and his poetic style by means of close examination). First the broad criteria confirm Teika as an eminently suitable candidate, and close examination of the knowledge of China shared by the tale and Teika corroborate this suitability in concrete and specific terms. Then the raw figures and the particular observations emerging from the study of style reveal sharp differences between Teika's and other poets' usage of poetic expressions found in the tale, not only verifying that Teika is the most likely candidate, but making it effectively unimaginable that the poetry in the tale could have been composed by any other hand.

Even where individual items of evidence are not capable of standing on their own, support for an argument can be strengthened by a convergence of a wide variety of evidence. In the present case, all of the evidence converges upon the same point with a consistency rarely encountered in studies of this nature, and some of that evidence is highly compelling even without the assistance of the rest. Furthermore, the point on which the evidence converges is none other than the one indicated by a contemporary reference to the tale explicitly indicating its author in a source that is generally accepted as reliable— *Mumyōzōshi*. The internal and external signs are in complete agreement.

Were there any forceful objections outstanding, one might still find reason for pause. However, a retracing of Ishida's steps, evaluating, updating, and expanding the study he conducted in 1940, has dissolved the doubts that had been left by the apparent irregularities in his method: whatever the lapses of detail, the overall argument and evidence are fundamentally sound. All other grounds on which Teika's authorship has been disputed are either based on false premises or have entirely plausible explanations.

Though some may yet wish to dissociate Teika from the tale because they find it unworthy of him in one way or another, there is no longer room for reasonable doubt that he was its author. It seems fair to say that in any further debate on the matter, the burden of proof rests on those who would disprove Teika's authorship rather than on those who would prove it. Until and unless compelling counterevidence is put forth, there need be no further hesitation to speak of Teika as the confirmed author of *Matsura no miya monogatari* with as much confidence as we speak of Murasaki Shikibu as the author of *Genji monogatari*.

Bibliography

The place of publication is Tokyo unless otherwise noted.

For periodicals, the month of publication is indicated in lowercase Roman numerals following the year. Short citations in the notes to the text give only the year, except as necessary to distinguish articles written in the same year.

The following abbreviations are used:

KBG   *Kokubungaku: Kaishaku to kyōzai no kenkyū*
KGKB   *Kokugo kokubun*
KGKBG   *Kokugo to kokubungaku*
KSKS   *Kokubungaku: Kaishaku to kanshō*
MN   *Monumenta Nipponica*
NKBT   *Nihon koten bungaku taikei*
NKBZ   *Nihon koten bungaku zenshū*

Abe Akio. 1966. *Nihon bungaku shi, chūko-hen.* Vol. 53 of *Hanawa sensho.* Hanawa Shobō.

Abe Akio, Akiyama Ken, and Imai Gen'e, eds. 1970–76. *Genji monogatari.* Vols. 12–17 of *NKBZ.* Shōgakukan.

Akahane Shuku. 1967.iv. "Teika no tabi no uta—dai-i no tsuikyū to iu ten kara." *Nōtorudamu Seishin Joshi-daigaku kiyō* 1:41–63.

―――. 1969.iii. "Teika no shūgaku-ki no uta (I)—Wakeikazuchi no Yashiro no utaawase, Shogaku hyakushu, Horikawa-dai hyakushu." *Nōtorudamu Seishin Joshi-daigaku kiyō* 3:21–50.

―――. 1974. *Fujiwara Teika zenkashū zenku sakuin, sakuin-hen.* Vol. 42 of *Kasama sakuin sōkan.* Kasama shoin.

Akita Sadaki. 1962.xi. "'Mōsu' to 'kikoyu'—Genji monogatari, Makura no sōshi o shiryō to shite." *KGKB* 31.11:19–43.

―――. 1964.iii. "'Mōsu' to 'kikoyu' hoi—Keitai no gawa kara." *Hokkaido Gakugei Daigaku gogaku bungakukai kiyō* 2:10–18.

―――. 1965.ix. "'Mōsu' to 'kikoyu'—Genji monogatari igo." *KGKB* 34.9:44–60.

Akiyama Ken, Jinbō Kazuya, and Satake Akihiro, eds. 1975. *Nihon koten bungakushi no kiso chishiki.* Yūhikaku.

Birch, Cyril, ed. 1965. *Anthology of Chinese Literature: From Early Times to the Fourteenth Century.* New York: Grove Press.

Borgen, Robert. 1982. "The Japanese Mission to China, 801–806." *MN* 37.1:1–28.

Bowring, Richard, trans. 1982. *Murasaki Shikibu: Her Diary and Poetic Memoirs.* Princeton: Princeton University Press.

Brower, Robert H., trans. 1972. "'Ex-Emperor Go-Toba's Secret Teachings': *Go-Toba no In gokuden.*" *Harvard Journal of Asiatic Studies* 32:5–70.

———, trans. 1978. *Fujiwara Teika's "Hundred-Poem Sequence of the Shōji Era," 1200.* Sophia University.

———. 1981. "The Reizei Family Documents." *MN* 36.4:445–61.

———, trans. 1985. "Fujiwara Teika's *Maigetsushō.*" *MN* 40.4:399–425.

Brower, Robert H., and Earl Miner. 1961. *Japanese Court Poetry.* Stanford: Stanford University Press.

———, trans. 1967. *Fujiwara Teika's "Superior Poems of Our Time": A Thirteenth-Century Poetic Treatise and Sequence.* Stanford: Stanford University Press.

Daijiten. See *Nihon kokugo daijiten.*

Dainihon shiryō, ser. 5, vol. 8. 1931. Tokyo Teikoku Daigaku.

Encyclopedic Dictionary of the Chinese Language. 1962–68. Taipei: The Institute for Advanced Chinese Studies.

Frank, Bernard. 1958. *Kataimi et kata-tagae: Etude sur les interdits de direction à l'epoque Heian.* Bulletin de la Maison Franco-Japonaise, n.s., 5.2–4.

Fujihira Haruo, ed. 1975a. *Kindai shūka.* Vol. 50 of *NKBZ.* Shōgakukan.

———, ed. 1975b. *Maigetsushō.* Vol. 50 of *NKBZ.* Shōgakukan.

Fujimoto Kazue, ed. 1983. *Goshūi wakashū.* 4 vols. Kōdansha Gakujutsu Bunko.

Fujioka Sakutarō. 1915. *Kamakura Muromachi jidai bungakushi.* Iwanami.

Fujioka Tadaharu, ed. 1971. *Izumi Shikibu nikki.* Vol. 18 of *NKBZ.* Shōgakukan.

Fujiwara Teika. See Brower, Robert H.

Fukui Kyūzō. 1960. *Makura kotoba no kenkyū to shakugi,* rev. ed. Ed. Yamagishi Tokuhei. Yūseidō.

Fukui Teisuke, ed. 1972. *Ise monogatari.* Vol. 8 of *NKBZ.* Shōgakukan.

Geddes, Ward, trans. 1984. *Kara monogatari: Tales from China.* Tempe: Arizona State University Center for Asian Studies.

Gotō Tanji. 1934.v. "Kinko shōsetsu no ni-san ni tsuite." *KGKBG* 11.5:58–62. Reprinted in his *Chūsei kokubungaku kenkyū.* Isobe Kōyōdō.

Hachisuka Fueko, ed. 1935. *Matsura no miya monogatari.* Iwanami Bunko.

Hagitani Boku. 1941.viii–ix. "Matsura no miya monogatari sakusha to sono kangaku-teki soyō." *KGKBG* 18.8–9.

———, ed. 1960. *Heian-chō utaawase taisei,* vol. 4. Dōhōsha.

———. 1969.viii. "Matsura no miya monogatari wa Teika no jikken shōsetsu ka." *KGKBG* 46.8:1–15.

———, ed. 1970. *Matsura no miya monogatari.* Kadokawa Bunko. (For corrigenda, see Hagitani 1975 and 1976.)

———. 1975.i. "Den Go-Kōgon-in shinkan-bon *Matsura no miya monogatari* chōsa hōkoku." *Nihon bungaku kenkyū* (Daitō Bunka Daigaku) 14:17–27.

———. 1976.i. "*Matsura no miya monogatari* hotei shūi." *Nihon bungaku kenkyū* (Daitō Bunka Daigaku) 15:126–27.

Haku Raku-ten shishū. 4 vols. 1929. Vols. 9–12 of *Zoku kokuyaku kanbun taisei.* Kokumin Bunko Kankōkai.

Harada Yoshioki, ed. 1969. *Utsuho monogatari.* 3 vols. Kadokawa Bunko.

Higuchi Yoshimaro. 1970.ii. "Ukinami monogatari kō." *KGKB* 39.2:1–22.

_____. 1970.iv. "Fukurozōshi, Mumyōzōshi no seiritsu jiki ni tsuite." *KGKBG* 47.4:81–96.

_____. 1978.x. "*Mumyōzōshi* no hottan." *KGKBG* 55.10:1–15.

_____. 1980.v. "*Matsura no miya monogatari* to *Monogatari nihyaku-ban utaawase* no seiritsu jiki ni tsuite." *KGKBG* 57.5:18–28.

_____. 1981.xi. "Monogatari to chūsei." *KSKS* 46.11:14–18.

Hirade Kōjirō. 1909. *Kinko shōsetsu kaidai*. Dainihon Tosho.

Hisamatsu Sen'ichi and Nishio Minoru, eds. 1961. *Karonshū, nōgakuronshū*. Vol. 65 of *NKBT*. Iwanami.

Hurvitz, Leon, trans. 1976. *Scripture of the Lotus Blossom of the Fine Dharma*. New York: Columbia University Press.

Ichiko Teiji. 1951. *Chūsei shōsetsu*. Shibundō.

_____, ed. 1973–75. *Heike monogatari*. 2 vols. Vols. 29–30 of *NKBZ*. Shōgakukan.

_____, ed. 1978. *Nihon bungaku zenshi*, vols. 2 and 3. Gakutōsha.

Ii Haruki. 1983. *Genji monogatari no nazo*. Vol. 98 of *Sanseidō sensho*. Sanseidō.

Ikeda Toshio. 1981.xii. "Minu Tōdo no yume—*Matsura no miya monogatari* o chūshin ni." *KBG* 26.16:80–85.

Imai Gen'e. 1954.x. "Ōchō monogatari no shūen." *KGKBG* 31.10:19–29.

_____. 1967. "Kyōju no mondai." In *Genji monogatari hikkei*, ed. Akiyama Ken. Gakutōsha.

Ishida Yoshisada. 1940.vi. "Matsura no miya monogatari no sakusha wa Fujiwara Teika ka." *KGKBG* 17.6:62–85. Reprinted with alterations as "Matsura no miya monogatari sakusha kō" in Ishida 1972.

_____. 1944.iii. "Mumyōzōshi sakusha kō." *KGKBG* 21.3:15–28.

_____. 1957. *Fujiwara Teika no kenkyū*. Bungadō.

_____. 1970.i. "*Matsura no miya monogatari* no Teika-teki igi." *Gakuen* 361:34–50, 136.

_____. 1972. *Shinkokin sekai to chūsei bungaku, jō*. Kitazawa Tosho Shuppan.

_____. 1979. *Yōen: Teika no bi*. Vol. 84 of *Hanawa sensho*. Hanawa Shobō.

Ishii Susumu. 1974. *Nihon no rekishi 7: Kamakura Bakufu*. Chūō Kōronsha.

Ishii Yukio. 1977.xi. "*Matsura no miya monogatari* ni okeru kōsō no hatan." *Kushiro ronshū* 9:1–23.

Ishikawa Tōru. 1958. *Kodai shōsetsushi kō*. Tōkō Shoin.

_____. 1980.i. "Monogatari no nagare." *KSKS* 45.1:6–16.

Jōkaku. 1956. *Waka iroha*. Vol. 3 of *Nihon kagaku taikei*, ed. Sasaki Nobutsuna. Kazama Shobō.

Kamens, Edward, trans. 1988. *The Three Jewels*. Ann Arbor: University of Michigan Center for Japanese Studies.

Kaneko Takeo. 1934. "Chūsei no monogatari bungaku gaisetsu—Kamakura jidai ni okeru shōsetsu." In *Nihon bungaku kōza*, vol. 3, 39–58. Kaizōsha.

Katagiri Yōichi, ed. 1972. *Taketori monogatari*. Vol. 8 of *NKBZ*. Shōgakukan.

Kawaguchi Hisao, ed. 1982. *Wakan rōeishū*. Kōdansha Gakujutsu Bunko.

Keene, Donald. 1971. *Landscapes and Portraits*. Kodansha International.

_____. 1989. "A Neglected Chapter: Courtly Fiction of the Kamakura Period." *MN* 44.1:1–30.

Kikuchi Hitoshi. 1978.iii. "Hamamatsu Chūnagon monogatari no zaitō kan—Genji monogatari kara no shōsha." *Kokugakuin zasshi* 79.3: 13–22.

_____. 1981.ii. "Monogatari sakka toshite no Fujiwara Teika—Matsura no miya monogatari no ichizuke." *Kokugakuin zasshi* 82.2:19–28.

Kitagawa Hiroshi and Bruce T. Tsuchida, trans. 1975. *The Tale of the Heike.* University of Tokyo Press.

Kitagawa, Joseph M. 1966. *Religion in Japanese History.* New York: Columbia University Press.

Kitamura Hideko. 1976.ix. "Matsura no miya monogatari ni okeru 'namamekashi' ni tsuite." *Shōin kokubungaku* 14:29–33.

Kokinshū, see Ozawa 1971.

Konishi Jin'ichi. 1953.vii. "Yōenbi—Bantōshi to no kōshō." *KGKB* 22.7:1–14.

_____, ed. 1976. *Shinkō roppyakuban utaawase.* Yūseidō.

Kōno Tama, ed. 1959–62. *Utsuho monogatari.* 3 vols. Vols. 10–12 of *NKBT.* Iwanami.

Kōno Yumiko. 1978.ii. "Matsura no miya monogatari kō—Yōenbi ni tsuite." *Kokugo kokubungaku kenkyū* 13:1–13.

Kubota Jun. 1969. "Kadan: Chūsei." In *Waka bungaku kōza,* vol. 3, ed. Waka Bungakukai, 94–128. Ōfūsha.

_____. 1973. *Shinkokin kajin no kenkyū.* Tokyo Daigaku Shuppankai.

_____. 1975.xi. "*Matsura no miya monogatari* no Tachibana Ujitada." *KBG* 20.15:166–67.

_____. 1980. "Shingi hikyo daruma-uta no jidai." In Kankōkai, ed., *Nihon bungaku kenkyū shiryō sōsho: Shinkokin wakashū.* Yūseidō. Reprinted with substantial revisions from Kubota 1973.

_____. 1981a.xii. "Kōki seijū no jidai." *KBG* 26.16:12–19.

_____. 1981b.xii. "Hyōgen-ron kara mita Teika no uta jisshu (kaidoku)." *KBG* 26.16:88–97.

_____. 1984. *Fujiwara Teika.* Vol. 9 of *Ōchō no kajin.* Shūeisha.

_____. 1985. *Yakuchū Fujiwara Teika zenkashū, jō.* Kawade Shobō Shinsha.

Kuge Hareyasu. 1981.xi. "Chūsei giko-monogatari no hassō to keisei: 'Monogataritori' no hōhō kara." *Heian bungaku kenkyū* 66:184–99.

Kuroiwa Ichirō. 1951.xi. "Teika no iu 'yōen'-bi ni tsuite." *Bungaku* 19.11:57–65.

Kurokawa (Sensōan) Harumura. n.d. *Ko monogatari ruiji shō.*

Kusano Michiko. 1979.xi. "Fujiwara Teika to Matsura no miya monogatari." *Waka bungaku kenkyū* 41:1–10.

Kuwabara Hiroshi. 1963.vi. "Takafusa to Takanobu—Heian-chō makki no monogatari aikō no seishin ni furetsutsu." *Heian bungaku kenkyū* 30:157–65.

_____, ed. 1976. *Mumyōzōshi. Shinchō Nihon koten shūsei.* Shinchōsha.

Kyūsojin Hitaku. 1955. "Teika jihitsu-bon monogatari nihyakuban utaawase no kenkyū." In *Monogatari nihyakuban utaawase to kenkyū.* Ser. 1, vol. 1 of *Mikan kokubun shiryō.*

_____. 1956. Introduction to *Nihon kagaku taikei,* vol. 3, ed. Sasaki Nobutsuna. Kazama Shobō.

Kyūsojin Hitaku, Higuchi Yoshimaro, and Fujii Takashi, eds. 1974–76. *Monogatari waka sōran.* 2 vols. Kazama Shobō.

Lammers, Wayne P., trans. 1982. "The Succession (*Kuniyuzuri*): A Translation from *Utsuho monogatari*." *MN* 37.2:139–78.

———. 1987. "A Poetic Ideal in a Narrative Context: Fujiwara Teika and *The Tale of Matsura* (*Matsura no miya monogatari*)." Ann Arbor: University Microfilms International (87–12158).

Levy, Ian Hideo, trans. 1981. *Man'yōshū*, vol. 1. Princeton: Princeton University Press.

Marra, Michele, trans. 1984. "*Mumyōzōshi.*" *MN* 39.2–4.

Maruyama Kiyoko. 1964. *Genji monogatari to Hakushi monjū*. Tokyo Joshi Daigaku Gakkai.

Matsumura Seiichi. 1973. *Tosa nikki*. Vol.9 of *NKBZ*. Shōgakukan.

Matsumura Yūji. 1980.i. "Matsura no miya monogatari." *KSKS* 45.1:52.

Matsuo Satoshi. 1963. *Heian jidai monogatari no kenkyū*, rev. ed. Musashino Shoin.

———, ed. 1964. *Hamamatsu Chūnagon monogatari*. Vol. 77 of *NKBT*. Iwanami.

Matsuo Satoshi and Nagai Kazuko, eds. 1974. *Makura no sōshi*. Vol. 11 of *NKBZ*. Shōgakukan.

Matsura no miya monogatari. 1933. Vol. 18–jō of *Zoku gunsho ruijū*. Zoku Gunsho Ruijū Kanseikai.

Matsura no miya monogatari. 1960. Vol. 16 of *Katsuranomiya-bon sōsho*. Yōtokusha.

Matsura no miya monogatari. 1981. *Gensō ei'in kotenseki fukusei sōkan*. Yūshōdō. Commentary by Yamamoto Nobuyoshi.

Matsura no miya monogatari. See also Hachisuka 1935 and Hagitani 1970.

Matsushita Daizaburō. 1925.vi. "Utsuho monogatari wa Kamakura igo no gisaku ka." *Kokugakuin zasshi* 31.6. Reprinted in Kankōkai, ed., *Nihon bungaku kenkyū shiryō sōsho: Heian-chō monogatari II*. Yūseidō, 1974.

———, comp. 1925–26. *Zoku kokka taikan*. 2 vols. Kigensha. (1931 reprint by Chūbunkan used for this study.)

Matsushita Daizaburō and Watanabe Fumio, comp. 1903. *Kokka taikan*. 2 vols. Kyōbunsha. (1931 reprint by Chūbunkan used for this study.)

McCullough, Helen Craig, trans. 1968. *Tales of Ise: Lyrical Episodes from Tenth-Century Japan*. Stanford: Stanford University Press.

McCullough, William H., trans. 1964. "Shōkyūki: An Account of the Shōkyū War of 1221." *MN* 19.3–4.

———, trans. 1968. "The *Asuma Kagami* account of the Shōkyū War." *MN* 23.1/2:102–55.

———. 1973. "Spirit Possession in the Heian Period." In *Studies on Japanese Culture*, vol. 1. The Japan P.E.N. Club.

McCullough, William H., and Helen Craig McCullough, trans. 1980. *A Tale of Flowering Fortunes: Annals of Japanese Aristocratic Life in the Heian Period*. 2 vols. Stanford: Stanford University Press.

Mills, D. E., trans. 1970. *A Collection of Tales from Uji: A Study and Translation of Uji Shūi Monogatari*. Cambridge: Cambridge University Press.

Minemura Fumito. 1968.v. "*Genji monogatari* to kōki karon, utaawase to no kakawari." *KSKS*:106–9.

———, ed. 1974. *Shinkokin wakashū*. Vol. 26 of *NKBZ*. Shōgakukan.

Miner, Earl. 1968. *An Introduction to Japanese Court Poetry*. Stanford: Stanford University Press.

———, trans. 1969. *Japanese Poetic Diaries*. Berkeley and Los Angeles: University of California Press.

Misumi Yōichi. 1974.ix. "*Matsura no miya monogatari* no shudai to kōsō." *Kōchi-dai kokubun* 5:1–9.

———. 1975. "*Matsura no miya monogatari* no ito o megutte." *Kōchi Daigaku gakujutsu kenkyū hōkoku—Jinbun kagaku* 24.1:1–11.

———. 1979. "'Oyako no naka' to Nijō Taikōtaigōgū no Shikibu." In *Genji monogatari oyobi igo no monogatari, kenkyū to shiryō*. Vol. 7 of *Kodai bungaku ronsō*. Musashino Shoin.

Mitani Eiichi. 1967. "Roman no tasogare." In *Nihon bungaku no rekishi*, ed. Kadokawa Gen'yoshi, vol. 5. Kadokawa.

Mitani Eiichi and Sekine Yoshiko, eds. 1965. *Sagoromo monogatari*. Vol. 79 of *NKBT*. Iwanami.

Mitoma Hirosuke. 1966.i. "Kaisetsu: '*Utsuho monogatari* wa Kamakura igo no gisaku ka.'" *Kokugakuin zasshi* 67.1:103–4.

Mizuno Haruhisa. 1940.vi. "*Matsura no miya monogatari* no seiritsu nendai to sakusha ni tsuite." *KGKBG* 17.6:53–61.

Monzen. 3 vols. 1921. Vols. 2–4 of *Kokuyaku kanbun taisei*. Kokumin Bunko Kankōkai.

Mori Katsumi. 1966. *Kentōshi*. Shibundō.

Morohashi Tetsuji, Kamata Tadashi, and Yoneyama Toratarō, eds. 1981–82. *Kōkanwa jiten*. 4 vols. Taishūkan.

Murayama Shūichi. 1962. *Fujiwara Teika*. Vol. 95 of *Jinbutsu sōsho*. Yoshikawa Kōbunkan.

Nagayama Isamu. 1968. *Kokugoshi gaisetsu*. Kazama Shobō.

Nagazumi Yasuaki and Nakata Takanao. 1963. "*Matsura no miya monogatari*." In *Zōho kaitei Nihon bungaku daijiten*, ed. Fujimura Tsukuru. Shinchōsha.

Nakajima Yōichi. 1966. *Nihon bungei riron ni okeru shōchōteki hyōgen rinen no kenkyū*. Kazama Shobō.

Nakamura Yoshio. 1962. *Ōchō no fūzoku to bungaku*. Vol. 22 of *Hanawa sensho*. Hanawa Shobō.

Nakano Kōichi. 1963.xii. "Kodai monogatari no dokusha no mondai: monogatari ondokuron hihan." *Gakujutsu kenkyū* 12.

———. 1964.xii. "*Genji monogatari* no sōshiji to monogatari ondokuron." *Gakujutsu kenkyū* 13.

———. 1967.iii. "Kodai monogatari no kyōju to hōhō." *Gakujutsu kenkyū* 15.

———. 1969.i. "'Monogatari idekihajime no oya' kō: *Taketori monogatari* no bungakushi-jō no chi'i." *Kaishaku* 15.1:20–25.

———. 1971a. *Monogatari bungaku ronkō*. Kyōiku Sentā.

———. 1971b. *Murasaki Shikibu nikki*. Vol. 18 of *NKBZ*. Shōgakukan.

———. 1981. *Utsuho monogatari no kenkyū*. Musashino Shoin.

Nienhauser, William H., Jr., ed. and comp. 1986. *The Indiana Companion to Traditional Chinese Literature*. Bloomington: Indiana University Press.

Nihon Gakujutsu Shinkōkai, ed. 1969. *The Manyōshū*, rev. ed. New York: Columbia University Press.

Nihon kokugo daijiten (Shukusatsu-ban). 1980. 10 vols. Shōgakukan.

Nihon koten bungaku daijiten. 1983–85. 6 vols. Iwanami.

Nishiki Hitoshi. 1988. "Teika to monogatari: *Matsura no miya monogatari* shiron." In *Ronshū Fujiwara Teika. Waka bungaku no sekai 13*, ed. Waka Bungakukai, 119–42. Kasama Shoin.

Nishio Kōichi. 1960. "*Matsura no miya monogatari*." In *Nihon bungaku kanshō jiten: koten-hen*, ed. Yoshida Seiichi. Tōkyōdō.

Nomura Hachirō. 1926. *Kamakura jidai bungaku shinron*, rev. ed. Meiji Shoin.

———. 1933. "Kamakura jidai no shōsetsu." In *Iwanami kōza Nihon bungaku*, vol. 8. Iwanami.

Ogi Takashi. 1961. *Kamakura jidai monogatari no kenkyū*. Tōhō Shobō.

———. 1973. *San'itsu monogatari no kenkyū: Heian, Kamakura jidai hen*. Kasama Shoin.

Ogihara Asao. 1973. *Kojiki*. Vol. 1 of *NKBZ*. Shōgakukan.

Oka Kazuo, ed. 1972. *Heian-chō bungaku jiten*. Tōkyōdō.

Okazaki Yoshie. 1969. *Bi no dentō*. Hōbunkan Shuppan.

Omodaka Hisataka, ed. 1957–70. *Man'yōshū chūshaku*. 21 vols. Chūō Kōronsha.

Ōta Seikyū (Hyōzaburō). 1968. *Nihon kagaku to Chūgoku shigaku*. Shimizu Kōbundō.

Ōtsuki Osamu. 1967.v. "*Matsura no miya monogatari* ni tsuite no oboegaki." *Gobun* (Osaka Daigaku) 27:22–27.

———, ed. 1979. *Ariake no wakare—aru dansō no himegimi no monogatari*. Sōeisha.

Oyamada Tomokiyo. 1829. "*Matsura no miya monogatari* kōshō." Reproduced in Hachisuka 1935, 101–8.

Ozawa Masao, ed. 1971. *Kokin wakashū*. Vol. 7 of *NKBZ*. Shōgakukan.

Philippi, Donald L., trans. 1968. *Kojiki*. University of Tokyo Press.

Po Chü-i. See *Haku Raku-ten shishū*.

Pollack, David. 1983. "The Informing Image: 'China' in *Genji monogatari*." *MN* 38.4:359–75.

Reischauer, Edwin O. 1955. *Ennin's Travels in T'ang China*. New York: Ronald Press.

Reischauer, Edwin O., and John K. Fairbank. 1958. *East Asia: The Great Tradition*. Boston: Houghton Mifflin.

Rohlich, Thomas H., trans. 1983. *A Tale of Eleventh-Century Japan: "Hamamatsu Chūnagon Monogatari."* Princeton: Princeton University Press.

Ruch, Barbara. 1977. "Medieval Jongleurs." In *Japan in the Muromachi Age*, eds. John Whitney Hall and Toyoda Takeshi, 279–309. Berkeley and Los Angeles: University of California Press.

Saigō Nobutsuna. 1972. *Kodaijin to yume*. Heibonsha.

Sakurai Hide. 1933.vii. "*Matsura no miya monogatari* no genten ni tsuite." *Bungaku* 1.7:76–86.

Sasaki Osamu. 1940.ix. "*Matsura no miya monogatari*—Mintan yōso to chūshin tēma." *Bungaku* 8.9:59–70.

Seidensticker, Edward G., trans. 1976. *The Tale of Genji*. 2 vols. New York: Alfred A. Knopf.

Shida Gishū. 1926.x. "Gunki-monogatari to giko-monogatari." *KGKBG* 30:13–33.

Shinkokinshū, see Minemura 1974.

Shinpen Kokka Taikan Henshū Iinkai, comp. 1983–87. *Shinpen kokka taikan*, vols. 1–5. Kadokawa. Further volumes continue to appear.

Sugiyama Keiichirō. 1929. "Mumyōzōshi kō." *Kokugo kokubun no kenkyū*, 35, 36, and 38.

Suzuki Hiromichi. 1965. *Nezame monogatari no kisoteki kenkyū*. Hanawa Shobō.

————. 1968. *Heian makki monogatari ron*. Vol. 62 of *Hanawa sensho*. Hanawa Shobō.

————, ed. 1970. *Kōchū Mumyōzōshi*. Kasama Shoin.

Tahara, Mildred M., trans. 1980. *Tales of Yamato: A Tenth-Century Poem-Tale*. Honolulu: University Press of Hawaii.

Takahashi Shōji, ed. 1972. *Yamato monogatari*. Vol. 8 of *NKBZ*. Shōgakukan.

Tamagami Takuya. 1950.xii. "Monogatari ondokuron josetsu." *KGKB* 19.3.

————. 1955.iii. "*Genji monogatari* no dokusha: Monogatari ondokuron." *Joshidai bungaku* 7.

Taniyama Shigeru. 1955.xi. "Shinkokin-teki yōen-bi to Heike ichimon no eiga." *KGKB* 24.11. Reprinted in Kankōkai, ed., *Nihon bungaku kenkyū shiryō sōsho: Shinkokin wakashū*, Yūseidō, 1980.

Teramoto Naohiko. 1970. *Genji monogatari juyōshi ronkō*. Kazama Shobō.

Tesaki Masao. 1940.vi. "Teika no monogatari sōsaku." *KGKBG* 17.6:42–52.

Tomikura Tokujirō, ed. 1954. *Mumyōzōshi hyōkai*. Yūseidō.

Torino Kōji. 1925.x. "Genji monogatari-chū no hikiuta." *KGKBG* 2.10:154–70.

Toyoshima Hidenori. 1976–78. "Fujiwara Teika to *Matsura no miya monogatari*." *Kikan kagaku* 3:23–32; 4:17–27; 5:31–39; 6:37–45; 9:23–28; 10:47–57.

————. 1980.iii. "*Matsura no miya monogatari* no kōzō to *Mumyōzōshi* no hyōgen." *Hirosaki Gakuin Daigaku gakkaishi* 6:8–17.

Tsuji Hikozaburō. 1977. *Fujiwara Teika Meigetsuki no kenkyū*. Yoshikawa Kōbunkan.

Utsuho Monogatari Kenkyūkai, ed. 1973–75. *Utsuho monogatari—honmon to sakuin*. 2 vols. Kasama Shoin.

Waley, Arthur, trans. 1923. *The Temple and Other Poems*. New York: Alfred A. Knopf.

Watson, Burton, trans. 1974. *Courtier and Commoner in Ancient China*. New York: Columbia University Press.

Yamagishi Tokuhei. 1933. "Nihon bungaku shomoku kaisetsu, Kamakura jidai, ge." In *Iwanami kōza Nihon bungaku*, vol. 1. Iwanami.

————, ed. 1973. *Mumyōzōshi*. Kadokawa Bunko.

Yasuda Ayao. 1975a. *Fujiwara Teika kenkyū*, rev. ed. Shibundō.

————. 1975b. *Saigyō to Teika*. Vol. 384 of *Kōdansha gendai shinsho*. Kōdansha.

Yoshida Kōichi. 1959.vii. "Matsura no miya no seiritsu nenji to sakusha ni tsuite no kōsetsu." *Heian bungaku kenkyū* 23:26–36.

Yoshizawa Yoshinori. 1952. *Shintei Kamakura bungakushi*. Vol. 5 of *Nihon bungaku zenshi*. Tōkyōdō.

General Index

Abe no Nakamaro, 113n.112, 141n.166; as model for Sekimaro, 72n.45
Abe no Sekimaro, 67; in China, 74, 113; model for, 72n.45
Aesthetic explosion, 37–38, 46, 50
Akiko. *See* Shōshi
Akirakeiko. *See* Meishi
Allusions. *See* "Ch'ang-hen ko"; *Genji monogatari*; *Hamamatsu Chūnagon monogatari*; "Kao-t'ang fu"; "Lady Li"; *Matsura no miya monogatari*; *see also* Index of First Lines of Poems Cited
Allusive variation. *See honkadori*
Ambassador. *See* Abe no Sekimaro
An Lu-shan, 98n.95, 101n.96, 129n.144
Antoku, Emperor, flight from Heian capital of: as date evidence, 12, 168; as model, 98n.95
Ariwara Narihira, 7n.9, 24, 24n.49, 30
Asuka, Princess (Ujitada's mother), 57; and the title, 5, 5n.3, 64–65, 69–72; welcomes Princess Hua-yang, 158; welcomes Ujitada home, 157
Asura(s), 151–52, 151n.186
Audiences. *See* Imperial audiences
Authorship evidence: detailed review of, 171–92; outlined, 10–12; pointing to male author, 26n.52

Borrowing: from *Genji monogatari*, 20n.43; from *Hamamatsu Chūnagon monogatari*, 45–46, 74nn.48, 50, 82n.62, 84n.65, 85n.68, 86n.69, 87n.71, 89n.78, 150n.182; Heian readers' attitudes toward, 19–21, 20n.42; from *Sagoromo monogatari*, 94n.87; from *Utsuho monogatari*, 58n.4, 67n.30, 80n.60, 94n.87, 95n.89

"Ch'ang-hen ko," 101n.96; allusion to, 116n.120
Cheng and Wei, music of, 149n.180
Chen-kuan era. *See* Jōgan
Chien-ko Path, 101n.97
Child emperor: accedes to throne, 96; as crown prince, 77; education of, 112–13, 120, 124; flees from capital, 98-99; formally installed, 112; as sage emperor, 113; and Ujitada, 77, 128–29, 141–42, 147, 148–50
Ch'i-mi, 44n.77
Chinese sources reflected in tale: nature of, 26n.52, 175–76; Teika's familiarity with, 176
Chin Mi-ti, 76n.52, 90n.80
Chin-yung Ch'eng, 111n.110
"Chōgonka." *See* "Ch'ang-hen ko"
Chrysanthemum Banquet, 59n.8
Chūnagon, 45, 82n.62, 84n.65, 89n.78
Ch'ün-shu chih-yao, 124n.135
Colophon, fictitious, 6–8, 162; date in, 6–8, 24–25, 162n.209; intent of, 21–22, 22n.46, 25–26; internal contradictions of, 23, 24n.48, 26n.52
Colophon, variant of, 6n.5, 25
Coming-of-age ceremony, 58n.4
Confessions of Lady Nijō, 14n.23
Court business. *See* Imperial audiences

Date evidence, 6–12, 163–72
Dazaifu, 70, 70n.39
Departure activities: in China, 155–57; in Japan, 67–71
Directional taboos, 85n.68
Dowager. *See* Empress dowager
Dreampath, 42, 47, 125–26, 135, 146, 153

Dreams: compared to *Hamamatsu Chūnagon monogatari*, 45; and reality, 24n.49, 28, 39–45, 47–48, 110, 128n.143, 133n.150, 137

Earlier *monogatari*. *See* Borrowing; *Genji monogatari*; *Hamamatsu Chūnagon monogatari*; *Kakuremino no monogatari*; *Sagoromo monogatari*; *Taketori monogatari*; *Utsuho monogatari*; *see also* Index of First Lines of Poems Cited
Embassy: arrives in Chinese capital (Ch'ang-an), 74; arrives in Ming-chou, 73; departs from Dazaifu, 71; departs from Japanese capital (Fujiwara), 67–69; size of, 70n.39
Emperor. *See* Child emperor; Hsüan-tsung, Emperor; Wen, Emperor
Empress dowager: clairvoyance of, 115, 118n.125; consults with advisors, 101–2, 107–9, 112–13, 130; as enlightened and benevolent ruler, 18, 24–25, 112, 124, 129–30; family background of, 129; model for, 108n.107, 112n.111; as mysterious lady, 42, 48; proposes ambush, 102; reveals true circumstances, 150–54; and Ujitada, 102–3, 114–20, 120n.129, 124–25, 129, 140, 148–55, 156–57, 160. *See also* Mysterious lady
Enchantment, 30, 31, 33–34, 38, 45; is broken, 36–37, 45–50
Ending, 21–26, 23n.47
Ethereal charm or beauty. *See yōen*
Experimental romance, 50–51

Fantastic, the. *See* Supernatural, the
Fiction, attitudes toward: Heian period, 50–51; Shunzei's, 51, 175; Teika's, 51–52, 175
First Chinese emperor. *See* Wen, Emperor
Five Phoenixes, Pavilion of the, 89n.77; scene at, 91–93
Flight from capital, 98–99, 98n.95, 101nn.96, 97
Forgery of ancient tale, 21, 57n.1; contradictions in, 59n.9, 72n.45, 73n.46, 83n.64, 142n.168

Fragmentation. *See Matsura no miya monogatari*, thematic coherence of
Fujiwara (place), 57n.1
Fujiwara Michinaga, 7
Fujiwara Shunzei, 8, 9n.14, 13–14, 51, 51n.85, 175
Fujiwara Takanobu, 9
Fujiwara Teika: allusions to tale by, 29, 30–31, 30n.63, 186–88, 190–91; as innovative poet, 13, 14; loss of interest in tale, 16, 22, 23n.47, 49–50; playfulness of, 26, 118n.125; poetics of, 11, 11n.19, 14–15, 44n.77, 46, 52; political sentiments of, 17–18, 18n.37; qualifications of, as author, 174–75; as scholar of prose texts, 13; Shōtetsu's view of, 13
Fujwara Yoshifusa, 7, 7n.7; and colophon, 26n.52
Fushimi manuscript, 53–54, 87n.70
Fūyōshū, 163–65, 170
Fuyuaki (Ujitada's father), 57, 58, 64, 69–72

Genji monogatari: allusions to, in tale, 20n.43, 68n.33, 86n.69, 128n.143, 134n.152, 136n.154, 146n.175; allusions to, in Teika's poetry, 28, 51; as model for later tales, 20; scenes from, compared, 32n.66, 58n.4, 128n.143
Gesaku. *See* Playful composition
Giko-monogatari, military figures in, 17
Go-Hanazono manuscript, imitation of, 6n.5, 53
Go-Kōgon manuscript, 53–54, 87n.70
Grievance boards, 130, 130n.145
Gunki-monogatari, 17

Haku Raku-ten shishū. *See* Po Chü-i, works
Hakushi monjū. *See* Po Chü-i, works
Hamamatsu Chūnagon monogatari: allusions to, 132n.148; dreams in, 45–46; title of, 5n.3; *Mumyōzōshi*'s view of, 20n.42. *See also* Borrowing
Hatsuse (or Hase), 92, 92n.83, 158–59
Heike monogatari, 98n.95
Hens that crow, 108n.106
Hero. See *Monogatari*, idealized heroes of

Index of First Lines of Poems Cited

ABOUT THE AUTHOR

Wayne P. Lammers received a doctorate from the University of Michigan and is currently Assistant Professor of Japanese at Lewis & Clark College in Portland, Oregon. In addition to his research on classical Japanese fiction, he is the translator of a forthcoming volume of short stories by the contemporary Japanese author Shōno Junzō.